Poecilia reticulata (Veiltail Guppy)

THE CONCISE ENCYCLOPEDIA OF

TROPICAL AQUARIUM FISHES

The Male Paradisefish inspects the bubblenest

This spectacular aquascape shows the quality of planting and decoration that can be achieved in the home aquarium.

THE CONCISE ENCYCLOPEDIA OF

TROPICAL AQUARIUM FISHES

Compiled by
Dick Mills

Crescent Books
New York

A SALAMANDER BOOK

Library of Congress Cataloging-in-Publication Data
Mills, Dick
    The concise encyclopedia of tropical aquarium fish

    1. Aquariums.   2. Tropical fish.   I. Scott,
Peter, Dr.   II. Sands, David.   III. Title.
SF457.M5617   1988   639.3'4   88-15022
ISBN 0-517-66776-2

h g f e d c b a

Xiphophorus maculatus (Red High Fin Platy)

CREDITS

Editor: Anne McDowall   Design: David Jones
Colour reproductions: Bantam Litho Ltd.
David Bruce Graphics
Chelmer Litho Reproductions
Contemporary Lithoplates Limited
Melbourne Graphics Ltd.
Rodney Howe Ltd.
Tempus Litho
Filmset: SX Composing Ltd.
Printed and bound in Belgium

AUTHORS

Dick Mills
Dick Mills is an experienced fishkeeper and author wih a very clear understanding of the needs and aspirations of beginners to the aquarium hobby. His ability to explain unfamiliar and often quite complex concepts in a clear way is put to good use in the first two parts of this book, which explain how to set up a tank and populate it with colourful tropical freshwater fishes. Dick has an excellent 'pedigree' in the fishkeeping world, having kept a wide range of fishes for over 20 years and pursuing an active involvement in the Federation of British Aquatic Societies, for which he regularly lectures and produces a quarterly News Bulletin.

David Sands
David Sands has prepared the specialist material on cichlids and catfishes in Parts Three, Four and Five. He is an acknowledged expert on these fishes and regularly writes for the fishkeeping magazines in the UK and USA.

Dr. Peter W. Scott
Dr. Peter W. Scott, a veterinarian with a special interest in fish, reptiles and amphibians, has contributed Part Six on livebearing fishes. He is the author of four books and a contributor to several others, particularly on the subject of fish health.

CONTENTS

Part Two
Popular Aquarium Fishes 78

A wide-ranging selection of 120 aquarium fishes, all photographed in colour and described in detail. They are presented in A-Z order of scientific name in logical 'popular-name' groupings.

Part Three
Central American Cichlids 196

In this, the first of our closer looks at particularly popular groups of fishes, our attention turns to Central America, a veritable 'cornucopia' for the fish enthusiast. Cichlids are among the most popular fishes around the world and the warm climes of Central America have much to offer.

Part Four
African and Asian Catfishes 214

Catfishes are fascinating subjects for the tropical aquarium and enjoy universal acclaim for their often strange appearance and secretive behaviour. This is the first of two sections in the book that spotlight a wide range of catfish species. The following families are featured:

Part Five
South American Catfishes 236

These are the most popular catfishes in the world, particularly the many species of *Corydoras,* which are usually easy to keep in the community tank. As you might expect, *Corydoras* catfishes, which belong to the callichthyidae family, feature strongly in the following selection, but there are plenty of other species to 'take the eye' of enthusiastic fishkeepers. Species are presented from the following families:

Part Six
Livebearing Fishes 270

As their name suggests, these fishes bear live young. (Most other fishes lay eggs.) The Guppies and Swordtails are among the easiest fishes to keep and breed and, not surprisingly, have earned a justifiable reputation as beginners' fishes. These are presented in Part Two of the book. Here, the more unusual livebearers are presented for the more 'adventurous' fishkeeper. Species from the following families are featured:

The distribution of some popular fish groups

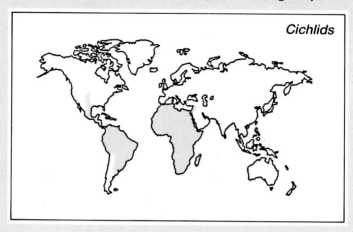

Cichlids

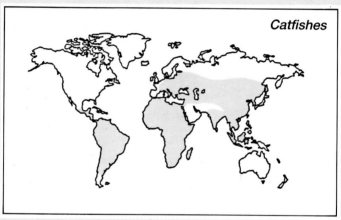

Catfishes

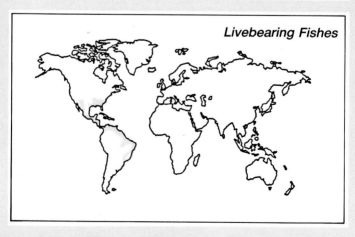

Livebearing Fishes

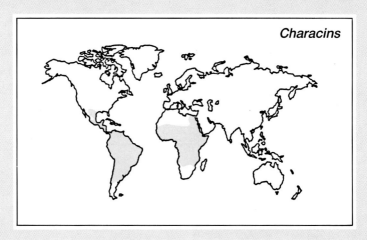

Characins

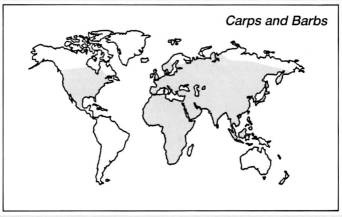

Carps and Barbs

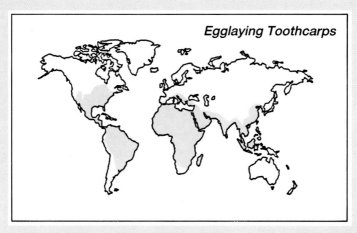

Egglaying Toothcarps

Part One
Practical Section

Above: Cichlasoma ellioti *is but one of the many colourful cichlids available from Central America.*

Modern fishkeeping has long since escaped from the pioneering days of 'hit and miss' technology; today's equipment is entirely reliable, foolproof and easy to install. Little technical knowledge is needed beyond the ability to connect an electrical plug: even youngsters (with a little adult supervision) may be safely encouraged to set up a freshwater tropical aquarium. The tanks themselves are no longer prone to rust, nor are they heavy unsightly angle-iron-framed glass boxes. Fishes, too, are also available in both larger numbers and in better health, thanks to the use of modern transportation methods and, of course, to the practical experience gained by breeders and exporters over the years. However, two things remain the same – the need for a clear understanding of your fishes' requirements and, just as important, the acceptance

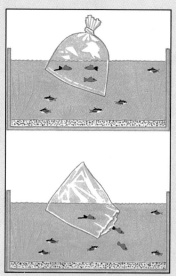

Above: *Float the fishes' carry home plastic bag in the aquarium to restore their water temperature to the correct level before their release, a vital tip to reduce stress.*

of the responsibility to provide and maintain these conditions. Learning about the characteristics of the fishes themselves comes at a later date and the satisfaction that this brings will reward your earlier work.

If you are just beginning in fishkeeping, please do not turn immediately to the fish illustrations and start planning your collection. The first part of this book is the most important, as the information contained in it is relevant to *all* the fishes described later; without a sound basic knowledge of how to set up and maintain a tropical freshwater aquarium, your success rate will be diminished. Compared to the effort required in maintaining other pets, that needed in fishkeeping is relatively minimal; once you have fully grasped the basic rudiments, such as water and dietary requirements, there only remains one more thing to do – enjoy your fishkeeping!

Above: *A fully furnished aquarium forms an attractive feature in the home, here as a room divider.*

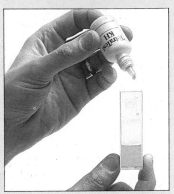

Above: *Checking water quality of the aquarium with suitable test kits is an important part of maintenance.* Left: *The vibrant Marigold Platy.*

Tank size

When choosing the size of the tank there are certain factors to be considered. Obviously, the number of fishes that can be kept in it will be uppermost in most fishkeepers' minds; there is also the question of how the overall dimensions of the tank fit in where you intend it to be sited. Again, some tank shapes are more pleasing than others and lend themselves better to aquatic 'landscaping' and furnishing when setting up the tank.

It is suggested that the minimum length of tank should be 60cm (24in) with a front to rear dimension of 30cm (12in) and a depth of 30cm (12in), but a better aquatic picture is provided with a tank depth of 38cm (15in).

Although tanks can be made to suit any required dimensions and to fit exactly into any awkward recess, it should be borne in mind that the tank will be the living quarters of our fishes; and although the dimensions of the tank may suit *our* requirements, it does not always follow that the fishes will be happy with this arrangement. For reasons that will be explained in a moment, the number of fishes that can be accommodated within any tank is governed by the length and breadth, and the depth of the tank affects only the water capacity.

Through their gills fishes absorb oxygen that is dissolved in water, and they exhale carbon dioxide. As the oxygen is depleted it is replenished via the water surface, the interface between water and air. Similarly,

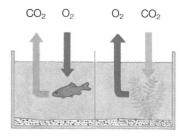

Above: *During the hours of 'tanklight' the fishes' and plants' respiratory needs and actions complement each other perfectly in the aquarium.*

carbon dioxide can be expelled only at the water surface, although we shall see later how aquarium plants can reduce the level of carbon dioxide in the water. So, to allow the tank to accommodate its full quota of fish, without discomfort and the danger of asphyxiation, a large water surface is required. Reference to the diagram will show you that although the two tanks hold the same volume of water, the one with the largest water surface can hold the largest number of fishes. The general rule is to allow 75cm^2 (12in^2) for every 2.5cm (1in) of fish body. (When measuring a fish do not include the tail.) For example a tank 60cm × 30cm (24in × 12in) will hold 24 fishes each 2.5cm long. This figure holds true no matter how deep the tank is, so in the case of our 60cm (24in) tank you may as well opt for the deeper 38cm (15in) dimension, and give your fishes more room to swim in

Below: *In two tanks of identical volume a higher number of fishes can be kept in the tank with the larger water surface area, shown at right.*

Above: *Careful planning and choice of species ensure that a varied, well-stocked aquarium makes use of all the space available, with fishes swimming at all levels. The three levels – (1) top (2) mid-water (3) bottom – form the divisions of the fish section later in this guide.*

and yourself more room in which to create your underwater world.

Another reason for choosing a 60cm (24in) tank is that within the confines of the aquarium the water conditions will fluctuate, particularly in small tanks. With this tank size (capacity 54-68 litres, 12-15 gallons) such changes will be more gradual and less likely to affect the fishes adversely. Similarly, temperature changes will occur more gradually.

A 'balanced' aquarium

Having selected a suitably sized tank, you can now fill it with fishes. The aquarium should present to the viewer a complete picture of an underwater world; fishes should be chosen that will naturally inhabit all water levels in the aquarium. Surface-swimming fishes tend to be fast swimmers, either to escape predators or to catch their own food, usually insects floating on the water surface. Mid-water swimmers can be more slow-moving; for example, the Angelfish (*Pterophyllum* sp.) inhabits

reedbeds and is quite a sedate fish, as are members of the Gourami family. Bottom-dwelling fishes are another characteristic group; many are nocturnal by nature, hiding away among plants and rocks by day (or tank-lit times). They are often relegated to the scavenger category by ignorant fishkeepers who do not realize that these fishes have a lifestyle of their own and deserve to be treated accordingly.

There are no set rules for the proportions of surface swimmers to mid-water fishes to bottom dwellers; obviously, species from one group will stray into the other two strata during their daily lives and not even the most inexperienced fishkeeper would expect it to be otherwise. Generally, the mid-water fishes outnumber the other two groups in the aquarium just as they do in nature. Some aquarists deliberately specialize in fishes from only one group, but that is a choice you can make as you progress in your own fishkeeping adventures.

13

Heating

In order to keep tropical fishes alive, the temperature of their aquarium water must be maintained at its natural level, i.e. around 24°C (75°F). This is easily accomplished and nothing for the novice fishkeeper to be unduly worried about.

Today's modern aquarium hardware is completely reliable, simple to install and safe to handle. It is not expensive to run, and an average-sized aquarium requires around 250 watts electrical consumption for its full operation. The heating apparatus is thermostatically controlled, and the lighting is not used at night, so the actual consumption is much lower than the estimate.

Aquarists owning many tanks may find it more economical to heat the room space instead of individual tanks; electrical or gas appliances can be used to good effect in this case, both being thermostatically controlled as required. Paraffin oil heaters can also be used, but care must be taken periodically to remove the film of oil that forms on the aquarium water surface with this form of heating.

Heat conservation (and fuel saving, too) can be achieved by insulating the outside of the side and rear walls and the bottom of the tank with expanded polystyrene sheets.

In the event of power failure, temperatures fall quite slowly (or very slowly in large tanks) and should not cause concern unless power failure is prolonged. Should this occur, bottles of hot water (heated by alternative means) can be stood in the tank (beware of overflowing) to restore the temperature to its required value again, or to prevent further heat losses. Cover the tank with a blanket to conserve heat in an emergency.

Temperature is easily measured by means of a simple aquarium thermometer, which may be of a floating or adhesive type. Again, modern technology has provided an up-to-date version in the form of a flat, liquid crystal display fixed to the outside of the aquarium glass.

The majority of aquarium heating is achieved by means of combined heater and thermostat units. Needing

Above: *Attach this basic type of thermometer to the inside glass at a convenient height for easy reading.*

Below: *Fix liquid crystal types (right) on the outside glass; sealed dial versions (left) on the inside glass.*

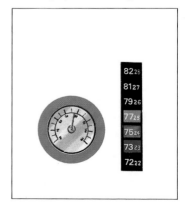

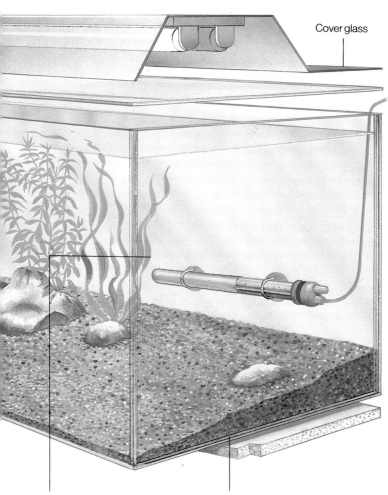

Cover glass

Above: *A combined heater-thermostat will prove adequate for most small and medium-sized tanks. Mount it as shown on the rear wall at an angle or nearly vertical in a corner.*

Above: *A thick piece of expanded polystyrene cut to size and placed underneath the tank will cushion any irregularities in the supporting surface and help to conserve heat.*

only the minimum of wiring and taking up less room in the aquarium, these trouble-free units have largely replaced the separate heater and thermostat arrangement favoured by fishkeepers for many years.

The heater/thermostat is housed in a watertight glass tube and is held in position in the aquarium by specially designed retaining clips; these clips,

of non-toxic plastics, are anchored by suction pads to the aquarium glass.

Where separate units are used, the thermostat may be one of two types – internal (submerged type), which looks very similar to a heater, or external (outside the aquarium), which is clipped to the aquarium side and senses the changes in water temperature through the glass.

Relatively recent developments have produced designs of thermostats that use microchip circuitry for even more accurate temperature control.

The aquarium heater should be the correct size for the tank. An approximate guide is to allow 10 watts per 4.5 litres (1 gallon) of aquarium capacity. Aquarium heaters are available in 'standard' sizes (50, 75, 100, 125, 150, 200, 300 watts) and the heater that most nearly matches your aquarium's needs should be chosen. In our earlier example, the 60×30×30cm tank (holding 54 litres/12 gallons) would require 120 watts of heating; a 125 watt heater would be ideal. Remember to take into consideration the lowest temperature which the room falls to (central heating systems are usually programmed to go off at night) and the aquarium heater must be able to cope with the extra demand during the winter.

An over-large heater in a small tank could lead to a very rapid rise in temperature if the thermostat got stuck in the 'ON' state. A small heater would be inadequate for a large tank, and could cause thermostat damage.

To provide an even spread of heat throughout large tanks (90cm/36in upwards) use two heater/thermostats (one at each end of the tank) totalling the required heat wattage.

Installation

1 To provide the most efficient heating, heaters should be installed in the lowest part of the aquarium water. Normal practice is to position the heater so that it will be hidden by plants or rocks, but there should be free circulation of water around the heater, so mount it clear of the gravel.

2 Combined units may be too long to be mounted vertically in one corner, in which case they can be used diagonally along the rear or side of the tank. Check whether adjusting controls are totally watertight or whether the unit must be installed semi-submerged.

3 Large tanks should have combined heater/thermostats at each end.

4 Make all electrical connections *outside* the tank away from water. A proprietary junction box called a 'cable tidy' will enable all connections to be made safely and neatly. If you are unsure of your electrical wiring ability, always consult a qualified electrician.

5 A heater must always be under water when switched on.

6 Thermostats, generally factory set at around 24°C (75°F), are adjustable a few degrees either way to allow for special temperature requirements.

7 Before making any adjustments to the heating system, or to any other electrical equipment associated with the aquarium, disconnect the equipment from the power supply.

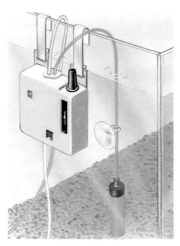

Left: *This external thermostat has microchip circuitry and a submerged sensor for precise heat control. Double-sided adhesive pads can be used as an alternative method of fixing the unit securely to the outside of the aquarium.*

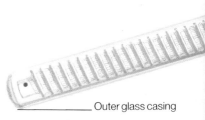

Outer glass casing

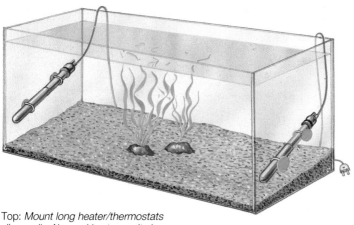

Top: *Mount long heater/thermostats diagonally.* Above: *Use two units in large tanks to spread heat evenly.*

Temperature adjustment knob

Wire heating element wound on ceramic core

Thermostat

Watertight cap

Neon power indicator

Mains lead

Above: *A submersible combined heater-thermostat. Position it in the tank so that the thermostat is above the heating element.*

Lighting

Besides making an aquarium look more attractive, light is also an essential stimulus to the plants and fishes. Aquarium plants need light to photosynthesize – a process by which they remove carbon dioxide from the water. In nature, fishes are lit from above by the sun, and any strong side-lighting tends to makes them lean over.

Light can be easily provided by means of lamps mounted in the aquarium cover, usually referred to as the hood or reflector. To simulate the fishes' natural light in brightness and intensity is difficult, given the restrictions imposed by the dimensions of the hood, but luckily the home aquarium appears to be able to function quite happily with much less light. Tungsten lamps, fluorescent tubes, or a combination of the two can be used, each system having both advantages and disadvantages.

Aquatic plants require certain wavelengths of light for optimum growth and special fluorescent lamps are available with these wavelength outputs emphasized. Many aquarists combine several fluorescent tubes of different colours to provide the type of lighting that they find works best, each tube being independently switched.

An approximate guide to the amount of light required is to allow 40 watts (tungsten) or 10 watts (fluorescent) for every 30cm (12in) length of the aquarium, and the aquarium should be lit for at least 10 hours each day. The exact amount and duration of light required is best found by trial and error – enough light to promote good plant growth, but not enough to encourage the unsightly (and often uncontrollable) growth of algae.

Aquariums are often very well furnished with plants – particularly those of Dutch aquarists, who practise 'underwater gardening' so expertly. These aquariums need a much higher intensity of light levels, perhaps four to six times higher than the requirements outlined above.

Cover glasses are necessary to reduce evaporation losses, and to stop dust entering the aquarium.

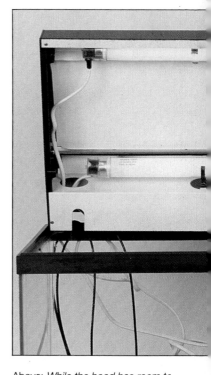

Above: *While the hood has room to incorporate different types of lights, fluorescent lamps are best. Tungsten lamps, although easy to install and inexpensive, run hot, are 'single-coloured', and consume a fair amount of electricity. Fluorescent lamps are more costly and need special starting circuitry, but they run cooler, are available in many 'colours', and produce an even light.*

They also protect the floating plant leaves from becoming scorched, and the light fittings from condensation damage, and they prevent fishes from leaping out of the aquarium. Cover glasses should be kept spotlessly clean to minimize light losses, and the reflector/hood should be equally well maintained. If tungsten lamps are used, the hood should be well ventilated to reduce a build-up of heat within the hood, which otherwise might shorten lamp life and even raise the temperature of the surface layers of the water to an unacceptable level. Such over-heating can kill fishes.

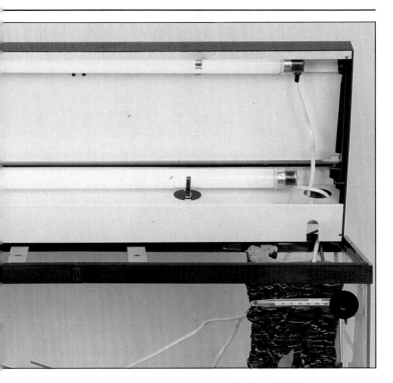

Below: *A centrally placed lamp casts shadows forward; to be avoided.*
Bottom: *A lamp at the front casts shadows away from the viewer; ideal.*

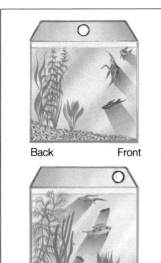

Back   Front

Installation of lighting

Modern aquarium hood/reflectors usually come with ready-made holes for tungsten lamp fittings, and in some more expensive hoods clips are provided for fluorescent tubes together with space for the bulky starter equipment. The use of waterproof connectors in either case is recommended. The aquarium cover glass will prevent water being splashed onto the hot lamps, but be careful (if fluorescent lighting is used) that the extra heavy hood is not dropped onto the cover glass or it may crack it. Fluorescent light starting equipment can be housed remotely from the tank if necessary.

Many hoods are hinged, or have feeding hatches built into them for ease of access at feeding times; a small aperture in the cover glass immediately below the hatch will make feeding even easier. The reflector can be painted white inside or lined with silver foil to give maximum efficiency, and the lamps positioned to give the correct lighting into the aquarium (see diagram).

19

Aeration

Novice fishkeepers often think it obligatory to have a column of air bubbles constantly rising through the aquarium water, as this condition is to be found in practically all aquatic shops. However, this is not completely necessary and the use of air in the aquarium is sometimes not fully understood.

The benefit of aeration is not quite as obvious as it seems. The belief that oxygen is somehow forced into the water by means of the air bubbles is a misconception. The value of aeration lies more in its ability to create turbulence at the water surface, and to assist circulation of water from the bottom of the tank to the top (something that the processes of heating and filtration and the movements of the fish also do to some extent).

Turbulence on the surface of the water effectively increases the water surface area, which, as we have already learnt, plays an important role in the replenishment of oxygen in the water and the removal of carbon dioxide from it. This, in turn, allows more fishes to be kept in the tank than theoretical calculations suggest (see page 13). However, the use of aeration should not be taken as an excuse for crowding more fishes into the tank.

for if the air supply fails for any length of time, the tank will become over-crowded, although the risk to the fishes is from possible asphyxiation rather than from sheer numbers of fishes together.

A supply of air is provided by an air pump, which is electrically powered; there are two types of air pump – vibrator and piston type. The most popular type of air pump is the simple vibrator design, which is available in many sizes. It is reasonably quiet in operation and needs little maintenance. Piston air pumps can be more expensive but some fishkeepers prefer their obvious 'mechanical' appearance. They require more maintenance but usually make less noise than the cheaper vibrator models.

Pumped air is fed to the aquarium by means of plastic tubing. The flow of air may be regulated either with clamps or with air valves. Some higher-priced air pumps have an air control fitted; this may be an air-bleed screw, or a potentiometer (or variable resistance) in the pumps voltage supply. The air is broken up into a column of bubbles by passing it through a submerged airstone, usually a block of porous ceramic material or hardwood.

Below: *The output from the air pump can be distributed to the various filters and airstones by plastic tubing and regulated independently by control valves. The check valve guards against back-siphoning of water. If* *you have many tanks, it may be more practical to use a large-capacity air pump (or compressor), feeding a 'ring-main' circuit system of air-tubing to all tanks, rather than a separate air pump for each tank.*

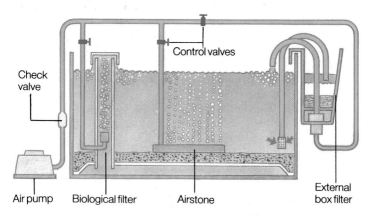

Control valves

Check valve

Air pump   Biological filter   Airstone   External box filter

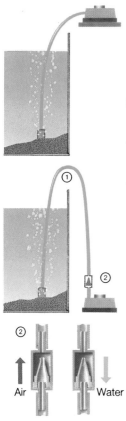

Air   Water

Above: *How to stop water siphoning back into the air pump by (top) placing the pump above water level or (centre) making an 'anti-siphon' loop (1) at least 5cm(2in) high. The lower diagrams show that a one-way check valve (2) allows air through (left) but closes against water pressure (right). The photograph shows an airline connected to a ganged valve. The air pump has a rotary control to regulate its output.*

Installing the air system

The pump should be placed, ideally, above the water level of the aquarium, to prevent water siphoning into the pump if the electrical supply fails. Alternatively, as most hobbyists seem to site their air pumps on a handy shelf below the aquarium, an 'anti-siphon loop' is made in the airline, looping it a few centimetres above the water level to prevent back-

siphoning. A commercially available 'one-way' check valve also prevents back-siphoning. If extra equipment is to be fed from the one air supply, the air is first fed into a multi-way ganged valve, which allows independent control of the air supplies; a spare position on this multi-way valve can also be used to bleed off excessive air from the system.

Some inexpensive vibrator pumps will have an annoying buzz to them. Enclosing them in a cupboard will deaden the noise somewhat, but a close-fitting, foam-filled box is better; ventilation holes should be left to prevent the air pump from over-heating and to allow a free passage of air. Most pumps have a felt-pad air filter mounted underneath – keep it clean! Piston pumps require regular oiling, and an oil-trap should be fitted in the airline to prevent oil reaching the aquarium and affecting the fishes.

Filtration

So far, sufficient space, oxygen, heat and light have been provided for the fishes in correct quantities, and we have arranged for these conditions to be held as stable as possible. However, the presence of living animals and plants in the aquarium will upset the stable environment we have created unless further steps are taken to prevent deterioration of the water's wholesomeness.

The living aquarium produces waste products from several sources. The fishes excrete liquid and solid matter which produces ammonia; plant leaves die and decompose; uneaten food also rots. The water takes on a slightly amber coloration and may even begin to smell. The action of the fishes often causes the water to be less than crystal clear.

Water in a natural environment is subject to change by the effects of wind, rain and – most important of all – a continuous water flow in streams and rivers. Without actually recreating a river course in our aquarium, we can attempt to purify the water (or at least minimize any pollution of it) by two simple means – partial water changes, and filtration.

Partial water changes are self-explanatory: every two or three weeks some 10-20% of the aquarium water is removed and replaced with fresh, ideally at the same temperature, although most fishes appear to enjoy the addition of slightly cooler water, as long as it does not lower the water temperature too drastically. The action will obviously remove some waste material (including dirt from the aquarium floor, if a siphon tube is used to good advantage), and the addition of clean water will dilute the waste products still remaining in the tank. Automatic water changers make this chore less tiresome.

Filtration equipment for the aquarium works in three simple ways: mechanical, chemical or biological. The majority of container-type filters (whether of internal or external design, or of air or electrical operation) are of the first two categories, using some form of medium to trap suspended material in the water flowing through it, and some other materials (such as

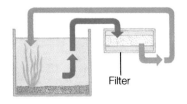

Above: *The principle of mechanical filtration. Dirty water is removed, cleaned and returned to the tank. Water is drawn into the filter by siphonic action and is returned via an airlift or electric impeller.*

activated carbon, peat, resins) to remove dissolved waste products or to alter the water's properties. Biological filtration is completely different in concept, relying on bacterial action to break down ammonia and nitrites into the less toxic nitrates.

Container-type filters

The general principle of these filters is to pass dirty aquarium water through a medium-filled container (where the dirt is removed) and return the cleaned water to the aquarium. The usual medium is some form of man-made fibre: dacron floss, nylon floss, etc. (Glass wool is not recommended, as tiny fragments of glass can be transferred into the aquarium with the risk of injuries to the fishes.) Some modern filters have tailor-made filter pads of foam material, but do not attempt to do it yourself with, say, polyurethane

Left: *This submersible internal power filter is held vertically in place in the corner of the tank by rubber suckers (not shown). Water enters through the vertical slots and passes through the white foam filter medium before returning to the tank via the single outlet hole (see top of motor module). An extra feature of this model is that the degree of aeration added to the stream of water returning to the aquarium can be varied. Be careful to ensure that the motor module is submerged at all times.*

Right: *External power filters, such as this one, can be sited alongside or underneath the tank. Be careful to ensure that all water hose connections are very secure before starting the filter, to avoid unseen leaks. Separate filter medium containers hold different media for various water treatments.*
Below left: *This motorized external box filter provides plenty of clean, well-oxygenated water. The filter medium is in the form of blocks, which are easy to change without causing undue mess in the process.*

foam, because such material may be toxic to fishes.

Filters containing activated carbon should not be used if any medication is to be added to the aquarium, because the medication will be adsorbed by the carbon. Aeration should be substituted, as some medicaments reduce the oxygen content of the water.

For a decorative or fully planted aquarium, an outside filtration system is best so that regular maintenance of the filter does not cause disruption to the planted tank.

The external, open-box filter *cannot* overflow (often a worry to

beginners). The siphon system into the box from the aquarium automatically stops when the filter box is full, and only when cleaned water is being returned to the aquarium does it start again.

'Power filters' – i.e. electrically powered 'open-box' or 'canister' types – may be used inside or outside the aquarium, and they have a far larger water flow rate. Check all tube connections thoroughly before operating, as a loose pipe can result in an empty tank and a flood elsewhere! This is particularly important where a canister filter is used remote from the aquarium.

Biological filtration

Using nature's own way of dealing with waste products, the biological filter makes use of the aquarium's gravel as a filter bed. The aquarium water is passed through the gravel and a colony of bacteria develops throughout the entire gravel bed. The virtue of this type of filtration is that the hardware is sited invisibly beneath the gravel and needs hardly any maintenance. The natural sequence of events is that waste products from the fish are first converted to toxic *ammonia*. This ammonia is converted to *nitrite* by Nitrosomonas bacteria, then Nitrobacter bacteria turn nitrite into *nitrate*, which is less harmful to fishes and which many plants use as a food material.

A biological filter (usually referred to by hobbyists as an undergravel filter) is generally operated by air from the air pump, although where an extra large water flow is required an electrical water pump can be fitted. If biological filtration is to be used in an aquarium containing fishes that dig or forage a lot in the gravel, then the undergravel filter plate must be protected and not allowed to become exposed. This can be done by putting a piece of nylon netting over the gravel bed one or two centimetres above the filter before the final layers of gravel are put in place.

The biological filtration process depends, as we have seen, on bacterial action, and the bacteria colony is sustained by the flow of oxygenated water through the gravel. For this reason, an undergravel filter should never be switched off, for as soon as the water flow stops, the bacteria colony will begin to die and the action of the filter will be lost.

Right: *This non-submersible electric water pump is mounted on the top of the biological filter's lift tube. This is a very efficient method of upgrading the water flow rate through the biological filtration system but it has a slight practical drawback; you will need to make some practical modifications to the tank hood in order to accommodate the motor assembly, which protrudes above the top of the tank.*

The airstone provides a stream of bubbles.

The biological filter plate should cover the base of the aquarium to provide the greatest area for the bacterial colony in the gravel.

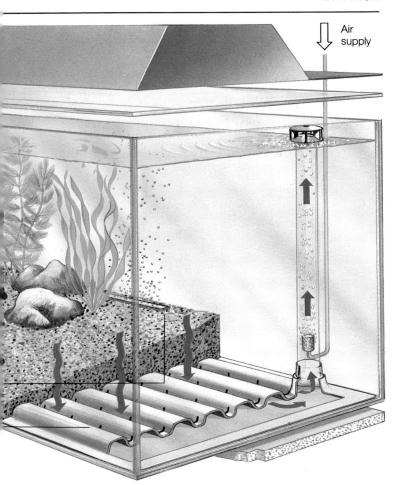

Air
supply

Below: *A power filter can be used to drive pre-cleaned water through the gravel bed of a reverse-flow biological filter. This will keep the gravel in the aquarium cleaner for a longer time than in usual 'downflow' systems.*

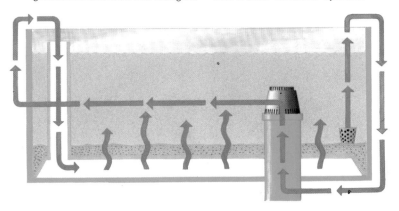

Installation of filters

Filters are best installed before the addition of various aquarium furnishings, such as rocks and plants, restricts working space.

Provision must be made for easy access to inside filters for maintenance purposes. Unless they are fitted with anchoring suction pads, inside air-operated filters have a tendency to float up, but a few pebbles in the bottom avoid this. A plastic bag slipped under the filter box before removing it from the tank for cleaning will also prevent dirty water spilling back into the tank.

Installation of outside box filters often means that the tank hood has to be modified to accommodate the siphon and return tubes. In large tanks, arrange them so that the returned clean water enters the tank well away (preferably at the other end of the tank) from the filter's intake siphon; this will provide a flow of water across the whole tank.

Where activated carbon is used in a filter system, it should not be the last material that the water passes through before returning to the tank. Activated carbon is often sandwiched between layers of filter floss – the first layer removes suspended dirt from the water, the second prevents particles of carbon being drawn into the aquarium. Alternatively, the carbon can be contained in a cloth bag if used in a filter alone.

Above: *Fit the biological filter first.*
Left: *Cover the plate with a layer of gravel at least 5cm(2in) deep.*
Below: *Slope the gravel from back to front and contour as you wish using rocks to maintain the slope.*

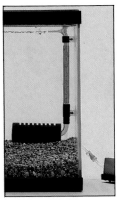

Above: *This sponge filter not only strains out dirt but, in time, also acts biologically.*

Above: *Examples of air-operated filters. The simple sponge filter (top) and the internal box filter (shown below it) are both ideal for using in fry-raising, unplanted tanks. Clean them regularly!*

Left: *External open-box filters that are more suitable for furnished tanks, where their regular maintenance will cause little disturbance to the fishes and the plant arrangements inside the tank. Both of these models are operated by pumped air.*

Below: *The conventional operation of an external power filter. Because the whole filter system is normally filled with water (the spray bar is shown above the water for clarity), you can, if you wish, locate the filter canister away from the tank. The water returning to the aquarium is usually under pressure and you* should fit the spray bar so that the water jets create turbulence aross the water surface. If you keep fishes such as Hatchetfishes, which are surface-water swimmers, you will need to turn the jets downwards so that the water surface remains calm.

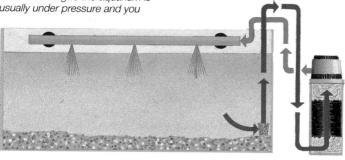

Right: *A powerful external canister-type filter. Water is drawn from just above the gravel bed and, once cleaned, returns to the aquarium through a horizontal spray bar that runs the length of the tanks. The guard on the end of the inlet pipe to the filter prevents fishes and larger particles of dirt entering, which may block the system. Because of their proximity to the aquarium lights, the holes in the spray bar may become clogged with algae – clean them regularly. Isolating taps can be fitted in the inlet and return pipes and cleaning the filter will be safer and less messy if you turn these off. You should, in any case, be sure to switch off the electricity supply before removing the motor module from the top of the filter.*

To prevent back-siphoning of water to the air pump, all air-operated filters' air supplies should have an anti-siphon loop in them similar to that suggested for airstones (see Aeration, pages 20-1).

Some electrically driven power filters allow air into the returning water, but care should be taken not to let in too much air, in case the motor-impeller runs 'dry', resulting in rapid wear. The makers' instructions usually make this point quite clear.

In addition to having optional aeration facilities, the sophisticated power filters also allow water flow to be adjusted and for the motor to be cooled by the aquarium water (which also means a saving on the heating bill, as the motor's warmth heats the aquarium water all the time the filter is operating). Other designs permit the easy addition of extra filter modules as required; some filters can even be cleaned and the filter medium replaced without switching off or removing from the tank.

Because of the increased water flow capability of this type of filter, the returning water is usually distributed through a spray bar. Some fishes may not appreciate the turbulent conditions set up by such filters.

Whatever filter material is used, it should not be packed so tightly into the filter body that the flow of water is impeded. Usually a poor water flow back from a filter indicates that it needs cleaning! (Filter floss can be used again after washing out, so it is in your own interest not to let it get too dirty in the first place.)

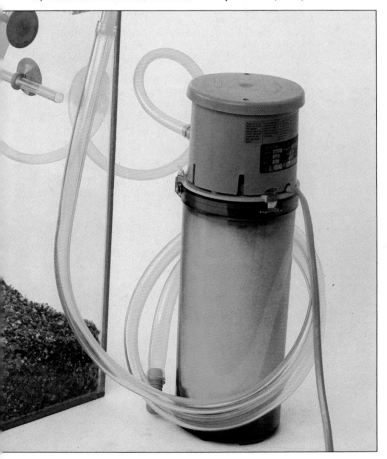

Tank furnishings

For the purposes of studying a fish's anatomy closely a small bare tank is ideal, but in order to study a fish's way of life with all its complexities of feeding, territorial possessiveness, breeding etc it is necessary for the fish to feel as at home in the aquarium as it would in its natural surroundings. Hence, the tank needs to be furnished with gravel, rocks and plants to provide the fish with shelter and a sense of security, for illogically the more retreats you offer a fish the less they seem to be used.

Gravel and rocks
One of the most reassuring environments a fish can have is a dark aquarium floor-covering; seen from above, the fish's dark top surface merges excellently with a dark background, whereas if light-coloured sand is used every fish is conspicuous. The usual gravel obtainable from aquarium dealers, of a dark to mid-brown/yellow

appearance, is quite suitable for a community collection. The particle size of 2-3mm (0.08-0.1in) is recommended, being neither too coarse (which would allow food to be trapped uneaten within its interstices) nor too fine (which would hamper plant root growth and also impede water flow through a biological filtration if this is fitted).

Many fishes, particularly nocturnal species, enjoy resting places, and rock caves provide ideal sanctuaries. In addition, rocks help to break up the uniformity of the aquarium, and by careful use of rocks different levels of gravel banks can be created and maintained. Only non-soluble, hard rocks with no evidence of metal ore-bearing veins should be used; limestones and calcareous rocks are not suitable. Slate, once any jagged edges have been removed, can be structured into layered outcrops (a dab of silicone adhesive will keep the desired shape in place), and if cave-

Below: *There is a wide range of natural and synthetic materials available with which to furnish the aquarium, some decorative and some functional for the fishes' needs.*

Right: *This furnished aquarium combines gravel, slate, synthetic logs and plastic plants to produce a striking and stable environment for its mixed population of fishes.*

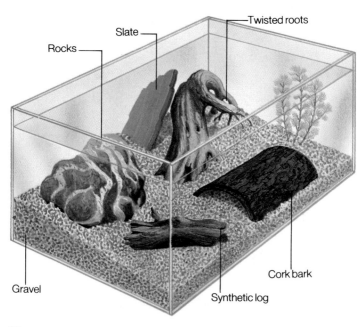

Twisted roots
Slate
Rocks
Gravel
Synthetic log
Cork bark

or rock-dwelling fishes are to be kept, this is an easy way to make sure that each fish has its own territory. To disguise the aquarium's boxiness the sides and rear walls can be covered with pieces of rock, again stuck on with silicone sealant. Another way to make the aquarium seem bigger is to build a rocky diorama which is fixed (and lit) behind the aquarium itself.

Other tank furnishings
Other fishes naturally inhabit reed-beds and areas where submerged tree roots offer refuge. Such conditions can be created within an aquarium by the use of wood and dead roots, preferably collected from a river bank where the waterlogging process has rendered them suitable for aquarium use. Any wood used in the aquarium must be free of decay and boiled in several changes of water before use; alternatively, wood can be given several coats of polyurethane varnish to seal it and prevent tannins from leaching out into the aquarium water.

Cork bark is another favourite aquarium decoration and can be shaped and cut easily. Natural-looking logs can be made from rolled cork, and can be persuaded not to float up by the use of a gravel-filled pipe or a base plate buried in the gravel on the aquarium floor.

Synthetic aquarium decorations may be easier to acquire than real logs, and these artificial but realistic-looking substitutes soon take on the appearance of the real thing as they become covered with living algae.

Decorating the aquarium is a compromise between the needs of the fishes and what satisfies your artistic needs; remember, you are trying to create a natural environment for the fishes rather than a work of art for yourself. However, if you put the fishes' requirements first, you will be even more pleased with the finished effect of your furnished aquarium. Only if the fishes are content can you expect success in fishkeeping.

Water

One of the attractions of keeping tropical freshwater fishes is the wide range of species available. Hardly any body of water anywhere in the world has escaped the collector's net, and supplies of fish are never more than a few hours away, thanks to modern air transport.

It follows that fishes come from many differing locations – streams, rivers, lakes, estuaries – and each location will have a different quality of water, in addition to whether it is flowing or static.

It says much for the hardiness and physical tolerance of aquarium fishes that, despite their various origins, most of them survive very well in the water we provide for them, usually from our domestic supply. To appreciate the fishes' problems, and to understand their requirements more fully so that we can provide suitable living conditions for them, we should take a little time to study water itself – the fishes' own 'atmosphere'.

The water cycle is the most important natural phenomenon on earth, regulating our weather and the growth of food crops. It has no starting or ending point but is a continuous process. For the purposes of our study, we can conveniently join the process at the sea, which covers nearly three quarters of the earth's surface. Water evaporating from the sea condenses into clouds, which deposit pure fresh water as rain over the land masses. This water then finds its way by rivers and underground percolation back to the sea, where the natural cycle begins again.

That is the bare bones of the story of water, but other conditions alter the purity of the water on its long journey back to the sea; as this journey will encompass the living areas of our freshwater fishes we shall follow it in a little more detail.

As rain water falls through the atmosphere it absorbs various salts and gases, and by the time it reaches ground level it is already fairly contaminated, generally being acidic in make-up. Its chemistry is further modified by the nature of the terrain on which the rain falls and over which the ground water subsequently flows.

Above: *The lakes of the Great Rift Valley in East Africa contain hard, alkaline water that supports unique populations of Cichlid fishes.*
Right: *A simplified representation of the natural water cycle. The rocks, terrain and vegetation all affect the final quality of fresh water. Rocks used as decoration will similarly affect aquarium water conditions.*

Water running across granite mountains will be quite different in composition from that seeping through chalk hills; water held in lakes in rocky basins will be different from that in rain-forest streams and rivers.

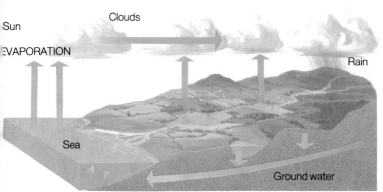

Sun

Clouds

EVAPORATION

Rain

Sea

Ground water

What is meant by 'different', and can it be measured? There are two types of differences, although they are often interrelated and often confused. They are *pH* and *hardness*.

The pH of water

The pH is simply a scale of values on which the relative acidity or alkalinity may be measured. The numbers on the pH scale (0-14) are logarithmic, so that an increase or decrease of pH 1 is in fact an increase or decrease of the power of 10. The pH 0 is the strongest acid and pH 14 is the strongest alkali.

The middle position, pH 7, is known as the neutral point, being neither acidic nor alkaline.

Fortunately, the range with which we are concerned is a relatively narrow one, between pH 6.6 and 7.5 for normal fishkeeping purposes. In nature, fishes can be found under more extreme conditions – from pH 5.5 (very acid, jungle streams with lots of decaying vegetation) to pH 9 (soda lakes in Africa's Rift Valley).

Water's pH is measured very easily with suitable test kits; these range from simple sensitized papers to elaborate electronic devices, and of course the accuracy is proportional to the cost! The middle-range liquid colour indicators are adequate for hobby purposes, and foolproof.

The manipulation of the water's pH, should it be thought necessary, is a complicated process involving knowledge of water chemistry to a degree impossible to explain here; it includes strict control of everything that may be put into the aquarium water, which may otherwise adversely affect the conditions so carefully created. This area of aquarium technology becomes more significant when attempting to breed those aquarium fishes generally considered to be 'difficult', which demand more attention to detail than the normal community collection.

There is a general relationship between the pH of water and its hardness. Acidic (lower than pH 7) water is usually soft, and alkaline (higher than pH 7) water is hard due to the amount of dissolved minerals.

The stability of pH in the aquarium is not constant and may vary from day to night as the plants' photosynthesis has effect. The water may be more acidic after periods of darkness, so it is a good practice to make any test of the water at the same time of day, and at the same water temperature. The differences in pH due to the natural activity of the aquarium's daily life will not be in excess of, say, 0.1 of a reading, but drastic changes of pH should be investigated – or, to put it the other way round, drastic alterations in fish behaviour or health may be due to changes in the pH. Make changes to water conditions slowly, to avoid stressing the fishes.

Below left: *This jungle stream in Sri Lanka is strongly acidic (pH below 7) because of the decaying vegetation that builds up in the water.*

Below: *This pH test kit uses liquid reagents. The colour change in the water sample is compared to a colour reference wheel to give a direct pH reading. The second phial compensates for water colour.*

Above: *Dissolved minerals, notably calcium and magnesium salts, make the water in Africa's Rift Valley lakes alkaline in nature. Fishes from such lakes like hard water.*

pH values

0 1 2 3 4 5 6 7 8 9 10 11 12 13 14

←—— Acid ——— | ——— Alkaline ——→

Neutral

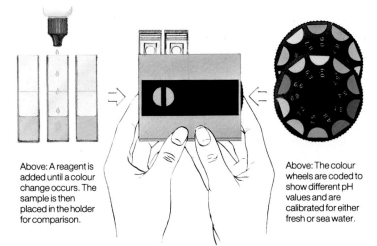

Above: A reagent is added until a colour change occurs. The sample is then placed in the holder for comparison.

Above: The colour wheels are coded to show different pH values and are calibrated for either fresh or sea water.

Hardness

Thanks to washing powder and detergent advertising, people are more conversant with water's other characteristic, hardness. Due to dissolved salts (usually of calcium and magnesium) hardness is of two types: temporary, and permanent. The temporary hardness may be removed by boiling, when the soluble calcium bicarbonate is deposited as calcium carbonate, the 'scale' in kettles. Permanent hardness can be removed only by chemical means, by ion exchange, or by distillation. Hardness as a whole can be reduced by dilution, using any known softer water in correct proportions to arrive at the required hardness figure. The calculations are simple: diluting 5 litres of hard water (12 degrees of hardness) with 5 litres of soft water, such as unpolluted rain water (0 degrees), will give 10 litres of water of 6 degrees of hardness.

Hardness can be added to any soft water by including pieces of chalk or limestone in the aquarium decoration, and (as we have already seen) the composition of the aquarium gravel may also harden the water (see Gravel and rocks, page 30).

Test kits are available for assessing water hardness; as with determining pH, a simple colour change process occurring in the sample of water to be tested gives an accurate figure.

A slight confusion may arise, because there are several different ways of measuring hardness, and

Above: *The Discus, or Pompadour, Fish needs soft, bacteria-free water, particularly when breeding.*

figures quoted in aquatic books may be from any system. The German fishkeeper measures general (or total) hardness in °GH, and carbonate hardness in °DH. (Hardness due to non-carbonates is calculated by subtracting °DH from °GH). English fishkeepers measure hardness by parts per million of calcium carbonate in water, and the figure is known as °Clarke. To add to the confusion, the German °DH is calculated on the amount of calcium oxide (in milligrams) in one litre of water.

Hardness can sometimes be reduced by using peat moss in the aquarium filter. Garden peat, to which chemicals may have been added, should not be used; natural sphagnum moss is recommended. Using peat will also tend to acidify the water (lower the pH) and such measures are often used by fishkeepers specializing in Egglaying Toothcarps (see pages 158-165).

Below: Labeotropheus trewavasae *is a colourful cichlid from the hard waters of Lake Malawi in Africa.*

Use of domestic supply water

Although water from the tap is primarily produced for human consumption, it is normally quite suitable for aquarium use provided one or two precautions are taken. Water that has been standing in copper pipes (particularly newly installed pipework) may be toxic to fishes, so let the tap run for a few minutes before using any water from it. Heavily chlorinated water should be strongly aerated to disperse the chlorine before the fishes are introduced. Some aquarists add dechlorinating additives, and the manufacturer's instructions should be closely followed for these.

The apparent problem of our fishes' needs for different water conditions can be put into perspective by realizing that many of our fishes do not come from where we think they do! Many are aquarium bred in commercial quantities, thousands of miles from their native homes. Added to this, the fishes at your local aquatic store will have been kept in similar water conditions to yours, before you buy them. A responsible dealer will give you all the information you need on the water conditions needed for his stock if this is different from the local supply.

Filling the aquarium

The aquarium, with gravel, rocks and any other tank decorations in place, and fitted with UNCONNECTED heating and filtration equipment, is now ready to be filled with water.

To prevent the water from destroying the contours of the gravel and washing away rock formations, take care when filling. A small jug or saucer standing on the aquarium gravel can break the force of the jet of water out of the hosepipe; the overflow will gently fill the aquarium.

Fill the tank to half way with cold water, then add warm water to bring the level up to three quarters full for planting. Water with the chill taken off will not shock the plants (or your hands) too much.

After planting, fill the tank with more warm water so that no waterline is showing below the tank frame or decorative trim. Any film of dirt on the water surface can be removed by drawing a lightweight sheet of paper slowly across the surface.

Below: *You can avoid disturbing your carefully contoured gravel when filling the aquarium by using a jar or saucer to break the initial force of the water. Alternatively, you can direct the water on to the surface of a large rock, which will have the same effect. However, you should ensure that the water pressure is not too high when you are filling up the tank or you run the risk of splashing water everywhere.*

Aquarium plants

Aquarium plants are available in many forms and contrasting shades. They look nice, and we have already discussed the important role they play in keeping the aquarium healthy; and plants also provide shade, refuge, spawning sites and (in some cases) food for the fishes.

The choice of plants is almost as wide as that of fishes. Plants can be selected to occupy different areas of the tank, from floating plants on the water surface to aquarium floor-covering miniature grasses. Leaf forms may be strap-like, feathery, or broad. Colours range from light to dark green, and some leaves have reddish purple undersides. Flowers in the aquarium are not rare either, and you can obtain seeds from certain species of plants, from which to grow fresh stock.

Most aquatic plants conform to the conventional idea of plants: a root system, above which grows the stalk and leaves. However, not all aquarium plants are rooted in the gravel, and many of those that are can also obtain nourishment directly from the water through their leaves. Some species cling to the surface of roots and submerged logs, but others have no fixed location, freely floating on the water surface, their trailing hair-like roots providing a sanctuary for tiny fishes.

Being totally submerged, the majority of aquatic plants reproduce by sending out runners or developing daughter plants on existing leaves. Many of the bushy, feathery-leaved plants can be multiplied by means of cuttings, where a top portion of the plant is removed and re-rooted in the

Right: *The diagonal arrangement of these plants of various colour and shape creates a sense of perspective.*

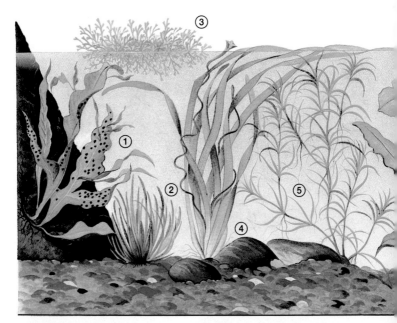

1 Microsorium pteropus
The rootstock clings to logs and rocks. Thrives in any light conditions.
2 Acorus gramineus var pusillus
Grows slowly in the aquarium. Prefers cool water conditions. A good choice as a foreground plant in the aquarium.

3 Riccia fluitans
Ideal for shading the aquarium and as a fry refuge. Some fish eat it.
4 Vallisneria natans
Excellent as a background plant.
5 Najas guadalupensis
Dense clumps ideal for spawning.

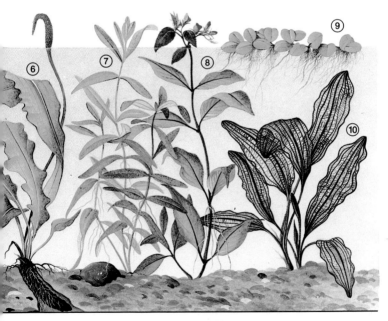

6 Aponogeton crispus
Grows from a rhizome. Will flower above the surface. Cool rest in winter.
7 Hygrophila polysperma
Fast growing. Easily propagated.
8 Nomaphila stricta
For hard water. May be eaten by snails.

9 Salvinia natans
Trailing roots provide excellent shelter for fry. Spreads quickly on surface.
10 Aponogeton madagascariensis
Needs bright light, water changes and a rest period to grow well.

gravel to grow as a new independent plant. Some species will develop roots from a single severed leaf, which will also provide a new plant.

When planting the aquarium, try to disguise the boxiness of the tank; careful planting can create an illusion of continuing space within the four walls of the aquarium. However, creating space is not done by planting regimented avenues of single plants in the manner of orchard trees. Plants should be grown in species clumps as they would occur in nature.

The mature aquarium should be capable of sustaining plant growth with nutrients generated within itself. A newly set-up tank can be given encouragement by providing additional liquid plant-food, by planting the plants in special nutrient-rich preformed plugs, or by adding peat, loam or clay to the aquarium gravel. Any such additions should be treated with caution, particularly by the newcomer, as early experiments in underwater horticulture do not always bring the hoped-for success.

The shape of a plant dictates its use in the aquarium. Tall, grassy plants such as *Vallisneria* and *Sagittaria* are ideal for the back and sides of the tank; even if the leaves grow taller than the water depth, their progress across the surface of the water brings shade to the fishes.

Bushy plants can be used to fill in corners and gaps between rocky outcrops. Cuttings taken from such plants encourage the original plant to develop more side-shoots. Typical species include water wisteria (*Synnema triflorum*, also known as *Hygrophila difformis*), *Hygrophila polysperma*, *Nomaphila stricta*, *Cabomba caroliniana*, *Ceratophyllum demersum*, *Ludwigia repens* and *Ceratopteris thalictroides*.

1 Sagittaria subulata
Popular plant; similar to Vallisneria.
2 Pistia stratiotes
The roots give shelter for young fish.
3 Hygrophila difformis
Leaves vary in shape depending on the strength of lighting. Roots easily.

4 Echinodorus bleheri
Very popular as a specimen plant. Plantlets form on long runners.
5 Cabomba caroliniana
Widely grown. An excellent spawning medium. Needs clean water to keep leaves sediment free. Roots easily.

Above: *The fishes and plants in this aquarium have been carefully chosen to contrast and complement each other. Note how the red of the fishes* at top centre reflects the colour of the plants at bottom left. The silvery shapes of the other fishes add sharp brilliance and movement to the scene.

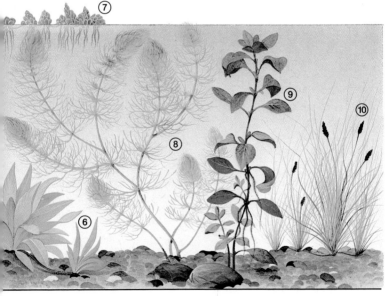

6 Echinodorus magdalenensis
An ideal foreground plant. Sends out many runners bearing young plants.
7 Azolla caroliniana
Floating plant with velvety leaves, often red-tinged. Provides a shady haven for young fishes. Shown raised.

8 Ceratophyllum demersum
Shown rooted but usually grows in a floating tangle. Grow from cuttings.
9 Ludwigia repens
A superb plant for bright aquariums.
10 Eleocharis acicularis
Interesting form; needs good light.

The floor of the aquarium can benefit from generous plantings of miniature species of *Cryptocoryne*, and larger varieties look well in front of rocks. There is no need to worry about these bottom-hugging plants being starved of light by their loftier neighbours, as they are quite used to lower light levels.

For spectacular specimen plants – often rivalling the fish for popularity – members of the *Echinodorus* and *Aponogeton* families are hard to beat. Such plants may be rooted in miniature flowerpots sunk in the gravel, where they can be pampered if necessary, as befits the 'stars' of the plant population.

Azolla, Riccia and *Salvinia* are all floating species of minute proportions, whereas *Pistia* is very large, often finding the cramped space beneath the hood rather limiting to its ambitious growth.

Above: *This preformed plant-plug will get specimen plants off to a good start. Bury plug in the aquarium gravel.*

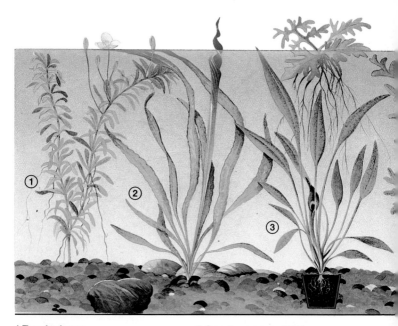

1 Egeria densa
Grows best in hard water. Absorbs nourishment through the leaves.
2 Cryptocoryne balansae
Long leaves make it ideal for a deep tank. Flowers above the surface in shallow water. Spreads by runners.

3 Cryptocoryne willisii
Variable in size. An extremely useful foreground plant shown here pot-planted, which allows it to be transplanted without disturbance. Will grow in shady locations and can be planted beneath taller plants.

Above: A lavishly furnished and stocked aquarium combining a wide range of fishes and plants from various tropical regions. Such 'aquascaping' is one of the many pursuits fishkeepers can enjoy.

4 Ceratopteris thalictroides
Can be grown rooted or as a floating subject with long trailing roots. A vigorous plant that thrives in warm brightly lit conditions, producing daughter plants on the surface of the leaves. Must be kept in check.

5 Cryptocoryne wendtii
Adaptable aquarium plant. Colour varies from one plant to another.

6 Vesicularia dubyana
A clinging moss with tiny leaves on long stems. Grow in good light and keep it clear of sediment and algae.

Planting

Planting is best done with the aquarium only three quarters filled with water (to avoid overflowing with water displaced by your hands and arms). Another advantage of this over planting the aquarium dry is that the plants take up their natural positions in the water and the effects of planting can be seen immediately.

Before planting, rinse each plant thoroughly, and inspect for snails' eggs, beetles or any other unwanted passengers. Species of plants can be laid out together in groups between layers of wet newspaper until required. Remove any dead leaves and trim back overlong roots.

Rooted species should be planted in the gravel so that the crown of the plant (the junction between roots and stem/leaves) is just above the gravel. Many plants take time to assume their

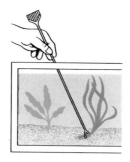

growing attitude and a few hours of tank-light may be needed before all the plants have finalized their positions. Clumps of cuttings may be anchored or weighted down with thin strips of lead twisted around the lower stems. Take care not to crush the stems when attaching the lead strips; bruising can be caused.

Some species of plants appear to be incompatible when grown together or expected to share the same tank. This is not surprising, for the plants come from many different localities and water conditions around the world. If you find that this is the case, a study of the plants' original habitats will enable you to select the species that should do well together.

Often biological filtration is blamed for poor plant growth, but this has not been conclusively proved. Usually a too shallow depth of gravel over the filter plate is the reason, and the simple remedy is deeper gravel.

Left: *Using a planting stick.*
Below: *Methods of propagation. Young plants developed on runners from the parent plant will self-root naturally or can be separated and replanted by hand. Take cuttings from the tops of bushy species, remove a few bottom leaves and replant in the gravel.*

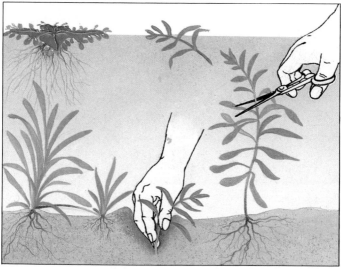

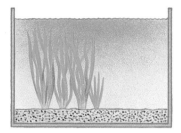

Background fillers

Sagittaria, Vallisneria. Tough leaves. Propagate by runners. These plants sometimes produce flowers.
Types of fish: *Angelfish, Gouramies, Cichlids, Headstanders, Killifish.*
Spawning value: *Negligible as sites, but these plants will provide a refuge for the female to escape the aggressive attentions of the male.*

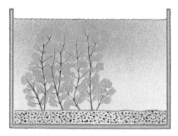

Space and corner fillers

Ambulia, Cabomba, Ceratophyllum, Egeria, Vesicularia. Soft leaves; may be browsed upon by some fishes. Can be propagated by cuttings.
Types of fish: *Barbs, Characins and Rasboras (except vegetarian ones).*
Spawning value: *Excellent aquarium plants for egg-scattering species and for some of the Killifishes.*

Specimen plants

Aponogeton, larger Cryptocorynes, Echinodorus. Tough leaves. Propagate by runners, division or, in some cases, from setting seed.
Types of fish: *All species.*
Spawning value: *Useful aquarium plants for some Cichlids, Rasboras and other species that deposit eggs on or under plant leaves.*

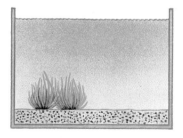

Low-level plants

Acorus, smaller Cryptocorynes, Microsorium. Tough leaves. Propagate by runners or division.
Types of fish: *Botia, the dwarf Cichlids, Corydoras.*
Spawning value: *Although these types of plants are of little value as spawning sites they may provide refuges for females or young fry.*

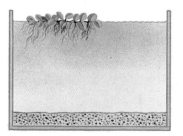

Floating plants

Azolla, Lemna, Pistia, Salvinia. Leaves floating above the surface; roots trailing down into the water.
Types of fish: *Danios, Gouramies, Killifishes, Live-bearers.*
Spawning value: *Often used in the construction of bubble-nests by Gouramies. Provide refuges for fry, especially newly born live-bearers.*

Starting up and running in

To complete the setting up, the heating, lighting, aeration and filtration equipment require final power connections to be made, but leave the moment of switching on until last. A convenient order of operations would be as follows.

Filters
External filters should be packed with layers of filter floss and activated carbon (see page 22). External filters should be filled with water by siphon action. The siphon inlet tube should be submerged until filled with water; a finger or starting stick prevents air from entering the top (short) end while the pipe is positioned over the tank edge into the filter box (keep the lower end of the siphon tube under water all this time). Remove your finger or starting stick, and water will flow into the filter box and stop automatically when the level of water rises to the same as that in the tank.

External canister-type power filters may be primed by a strong suck at their output pipe; when water flows out of this pipe, reconnect the flow pipe back to the aquarium.

Internal filters are self-priming and only need connecting to an air supply or electrical point in order to start.

Biological filters will already have their airlines connected when fitted.

Air pump
The airline from the pump should be connected to one end of the ganged control valve. Individual airlines are then connected from the control valve outlets to the airstone (if fitted) and to the air-operated filters, making sure that, if the air pump is not situated above the water level, the airline is looped above the water level for a few centimetres (see the anti-syphon loop described on page 21).

Right: *This schematic drawing shows how an air pump should be connected to a ganged control valve, which then supplies air to various pieces of equipment in the tank. The check valve and anti-siphon loop in the plastic tubing both act to prevent back-siphoning of water into the pump should the electricity supply accidentally switch off or fail.*

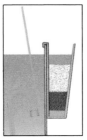
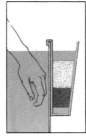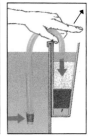

Above: *Priming filters.* Top: *Use a starting stick over the top end of the inlet tube with the bottom end still submerged.* Centre: *A finger does the same.* Bottom: *Prime power filters with water, then fix return hose.*

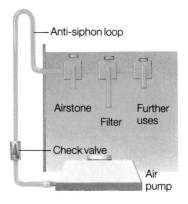

Anti-siphon loop

Airstone

Filter

Further uses

Check valve

Air pump

46

Thermometers

Fix the thermometer in a conveniently visible position (liquid crystal types are fitted to the glass externally).

Electrical connections

The supply wires to the air pump, electrically powered filter (if fitted), lighting and thermostat can now be connected to their respective terminals in the junction box or cable tidy. Note that the thermostat terminal connection is not switched whereas the air pump, lighting and other spare terminals can be switched. (The thermostat circuit must be live at all times, to maintain the heating circuit.) The wire from the separate heater is joined to the thermostat independently of the cable tidy; a combined heater/thermostat unit is wired directly to the cable tidy.

When all is finished within the tank, fit the cover glass and put the reflector/hood in place. Check that all electrical fittings are secure and watertight, and that tungsten lamps and/or fluorescent tube are fitted.

The supply wire to the cable tidy can now be connected to the mains supply and the power switched on. Hopefully, everything works!

Above, from left to right: *A dial-type thermometer that sticks to the inside glass. A conventional type attached to the inside glass by a rubber sucker. A flat liquid crystal type stuck on the outside surface of the tank. A colour change shows the temperature.*

Below: *A close-up of the cable tidy that acts as junction box for the electrical connections to aquarium equipment. Two switches and a neon warning light can be seen. The thermostat circuit is not switched but accessories' circuits may be.*

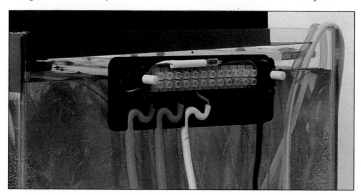

Operation

The heater circuit can be checked visually; the neon light in the cable tidy will glow as a warning that the electricity supply is connected. Neon lamps fitted to thermostats may show different information according to design. Refer to the manufacturer's instructions. If something is wrong, disconnect the power supply before investigating. Should the lights, air pump or power filter not operate, check that the switch on the cable tidy is not in the 'off' position.

If the air pump is servicing airstones and filters, or maybe an external filter and an internal biological filter, it is often the case that one will work and not the other. In this event, adjust the valves controlling the air supply to each device until a balance occurs and each piece of air-operated equipment functions correctly.

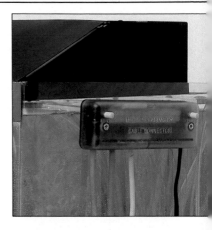

Above: *A neon lamp glows through the cover of the 'cable tidy' junction box to clearly indicate that the mains electricity supply is 'on'. Switch off supply before removing the cover.*

Very often external power filters do not pump water immediately. This is normally due to an air lock in the system, usually at the top of the filter body. A gentle shake usually persuades the trapped air to escape up the return pipe and the water flow commences quite readily.

Running in
It will be some time before the aquarium settles down. The biological filter will take time to mature its colony of bacteria (see page 28), and ihe plants also need time to become established. A few hardy fishes may be introduced, to provide waste ammonia for the bacteria to get started on, and to provide interest for you while you wait!

After a few days the plants will have taken up their normal attitudes and the water temperature will have stabilized. If no fishes have been introduced, the aquarium should be operated normally with the lighting hours observed just as if fishes were present. Of course, no food needs to be added until fishes are introduced.

Don't judge fishkeeping by your experiences in the first few weeks – you and your aquarium need to get to know each other, but the fun and real enjoyment is in the learning.

Below left: A cover glass protects the light fittings from condensation and prevents plant leaves from being scorched. You will need to ensure that it is kept scrupulously clean.

Below: These handy hints will help you through any early 'teething troubles'. Refer to the table on page 56 for a checklist of practical maintenance tasks.

PRACTICAL HINTS

Filters A tank stocked with large fishes with hearty appetites will need heavier filtration than one with small decorative tetras.

Don't pack the filter medium too tightly; it will restrict waterflow.

Airpump Mount the pump above the water level or fit a 'non-return' valve and/or an 'anti-siphon loop' (see page 21) in the airline. This will prevent water siphoning into the airpump.

Thermometer Mount thermometers where you can see them easily. External liquid-crystal types can be affected by ambient room temperatures and direct sunlight, and may give false readings.

Electrical connections Use a cable-tidy for safe, neat connections.

DO NOT switch on the power until the equipment is set up.

NEVER switch on the heater unless it is submerged in water.

ALWAYS switch off the electrical supply when making adjustments.

Operation Adjust the relevant air valves to balance the airflow to each piece of aquarium apparatus; excessive airflow through the filter airlifts only results in extra noise. A fairly slow stream of regularly ascending bubbles will be quite adequate.

Clear airlocks in power filter systems by gently rocking the filter.

Check that the heater is functioning by observing the neon indicator in the thermostat body.

Running in Let the aquarium function for at least two to three weeks before you add the fishes. This allows plants to root and the biological filter bed to develop. Add fishes gradually over a period of months so that the filterbed is not suddenly overloaded.

Introducing the fishes

Having carefully provided the ideal environment for the fishes, you owe it to them (and your own chances of success) to select the very best healthy stock, in correct numbers. This is not just a matter of calculating the theoretical numbers to suit the tank's fish-carrying capacity, but also involves purchasing a reasonable number (say six or more) of a species of fish that naturally lives in a shoal. Similarly, the total 'population' should be sub-divided into groups of fishes that occupy top, middle and lower levels of the aquarium water, thus ensuring that all the tank space is utilized, to give maximum room for the fish and maximum enjoyment for you as a 'viewer'.

When assessing a possible purchase, reject without hesitation any fish that:

1 cannot swim effortlessly, or maintain a steady position in the water.
2 has a very thin cross-section or a hollow belly.
3 has folded-down, split or frayed fins.
4 has obvious pimples, spots, wounds or other body damage.
5 is not eating regularly. (Ask the dealer; being *given* food regularly is not the same thing.)
6 has not been quarantined, or comes from a dubious source.
7 is of an extreme size, small or large, compared to its intended tankmates. (One may either eat, or be eaten by, the other.)
8 is very expensive, until you are sure that you can keep it successfully; it may need special conditions.

The change from shop tank to your tank is a traumatic experience for the fish, and it is therefore necessary to make this changeover as gentle a process as possible.

By the time the journey is completed there may be a difference in temperature between the water that the fish is in and the water in your aquarium. The bag or jar containing the new purchase should be floated in the aquarium until the water temperatures are equal, at which time the fish can be released. A recent school of thought prefers all new fishes to be transferred to an open jar before floating to equalize temperatures, as prolonged imprisonment in a plastic bag may cause a build-up of toxic gases. One advantage of using an open jar (or even an open plastic bag) is that increasing amounts of aquarium water may be added progressively during the floating period to acclimatize the fish to the quality, as well as the temperature, of the aquarium water. A special floating tank that allows gradual mixing of aquarium water to the fish's transit water is commercially available.

Many fishkeepers switch off the aquarium lighting when introducing new fishes, and even give the existing tenants a pinch or two of food to take their minds off the newcomers.

Below: *Floating the fishes' carry home plastic bag in the aquarium restores their water temperature to the correct level before they are released.*

Below: *After 15-20 minutes the fish can be released. Give the existing inmates of the aquarium some food to take their minds off the newcomers.*

This selection of fishes would be suitable for a mixed community aquarium. They will make use of all levels in the tank and provide a variety of shape and colour. Avoid mixing boisterous and timid fishes.

Above: *When selecting fishes for your aquarium from the bewildering display at your local dealer's, you should always look for healthy, sociable stock. If you are in doubt, ask your dealer for advice.*

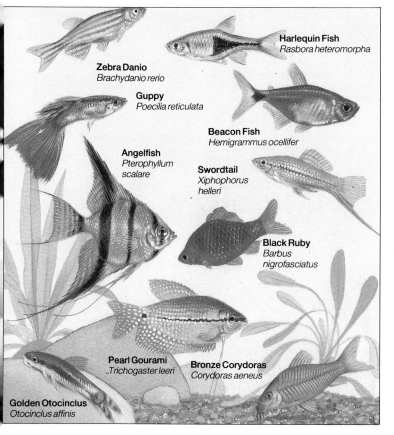

Harlequin Fish
Rasbora heteromorpha

Zebra Danio
Brachydanio rerio

Guppy
Poecilia reticulata

Beacon Fish
Hemigrammus ocellifer

Angelfish
Pterophyllum scalare

Swordtail
Xiphophorus helleri

Black Ruby
Barbus nigrofasciatus

Pearl Gourami
Trichogaster leeri

Bronze Corydoras
Corydoras aeneus

Golden Otocinclus
Otocinclus affinis

Feeding

Thanks to years of research and development, fishes in captivity are probably better fed than their relatives in the wild, and do not have to expend half as much energy in getting their food. Aquarium fishes receive their food by courtesy of the fishkeeper, and the responsibility for the quantity and quality of the food is entirely his. A fully varied diet is as necessary for, and appreciated by, the fishes as it would be for us, and such a diet ensures that they receive all the proteins and vitamins they require, which might be lacking in a more restricted diet.

In understanding fishes' dietary needs, we should also take note of how each species takes its food and from what position in the water. Surface swimmers use their upturned mouths almost like a scoop, their forward movement forcing food into their mouths as they patrol just beneath the surface. Fishes with terminal mouths may well snatch their food from the surface in isolated dashes but generally food is taken (often greedily) as it sinks through the water. An underslung mouth is best for foraging around the aquarium floor or for browsing on algae-covered rocks or aquarium glass.

With these feeding habits in mind

(and there will be some of each within the community collection) it will be quickly appreciated that no one food will suit all fishes. A floating food will never reach the bottom-dwelling fishes, and a rapidly sinking food will be lost to surface swimmers. A compromise can be easily reached by using different types of food – flake, granular or tablet – spread between the different feeding times. It is no use giving one heavy feed of all types of food and hope the fishes will somehow sort it all out and even save some for later.

Now is the time to learn probably the most important basic rule in fishkeeping: DO NOT OVERFEED.

Manufactured foods

The majority of food given is manufactured, not living, although we shall be looking at live foods shortly. Manufactured foods have one drawback among their many excellent advantages; they

Below: *These vivid male Guppies are feeding from a freeze-dried Tubifex cube stuck to the aquarium glass. Use more cubes (stuck at any depth) for a larger population of fishes. Other types of freeze-dried foods are available to supplement their diet.*

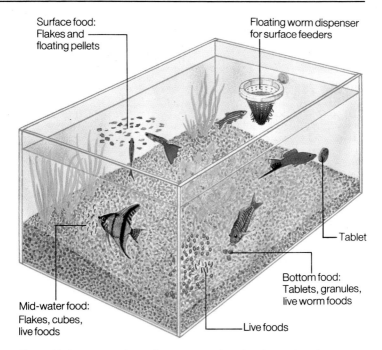

Surface food:
Flakes and
floating pellets

Floating worm dispenser
for surface feeders

Tablet

Bottom food:
Tablets, granules,
live worm foods

Live foods

Mid-water food:
Flakes, cubes,
live foods

Above: *Various types of aquarium foods have been developed to suit feeding habits of different fishes. Flake foods float for a short time before sinking slowly. Pellets do not sink. Freeze-dried cubes can be* stuck to the glass or kept in weighted plastic baskets for bottom feeders. Floating worm dispensers can be used to provide a supply of live worms (Tubifex) at the water surface for the top-swimming fishes.

decompose in water if left uneaten. This decomposition leads to pollution of the aquarium water, which will eventually kill the fishes. Fishes should be given only as much food as they willingly eat in 3-4 minutes, and this amount is very small. It is better to give little and reasonably often, and a hungry fish is always healthily on the lookout for food.

Feeds are usually given at the convenient times of morning and early evening to coincide with the fishkeeper's visits to the aquarium before and after the working day. A little more food, last thing at night, of a suitably fast-falling variety, will provide an almost exclusive meal for nocturnal bottom-dwelling fishes. Incidentally, all fishes should be treated as equals. Many bottom dwellers are kept in the belief that they will tidy up the aquarium floor, and this they will do, but they should also be

considered worthy of having food given especially for them.

Live foods
So far, we have discussed manufactured foods but obviously fishes in the wild are more used to taking living food – insects, waterborne crustaceans, larvae and smaller fishes. Aquarium fishes may also be given live foods and these fall into two groups, those that are naturally aquatic and those that are not, such as earthworms.

Aquatic-living foods include the water-flea, *Daphnia*, mosquito or gnat larvae, *Tubifex* worms and numerous other tiny inhabitants of pond or rainbutt. Any wild-caught live foods should be carefully checked for unwanted 'visitors' among their numbers before being put into the aquarium. Larvae of the dragonfly, water boatman, great diving beetles, leeches and, of course, snails should be looked for and removed. There is also a danger that living food caught from fish-populated waters may also carry fish diseases.

Non-aquatic live foods include a number of worms of the Enchytreidae family. These range in size from tiny hair's-breadth proportions up to stout thread size; known to fishkeepers as micro-worms, grindal worms and white worms (in ascending size order) they can be cultured in boxes and fed usually on cereal-based foods. As one culture nears the end of its useful life (your nose will tell you when!) a new culture can be started with a seeding of worms from the preceding culture.

Earthworms (small ones whole, or large ones chopped up!) are relished by fishes. Earthworms are best collected from beneath a damp sack laid in a corner of the garden, or from a compost heap. Do not use worms collected from any part of the garden which has been treated with weedkiller or other garden chemicals.

Cultures of wingless fruit flies (*Drosophila*) make good food and are snapped up as they float on the surface. Supplies of this food may sometimes be difficult to obtain, but usually a member of the local aquarist society will have a culture or know the whereabouts of one.

Some aquarium dealers sell live *Mysis* shrimps, which provide an occasional treat for your fishes.

Modern technology has also developed an alternative means of preserving fish food – freeze-drying. In this way, live foods can be collected on a large scale and freeze-dried, and thus their inherent nutritious content can be given to the aquarium fishes whenever convenient, and not be restricted to seasonal catches. Just what advantages are lost by the fact that the freeze-dried foods are dead has not been discovered, as the fishes cannot tell us whether or not they prefer the real (living) thing.

Another source of food is the kitchen. Fishes will take all manner of household scraps including raw lean meat, peas, lettuce, spinach, pieces of raw fish, cod's roe, potato, cheese etc. Introduce new foods gradually to

Above: *The worm dispenser is best fixed in position by a rubber sucker rather than allowed to drift around the surface of the aquarium. Use one in tanks that do not contain bottom feeders to dispense worms conveniently and prevent pollution should the worms die in the gravel.*

Above: *The top part of the worm dispenser can be used independently as a feeding ring to keep floating foods conveniently in one place. Alternatively, you can make a feeding ring quite simply using a circle of airline tubing sealed with aquarium silicone sealant.*

your fishes; try them first on hungry fish. Avoid all fatty foods. Remove any uneaten food; chunky foods can be dangled in the aquarium on a piece of thread for easy removal.

Foods for young fishes
Feeding newly born fishes used to be a messy and smelly business. Cultures of microscopic life (*Infusoria*) were encouraged by pouring boiling water over such things as chopped hay, crushed lettuce leaves, banana or potato skins etc. The resulting liquid was then supposed to burst into life with teeming millions of

Left: *Whiteworms can be cultured in a ventilated box of good moist soil with cereal or bread as food. Different types of worm require different culturing temperatures: whiteworms need cooler conditions than Grindalworms, for example.*

Right: *Separate the worms from the food and soil in some water. Only feed clean worms to the fishes.*

Below: *Hatching brine shrimps. The dry eggs (1) should be added to a solution of sea salt and agitated by an airstone (2) until hatching occurs. The live shrimps (3) should be strained through a net (4) and further rinsed with fresh water before being used as a food. The salt water can then be used again to hatch more eggs.*

infusoria after a day or two's exposure to air and sunlight (a kitchen window ledge was a favourite advocated position). All that most fishkeepers got was the smell and a talking to by other members of the family! Nowadays, young fishes can be well catered for by both manufactured and live foods.

Manufactured foods are formulated in liquid, paste and powdered forms, for egg-laying or live-bearing young fishes. Food for young fishes should not be given until they are free-swimming (see Breeding, page 76) and can take the food, otherwise pollution occurs.

The best live food, especially for tiny fishes, is the newly hatched nauplii of the brine shrimp *Artemia*

salina. Eggs of the brine shrimp can be stored indefinitely in a dry state, and when immersed in a saltwater solution (30gm/litre or 5oz/gallon sea-salt crystals) will produce tiny baby shrimps, which can be fed to young fishes. Again, progressive cultures should be made of these, to ensure a continuous supply of this nutritious, disease-free first food. The nauplii can be raised to bigger sizes for feeding to larger fishes; the food used to do this is normally yeast-based and convenient to handle. Research into improving methods of rearing brine shrimp has led, in recent years, to the eggshells being stripped before storage (in liquid). This process is thought to result in better hatchings.

Maintenance

The claim was made at the beginning of this book that relatively small effort need be exerted by the fishkeeper to maintain an aquarium in good health. Having the aquarium furnished with the first fishes swimming around is only a start, but what may be seen as chores are not too arduous.

Fish watching becomes addictive, but you should watch with a purpose as well as for pleasure. At feeding time, do a spot check on the number of fishes. Any repeated absentee should be searched for; it may be a normally nocturnal species having a sleep during the hours of 'tanklight', but the cause may be more serious. A dead fish undetected will pollute the tank and, if diseased, may posthumously infect the rest of the tank's inmates.

Water temperature can be monitored with a glance at the conveniently placed thermometer, although you will soon become expert at knowing the water temperature by the touch of your hand on the front glass.

Plants may need attention, too; remove dead leaves, prune the more rampant species, and start new plants from the cuttings. Specimen plants may be given regular food tablets to promote healthy growth.

MAINTENANCE CHECK	Daily	Weekly	Monthly	Periodically
Check water temperature and number of fishes	●	●	●	●
Water condition Check pH				●
Partial change of water			●	
Filters Box filter: Clean and replace medium according to amount of use and state of aquarium				●
Undergravel filter: Rake the aquarium gravel gently				●
Plants Remove dead leaves and excess sediment on leaves; thin out floating plants		●	●	●
Prune; replant cuttings and runners as necessary		●	●	●
General Check air supply carefully; clean air pump valves and air pump filter				●
Clean cover glass				●
Remove algae from front glass of aquarium				●
Check fishes for symptoms of diseases				●

Note: If your fishes start to behave oddly, it may be worth checking over the tasks outlined above – regular aquarium maintenance can keep them healthy. Any neglect on your part will eventually lead to problems.

Water conditions are kept stable by regular partial water changes, 10-20% being replaced every 2-3 weeks. Tests to check pH and hardness levels are not obligatory but should be made if sudden fish losses occur for any unexplained reason. When you set up an aquarium for breeding purposes, attention to water conditions may be more vital.

Any growth of algae on the front glass should be removed, but not those on the rear and side walls of the aquarium; vegetarian fishes will do this job for you and benefit into the bargain.

The sudden switching off or on of the aquarium lights may shock some fishes, which often dash about aimlessly in the tank as a result. Short of fitting dimmer controls, the best way of avoiding this risk is to leave the room light on for a few minutes after switching the aquarium lights off. Similarly, switch the room lights on for a few minutes (unless daylight is present) before switching the tank lights on again in the morning.

Keep cover glasses scrupulously clean, and replace any defective lamps. Filter medium replacement should be a regular, unneglected commitment. When servicing external power filters, pay particular attention to the secureness of the hose connections. Filters on air pumps and in airlines should also receive regular attention. Blocked airstones should be replaced, although sometimes boiling them cleans them out again.

The behaviour of the fishes, although not quite so relevant in a maintenance scheme, should also be noted. Transfer any ailing fish at once to a hospital tank (and make sure the tank components are serviceable, too). This hospital/quarantine tank can also be on standby to act as a breeding tank if fishes show signs of courtship behaviour.

The accompanying table gives a guide to the normal maintenance schedule. Itemized operations may be omitted or re-scheduled according to your particular set-up of aquarium equipment and the type of fishes that you keep. Remember, the fishes depend on you!

Useful equipment

Servicing an aquarium can almost be done with the bare hands, but there are implements available which make some routine jobs easier, quicker and a lot less messy – a siphon tube and bucket are essential!

Items used when setting up the aquarium will be of use also during the normal maintenance of the aquarium.

Planting sticks, despite their name, seem to be of more use *after* the tank has been planted and become established. During the original planting, it always seems easier to use one's fingers, probably because clumps, and not many individual plants, are being put into position.

Above: *The simplest way to make partial water changes is to siphon water from the floor of the aquarium using a length of tubing; detritus is removed at the same time.*

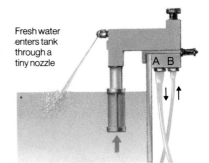

Fresh water enters tank through a tiny nozzle

A B

Above: *An automatic water changer that works by water pressure alone. Fresh water (B) enters via a nozzle as a preset amount of old water (A) drains; the level remains constant.*

Later on, however, the thin planting stick is more easily used in a thickly planted tank, where bulkier fingers might do more damage. Some planting sticks double as algae-scrapers, having a razor blade fixture at the other end. (A razor blade is always useful – for cutting airline to length, chopping up meaty foods, trimming plant roots, etc. – and it is handy to know where one is to be found for these jobs.)

The hose that was used to fill the tank can equally be used to empty some of the water out during partial water changes. This water should be drawn from the floor of the aquarium, so that any detritus is removed at the same time. Detritus can also be removed by the use of what can only be described as an aquarium vacuum-cleaner – an air-lift device (operated from the aquarium air pump) which discharges into a cloth bag where the dirt is trapped, the water running through back into the aquarium.

Nets of various sizes will also be needed. Square-shaped nets, with cranked handles, make the capture of obstinate fishes simpler, particularly when they flee into the corner of the aquarium and refuse to budge. Often the combined use of two nets (the larger one held stationary) brings better results. Fish nets should be made of soft material, which can be silk (for small nets for very young fishes), muslin (for catching live foods), or the more usual netting material found on commercially available fish nets. A widely opened plastic bag (invisible under water) is used by many fishkeepers to capture large fishes without damaging their scales.

Magnetic algae-cleaners have the advantage of being 'self-parking' in the aquarium; their only drawback is that if they are big enough to do the job quickly, they are unsightly when parked. Be sure to keep them well away from the thermostat; they can disrupt its functioning and cause temperature fluctuations in the water. Long-handled abrasive pads also do a good job in removing algae, or a nylon (not copper) pot scourer or steel wool (not the soap pad variety)

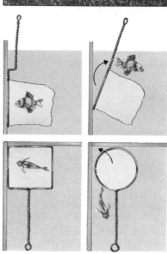

Above: The left-hand drawings show the benefits of cranked handles and square-shaped nets over the more traditional types shown on the right. Use soft nets for young fishes.

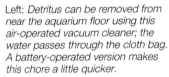

Left: *Detritus can be removed from near the aquarium floor using this air-operated vacuum cleaner; the water passes through the cloth bag. A battery-operated version makes this chore a little quicker.*

Above: *These self-parking abrasive pads are magnetized; as you move the outer pad the inner one clears the glass of unsightly algal growths. Be careful to avoid thermostats.*

Above right: *An abrasive pad on a long handle can be useful for cleaning the aquarium glass. Leave some of the green algae on the rear and side walls as food for the fishes.*

may be used instead for this job.

Unsightly growths of algae blanketing the plants may be removed by twirling a planting stick through the growth and collecting it like candy-floss. Chemical cures are also available, which kill the algae, but it is better to attack the cause. Algae can be encouraged by too much light or, conversely, by too few aquarium plants. Over-feeding often produces excess nutrients in the water for algae to feed and multiply on. And spores of algae may be inadvertently brought into an aquarium together with wild-caught live foods.

A spiral brush fitted onto a long wire is indispensable for cleaning out long external hoses on power filters or for unclogging an undergravel filter's airlift pipe very effectively.

Breeding traps are divided floating containers in which gravid (pregnant) female live-bearer fishes are placed to give birth; the young fishes swim into another compartment to escape from 'mum'. Unfortunately, these devices have two drawbacks: the gravid female is often disturbed by the confinement of the trap and will give birth prematurely to young fish who may not survive; and breeding traps floated in the aquarium directly beneath the aquarium lights will be in the warmest region and the high temperatures often account for many losses of fish kept in traps.

Test kits for pH, hardness and nitrites can be relied upon to give the fishkeeper accurate information as to the stability (or instability) of the aquarium water. For the beginner these kits are not absolutely necessary; for the technically curious they are mildly interesting (until the novelty wears off); but for the experienced aquarist trying to establish certain water qualities in order to breed a particularly demanding species, they are indispensable.

Automatic feeders, lighting dimmers and time clock controllers are very much *de luxe* pieces of equipment that only affluent fishkeepers have; for the average fishkeeper's absence from the aquarium during holidays (and you will not want to be away any longer than necessary), the expense of such equipment hardly merits its use, because it is much more fun to do it yourself as a *practical* fishkeeper.

Fish anatomy

Not every fish conforms to the traditional torpedo shape, and body shape reflects individual living and feeding habits. Ultra-streamlined bodies indicate fast-swimming, open-water predators, whose large tail fins are often complemented at the other end by a large tooth-filled mouth. Laterally compressed fishes such as the Angelfish (*Pterophyllum* sp.) inhabit slower flowing, reed-filled waters; and vertically compressed specimens live on the river bed itself.

The position of the mouth often indicates in what level of the water the fish generally lives. An upturned mouth indicates a swimmer just below the surface, whose mouth is ideally structured for capturing insects floating on top of the water. These fishes usually have a straight, uncurved dorsal surface. Fishes whose mouths are located at the very tip of the head, on a horizontal line through the middle of the body, are mid-water feeders taking food as it falls through the water, although they can feed equally well from the surface or from the river-bed, should the mood take them. Many other fishes have underslung mouths; and this, coupled with a flat ventral surface, clearly shows a bottom-dwelling species. But those fishes whose underslung mouths are used for rasping algae from rock surfaces (and the sides of the aquarium) may not be entirely bottom-dwelling. Some bottom-dwellers have whisker-like barbels around the mouth, which are often equipped with taste buds, so that the fish can more easily locate its food as it forages.

The scales

A fish's scales provide not only protection for the body but also streamlining. A variation from a scale covering is found in the Armoured Catfish group (Callichthyidae), whose bodies are covered with two or three rows of overlapping bony scutes. Some catfishes, particularly the Mochokidae and the Pimelodidae, are 'naked' and covered in neither scales nor scutes.

The fins

The fish uses its fins for locomotion and stability, and in some cases as spawning aids either during courtship or in the hatching period of the eggs. Fins may be either single or paired. The caudal fin provides the final impetus to thrust the fish through the water, and fast swimmers have a deeply forked caudal fin. The Swordtail (*Xiphophorus* sp.) has an elongated lower edge to the caudal fin, in the male fish only.

The dorsal fin may be erectile (as in the Sailfin Mollies – *Poecilia velifera*, *P. latipinna*) and will often consist of hard and soft rays. In some species two dorsal fins may be present, but these should not be confused with the adipose fin, a small fin (usually of a fatty tissue) that is found in some species, notably the Characoid group, between the main dorsal fin and the caudal fin.

The anal fin is another single fin

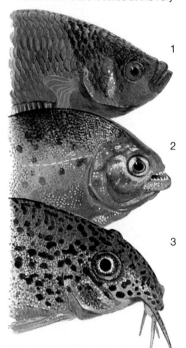

Above: *Mouths for all feeding purposes. (1) Upturned, as in top swimmers. (2) Terminal, typical of mid-water feeders. (3) Underslung, as in bottom-feeding fishes. The barbels have sensitive taste cells and lips may have bristles to rasp off algae.*

mounted under the body just forward of the caudal fin. Mostly used as a stabilizer, in the male live-bearing fishes it has become adapted to serve as a reproductive organ. In some Characoid fishes the anal fin of the male carries tiny hooks that help to hold the two fishes together during the spawning embrace.

The pelvic, or ventral, fins are

Below: *This characin (Moenkhausia pittieri) has the usual seven fins plus an extra one. Can you spot it? Yes, it's the small adipose one. This fish's white-edged fins will be seen to advantage against a background of sunken logs or dark green plants.*

paired and are carried forward of the anal fin. In many of the Anabantid fishes (Gouramies) these fins are filamentous and are often used to explore the fish's surroundings. The Angelfish also has narrow, elongated pelvic fins, but these are not so manoeuvrable, nor are they equipped with tasting cells. The Armoured Catfishes in the *Corydoras* genus use their pelvic fins to transport their eggs to the spawning site.

Pelvic fins in some species of Gobies are often fused together to form a suction cup that anchors the fish to the river bed and prevents it from being swept away by the action of the fast-moving water currents.

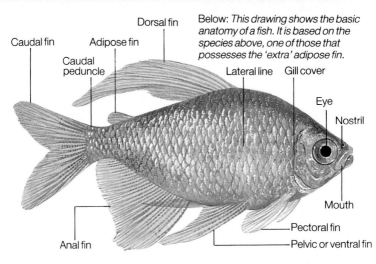

Caudal fin

Caudal peduncle

Adipose fin

Dorsal fin

Below: *This drawing shows the basic anatomy of a fish. It is based on the species above, one of those that possesses the 'extra' adipose fin.*

Lateral line   Gill cover

Eye

Nostril

Mouth

Pectoral fin

Pelvic or ventral fin

Anal fin

Pectoral fins emerge from just behind the gill cover (*operculum*). Primarily used for manoeuvring, pectoral fins have also been adapted for other uses. The Hatchetfishes emulate the marine Flying Fishes as they skim across the water surface by means of their well-developed pectoral fins. The marine Gurnard literally walks across the seabed on 'legs' formed by modified rays of its pectoral fins.

Many aquarium fishes have over-long, decorative fins. Fish breeders developed these exaggerated fins through deliberate breeding programmes and such fin developments are not found in their wild counterparts.

The fish's senses
The fish has the same five senses that a human being enjoys – sight, touch, taste, smell and hearing. Of these, the last two are more highly developed than those of humans. Many fishes detect food through smell, often over great distances. A fish's nostrils are not used for breathing, only for smelling. It is debatable where the sense of actual hearing ceases and the detection of low frequency vibrations begins in the fish world. This is because fishes are equipped with a sixth sense, the lateral line system. Through perforations in a row of scales, the fish's nervous system can detect minute vibrations in the surrounding water. This warns of other fishes or obstacles nearby. The Blind Cave Fish (*Astyanax mexicanus*) copes quite easily with life in an aquarium, navigating solely by

Above: *The eyes of this Blind Cave Fish have degenerated quite naturally; they would be redundant in its underground cave habitat. The fish can navigate successfully using its pressure-sensitive lateral line nervous system.*

means of its lateral line system.

Some fishes have developed sophisticated aids to help them cope in darkness or in murky waters, and these include the ability to generate a weak electromagnetic field. The Electric Catfish (*Malapterurus electricus* sp.), although scaleless, needs little protection against predators, because it packs a hefty electric shock. It is thought that it also uses this shock to stun smaller fishes.

The swim-bladder
A feature exclusive to fishes is a hydrostatic buoyancy organ known as a swim-bladder. This enables the fish to position itself at any level in the water, automatically giving the fish neutral density. Some fishes, notably the marine sharks, lack this organ.

Colour
Apart from attracting fishkeepers, colour plays an important role in the fish world. It serves to identify the species in general and the sexes in particular. It camouflages a fish from predators or gives clear visual warning that a species may be poisonous. Colour presents false targets to an attacker and gives some clue to a fish's disposition, showing that it may be frightened or angry.

Colour is determined by two

methods – by reflection of light, and by pigmentation. Those silvery, iridescent hues seen on the flanks of many freshwater species are due to reflective layers of guanin. Guanin is a waste product that is not excreted from the kidneys and body, but stored just beneath the skin. The colour seen depends upon the angle at which light hits and is reflected from these crystals. Many fishes, when lit by light coming through the front glass of the aquarium, seem to be coloured differently than when lit from directly overhead. This also explains why light-coloured gravel appears to wash out the fishes' colouring.

Fishes with deeper colours have pigment cells in their bodies, and some species are able to control the amount of colour they display. This can be seen quite easily in those species that tend to rest on the gravel surface or on rocks, where their colours are adapted to suit the background. Other fishes take on nocturnal colourations. The popular Pencilfishes (*Nannostomus* sp.) are notable examples and the hobbyist may be initially surprised at finding these fishes a different colour pattern each morning. Fishes effect such colour changes by contracting or expanding the pigmented cells (*chromatophores*) to intensify or dilute the colour showing through the skin.

Colour intensity is likely to be heightened in the male fish during the breeding period in order to attract a mate, and some female fishes within the Cichlid group may also have their colours exaggerated in order to be recognized by their subsequent offspring. A good example of this is seen in the *Pelvicachromis* genus, where the females are often more colourful during breeding than the male fishes.

It is possible to intensify fishes' colours by feeding them so-called 'colour foods'. These contain additives, such as carotin, that will accentuate colours. The Tiger Barb (*Barbus tetrazona*) is a favourite fish that responds quite startlingly to colour feeding, each scale becoming edged with black, giving a netted appearance. Unfortunately, in fish competitions the judges are quick to notice such artificial practices, and colour-fed fishes are likely to be down-graded for not complying with the natural colours of their species. The use of colour-enhancing lamps will also give the impression of more brightly coloured fishes, but naturally the fishes will regain their normal colours when removed to more normally lit environments using standard lamps in the hoods.

Below: *The sparkling colours of this Congo Tetra are produced by light reflecting from the guanin crystals just beneath the fish's skin. Many iridescent fishes look their best when illuminated with side-lighting, or when early morning sunlight shines through the aquarium glass.*

Diseases

Fishes will succumb to disease from time to time, but most diseases are easily recognized and successfully treated. However, the fishkeeper can do much, by following a few simple guidelines, to ensure that his fishes do not contract disease. The best deterrents to poor fish health are careful choice of original stock, quarantine and good aquarium hygiene at all times.

The selection of healthy stock is described elsewhere (page 58), but even apparently healthy additions to the aquarium should be quarantined. Isolate new stock in a spare tank for 2-3 weeks, during which time any latent disease should manifest itself. If any disease does occur, the quarantine tank can immediately be converted into a hospital tank.

Aquarium plants can also introduce unwanted guests into the aquarium and new plants should be thoroughly rinsed before use; a bath in a weak solution of potassium permanganate will destroy any minute aquatic life on plant leaves.

External factors should also be considered. Fumes from paint, cigarette smoke, air sprays and furniture polish can all be carried into the aquarium through the air pump. Avoid using materials giving off strong fumes or vapours near to the aquarium, and do not put hands recently washed with strong soap (or dirty hands not washed at all!) into the aquarium water.

Aquarium nets can spread diseases from tank to tank, so each tank should be allocated its own net, which must be disinfected after each use. Moving fishes from tank to tank if there is any suspicion of disease is asking for trouble.

Wherever possible, avoid any metal/water contact. The metal spring clip holding on an external thermostat can be covered with a length of airline to prevent contact with the water.

Be sure to maintain correct water temperatures, clean filters regularly and make partial water changes a habit. These actions, together with a full varied diet, will ensure that your fishes remain at the peak of fitness and highly resistant to disease.

Treatments

Treatments for disease range from individual baths to medication of the whole tank. In some cases, treatment can be administered internally by soaking the fish's food in the medication before feeding, but gauging the amount taken is somewhat difficult! Occasionally, a fish may be treated out of water, when dealing with a wound or a parasitic infection large enough to be treated in this way.

Filters used in any tank that is to be treated should not contain carbon, as it will adsorb the medication; and extra aeration should be used, because medicaments often reduce the level of oxygen in the water. Aquarium plants are sometimes adversely affected, and fine-leaved

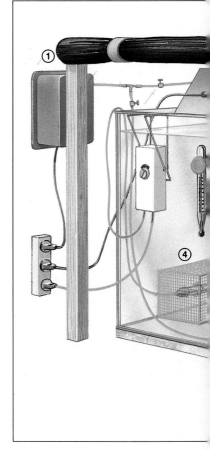

species suffer most.

At the end of any treatment the fishes should be acclimatized gradually to normal water conditions by the partial replacement of medicated water with fresh clean water over a period of days.

Below: A fish carrying a parasitic anchor worm (Lernaea) on its back. Large parasites such as this are easy to see and deal with.

The hospital aquarium (Below)

1 *The blinds can be lowered to prevent light reaching the aquarium and affecting the medication. The hood lights would be turned off.*
2 *A simple internal box filter is used containing no activated carbon that would adsorb medications.*
3 *A few flowerpots and plastic plants give the fishes a feeling of security. Plastic plants are used because live ones could be damaged by some medications being given.*
4 *The heater is controlled by an easily adjusted external thermostat and caged in to prevent damage to fishes sheltering nearby.*
5 *The airstone provides a bubble stream to circulate warmth and keep the oxygen level high in the tank; necessary during treatment.*

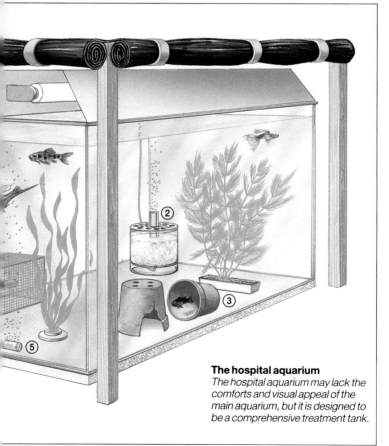

The hospital aquarium

The hospital aquarium may lack the comforts and visual appeal of the main aquarium, but it is designed to be a comprehensive treatment tank.

Fish diseases

Illustrated here are some of the more common ailments that befall fishes in the aquarium. Some are due to parasites introduced into the aquarium with live foods or plants from other waters; others are bacterial infections brought about by poor aquarium hygiene and lack of maintenance.

Tailrot/Finrot

These very obvious symptoms appear on fishes of poor health. Low temperatures, physical damage, and unhygienic conditions in the aquarium all encourage the harmful bacterial action.

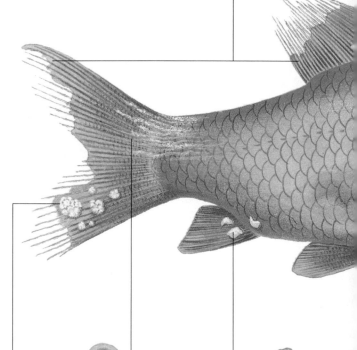

Lymphocystis

This conditions causes cauliflower-like growths to appear on the fins and the skin. At the same time the fish loses weight. Individual cell growth is rapid. This condition is rarely found among freshwater fishes.

Fungus

Fungus *(Saprolegnia)* attacks fishes already weakened by physical damage, parasites, or poor conditions. Also liable to affect fishes if they are transferred to widely differing aquarium waters.

Pox

White spots join to form large patches. Affected fishes become emaciated and are often left twisted. Faulty diet and lack of vitamins are likely causes. May heal itself under good aquarium conditions.

White spot
Tiny white spots cover the fins and body. A very common parasitic ailment that some aquarists believe lies dormant in every aquarium ready to afflict weak fishes.

Velvet disease
Infected fishes have a dusty appearance. Caused by a parasite *Oodinium*, which goes into an encystment stage. Will respond well to widely available proprietary cures.

Skin flukes
The *Gyrodactylus* parasites burrow into the fish's skin and stay near the surface. Affected fishes lose colour and become feeble. Responds well to treatments.

Eye infections
Cloudy eyes (below) are often due to eye fungus or to worm cataract, *Proalaria*. Protruding eyes (main illustration) usually suggest that other diseases are present as well.

Mouth 'fungus'
The slime bacterium *Chondrococcus* causes this. It is unrelated to body fungus.

Slimy skin
Fishes afflicted with this condition develop a thin grey film over the body. The parasites *Cyclochaeta* and *Costia* (shown at above left, right) cause the fish to produce excessive amounts of slime.

Dropsy
The scales protrude noticeably due to accumulated liquid in the body. The fluid from infected fish may infect others. To prevent this happening remove any sick fishes from the aquarium promptly.

Gill flukes
The flatworm *Dactylogyrus* attaches itself to the delicate gill membranes and causes an extremely obvious inflammation. Affected fishes develop an increased respiration rate and gaping gills.

White spot disease
(Ichthyophthiriasis) This is the most
common parasitic ailment and
probably the easiest to diagnose. The
fish's body is covered with tiny white
spots, which extend to cover the fins.
The disease is of a cyclic nature: the
parasite leaves the fish's body to form
cysts on the aquarium floor and upon
hatching the parasite is then free-
swimming, seeking a new host. It can
be attacked by treatment at this
stage. As the disease is likely to affect
all the fishes in an aquarium, the
whole tank should be treated.
Proprietary cures are readily
available, simple to administer, and
extremely effective.

Velvet This disease is also fairly easy
to diagnose. The fish appears to be
covered by a layer of fine golden dust,
giving it a velvety look. The parasite
responsible, *Oodinium limneticum*,
undergoes an encystment stage
similar to that of the white spot
disease parasite. *O. pillularis* is
reponsible for another 'velvet'
disease, where the colour is more of a
brown colour. Established long-term
bath cures included methylene blue
and acriflavine, but these have been
largely superseded by broad-
spectrum proprietary remedies.

Fungus *(Saprolegnia)* In this disease
outbreaks of cotton-wool-like tufts
appear on the fish's body, or it may be
covered completely with a fine layer of
cobwebby or dusty fungus. An
outdated treatment was to immerse
the suffering fish in a salt bath.
Proprietary treatments, such as
Liquitox and Furanace, are much
more effective.
   Often confused with body fungus is
mouth fungus, which is caused by a
slime bacterium, and may not be
cured effectively by all treatments
suggested for body fungus.
Phenoxethol has been successful.
Antibiotics can be used but these
must be obtained from a qualified
veterinarian.

'Shimmying' The symptoms are
aptly described; the fish makes rapid
undulating movements without any
forward movement occurring. One

Above: *The infection cycle for white
spot disease.* **1** *The afflicted fish
shows the symptoms and the
parasites leave the body.* **2** *Cysts
form on the tank floor.* **3** *The cysts
produce free-swimming parasites.
Successful treatment is only
possible during stage three.*

cause of this ailment is a drop in water
temperature, so that the fish
becomes chilled. The obvious
remedy is to check the aquarium's
heating system for any malfunction
and to raise the temperature to the
correct level. One species in
particular seems prone to
'shimmying' – the very popular Black
Molly (*Poecilia* hybrid).

Dropsy Occasionally a fish's body
becomes bloated to such a degree
that the scales protrude outwards.
This is due to the body cavities filling
with liquid. There is some confusion
as to what causes this. It is difficult to
cure and can be contagious, so
isolate the affected fish until it
recovers or has to be destroyed.

Finrot Degeneration of the tissue
between individual rays of the fins is
caused by bacterial infection, often
encouraged by poor water
conditions. The fins may have been
damaged by bad handling
techniques, or by a bullying fish. This
allows the bacterial infection to gain a
hold on the injured fins. A general

clean-up of the aquarium water is required, together with better aquarium management in the future. Proprietary cures will assist rapid recovery to full fin health, but these medicines cannot overcome neglect.

Gill flukes Fishes are sometimes seen scratching themselves on rocks or plants, accompanied by an increased respiration rate with the gills gaping and obviously inflamed. Such fishes are infected with *Dactylogyrus* or *Gyrodactylus* parasites, which burrow into the skin or collect on the delicate membranes. The parasites may be removed by bathing the fish in well-aerated solutions of proprietary treatments specially formulated for parasitic control, such as Paratox and Clout.

The parasites cannot survive without a fish host, so if the aquarium is left uninhabited for a few days while the fishes are being treated with proprietary medicaments, the parasites will be eliminated.

It is often easy to jump to the wrong conclusion. Fishes panting at the surface may not be afflicted by parasites at all, but gasping for oxygen because of an excess of

Above: A Neon Tetra (Paracheirodon innesi) *with abdominal dropsy, where fluid has accumulated in the body. Affected fishes may recover without treatment – or die despite it!*

carbon dioxide in the water. Immediate relief can be provided by extra aeration, but better aquarium management is the real answer.

Serious diseases
More serious ailments result from internal causes such as tuberculosis, threadworms and tapeworms, which are unseen by the fishkeeper. Usually when the symptoms become apparent it is too late to effect a cure. Diagnosis of these conditions can be done only by examination of the organs of the diseased fish (which in practical terms means a post-mortem) and this aspect of disease is beyond the capability of the beginning aquarist.

There are several diagnostic services available, but as these will only reveal the cause of death (from examination of the corpse), this course of action, which can be rather expensive, may be regarded as a little too retrospective in most cases.

Breeding

A large proportion of fishes kept in captivity will breed, often despite the conditions under which they are kept. These spontaneous breedings may go unnoticed by the aquarist, who may assume that, because the fish population's total number has not increased, nothing has been happening in the aquarium.

In the activity of the community tank, a pair of fishes may have difficulty in finding a territory in which to raise a family. Eggs from a spawning of egg-scattering fish will be accepted as a meal by the other occupants of the tank; and newly born live-bearer fry will also be harassed by more adult fishes. In order to survive, young fishes need protection, and that means a separate breeding tank with the fishkeeper playing a major role to ensure successful breeding.

There are three phases in fish breeding: pre-spawning activity, the actual spawning, and the raising of the young fry to maturity. It helps if the fishkeeper has some advance knowledge about the probable sequence of events so that appropriate arrangements can be made. The fishkeeper should know what method of spawning any of his fishes will use, how to prepare a suitable aquarium for them, and how to look after the young fry.

Methods of spawning
The majority of aquarium fishes are egg-layers, and external fertilization of the eggs occurs in several different ways. Parental care of the young is sometimes practised.

A small number of fishes are live-bearers; internal fertilization and development of the eggs occur within the female fish's body. The young fishes are born as free-swimming miniatures of their parents.

Egg-laying species
Fishes in this group fall into five categories; egg-scattering, egg-burying or egg-depositing fishes, nest-builders and mouth-brooders. Their parental care ranges from the non-existent to utter devotion.

Egg-scattering species normally inhabit flowing waters where their fertilized eggs are swept away upon release. In an aquarium the lack of water movement makes the eggs easy prey for the spawning adult

---

Egg-scatterers
The Zebra Danios (Brachydanio rerio) scatter their eggs and will eat them before they fall out of reach.

Egg-buriers
The egg-burying Argentine Pearlfish (Cynolebias bellotti) needs a deep layer of peat on the aquarium floor.

fishes, who will not hesitate to eat their own eggs. To overcome this otherwise abrupt halt in the breeding process the fishkeeper needs a breeding aquarium that will prevent the fishes from reaching their own eggs. Details of such designs can be found on pages 74-5.

Egg-burying species are native to waters that totally dry out each year; only by laying their eggs in the mud (where they await the rainy season before hatching) can the species guarantee further continuance. The aquarist has to provide a layer of peat on the floor of the aquarium to allow these fishes to spawn in their accustomed manner.

Egg-depositing fishes may be secretive spawners or open water spawners. The former choose small caves (or flowerpots, in an aquarium) in which to deposit their eggs; the latter are quite happy with flat rocks, broad-leaved plants or hollows dug out of the gravel. In all cases, the site is pre-cleaned and defended; the eggs are guarded, cleaned and often moved to other pre-cleaned sites before hatching occurs. When free-swimming, the fry are guarded and escorted around by their parents, who drive off any other fishes that venture too near.

Nest-builders need no help from the fishkeeper, building their nests from bubbles of saliva blown by the male fish, and often incorporating fragments of water plants in the nest construction. The aquarium should be densely planted to offer some shelter to the female, who may be harassed severely by the male fish after spawning is completed.

Mouth-brooding species have a two-stage spawning act. The eggs are laid by the female, usually in a depression in the gravel, and then fertilized by the male. The eggs are then picked up by the female, who incubates them in her buccal cavity, during which time she takes no food.

Live-bearing fishes
The popular species within this group will produce young at approximately monthly intervals. A single mating can produce successive broods, as the female can store the male fish's spermatozoa within her body. Other

Egg-depositors
'Kribs' (Pelvicachromis pulcher) *are secretive spawners and prefer the privacy of a flowerpot or rocky cave.*

Bubble-nest builders
Siamese Fighters (Betta splendens) *lay their eggs in a mass of bubbles they produce at the water surface.*

Left: *Spraying Characins* (Copella arnoldi) *spawning on the underside of a leaf above the water's surface. The male and female swim vertically to the surface, flick their tails and leap as much as 6cm(2.4in) up to a leaf. The female lays between five and eight eggs and these are immediately fertilized by the male. This procedure is repeated many times until hundreds of eggs have been eventually laid on the overhanging leaf.*

Left: *The female live-bearer's anal fin is fan-shaped; the male's is modified (fully or partly, depending on genus) into a functional reproductive organ.*
Right: *Jewel Cichlids* (Hemichromis bimaculatus) *spawning on a piece of wood. Both parents guard the eggs and tend the young.*

Mouth-brooders
The female Egyptian Mouth-brooder (Pseudocrenilabrus multicolor) *incubates the eggs in her mouth; a safe retreat for the fry. She will take no food until they hatch.*

species of live-bearers do not share this facility and require mating to occur for each brood. A thickly planted aquarium is recommended as a nursery tank for the pregnant female and her subsequent brood

Preparation for spawning
Whichever species you hope to breed you must start by selecting a true pair – a male and a female fish. Fortunately, this is straightforward in the live-bearing fishes, because the male fish has the anal fin modified into the reproductive organ known as the *gonopodium*. The female's anal fin is the normal fan-shape. The sex of egg-laying species can be determined by educated guesswork or by observation of the fishes' behaviour; usually, the male fish is slimmer and more colourful, and often has more elongated fins. Alternatively, particularly with egg-depositing species, the behaviour of the fishes may be more informative; if two fish constantly keep together,

and drive away other fishes from their locality, it is likely that they are a true pair, but finding out which sex is which is still a problem.

Fishes chosen for breeding must be healthy and full of vigour. The two sexes should be separated, and fed especially well on live and high-quality dried foods. This separation need not be practised with fish that have spontaneously paired off – all they need is good food and a little privacy.

If tank space is limited, a tank can be subdivided into two separate compartments to accommodate the prospective parents. It is usual to introduce the conditioned female into the breeding tank first, before the male; in this way he has to court her in her own territory. Otherwise, if the reverse procedure is followed, she may be liable to attack.

Slightly different factors arise with live-bearing species, who will mate with complete abandon regardless of colour variety within the same species. Very careful isolation of sexes and colour varieties is required to prevent the purity of the strain from becoming unstable. The gravid (pregnant) female should be moved to the densely planted nursery tank well before her estimated delivery time to prevent premature births. Leave the female in the nursery tank following delivery of young to recuperate for a few days before returning her to the main aquarium.

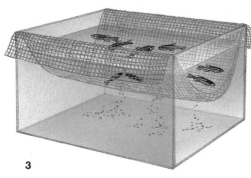

These illustrations show techniques fishkeepers can use to aid the breeding process in a wide range of fishes.

1 Separating the male and female for two or three weeks and feeding them with high quality and live foods ensures that both fishes are in peak condition for spawning and are keen to do so. They can be reunited simply by removing the clear partition between them.

2 A layer or two of marbles on the tank floor provides a fish-proof egg trap to prevent the adult fishes – in this case Tiger Barbs (Barbus tetrazona) – from eating the eggs. The shallow water level reduces the time that the falling eggs are at risk. Remove the eggs once spawning is over.

3 Another egg-saving device is a net draped in the water, through which the eggs fall to safety. Zebra Danios, shown here, may be spawned as a shoal.

4 Tetras lay adhesive eggs that may be trapped in a dense clump of plants where the female has been vigorously driven by the male fish to spawn.

5 Some Killifishes bury their eggs. There should be a deep layer of peat to accommodate such species as Cynolebias, shown here. After spawning, the peat (complete with the fertilized eggs) can be removed and stored almost dry for a few months. The hatching process is activated by immersing the peat in the aquarium water.

6 *Other Killifishes (such as the* Aphyosemion *shown here) lay their eggs on artificial mops, from which they can be collected and hatched in separate shallow dishes.*

7 *Depending on the species, Cichlids will require rocks, pieces of slate, flowerpots or broad-leaved plants as spawning sites. If the fishes lay their eggs in rocky caves or in flowerpots the hobbyist may not be aware that spawning has taken place until the parents bring their free-swimming youngsters out into the open.*

8 *Live-bearers can give birth in breeding traps. The fry escape to safety and should be raised in a separate, heavily planted nursery tank.*

9 Top: *A floating breeding trap that can be floated in the main aquarium. After giving birth, the female should be rested for a few days before being released into the main tank.* Bottom: *Two pieces of glass quickly convert a spare tank into a live-bearer's nursery.*

5

6

7

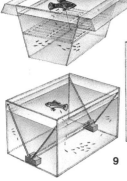

9

8

Spawning and after

Spawnings should be supervised, not just to see what occurs but also to protect the eggs or the female fish. Many male fishes will continue to harass the female after spawning; other males may not even accept the female as a partner at the outset, and she must be rescued from his violent attacks. The adult egg-scattering fishes should both be removed from the breeding tank after spawning is completed.

The eggs of the egg-burying species should be collected – still in the substrate or peat layer – and stored until re-immersing in water commences the hatching process.

Eggs deposited in plants or artificial spawning mops should be picked from the spawning medium and hatched in shallow water. Egg-depositors should be given the chance to rear their own young, but if they prove to be irresponsible parents the eggs can be hatched by using an airstone to substitute for the parent fishes' fin-fanning actions after the adults have been removed.

The male fishes of nest-building species take over the guarding of the nest and fry; the female should be removed for her own safety.

The female live-bearer should have a few days' rest after giving birth, before being returned to the community tank, to avoid undue early harassment by male fishes.

Care of the young fishes

Until the young fish swims freely it obtains nourishment from its attached yolk-sac, and it will not need food from the fishkeeper until that time. First foods can be proprietary liquid or powdered foods, formulated for either egg-layer or live-bearer young. Green water, micro-worms and grindal worms can be offered, but the best food is brine shrimp (see Feeding, page 55). As the fishes grow, the size and amount of the food should be increased. Aeration in the rearing tank should be used to keep the food moving; a simple sponge filter (as shown on page 27) is safest and will not trap fry. Weak, malformed young fishes should be removed. Aim to raise quality, not quantity.

Above: *Rosy Barbs spawning. The reddish male nudges the female until they are side by side, when the eggs are released and then fertilized.*

Final note: Keep a written record of breeding attempts, successful or not (particularly with different species). You want to be able to remember what you did wrong and when, and how, you eventually got it right!

Above: *The male Paradisefish (Macropodus opercularis) inspects the bubblenest as the female turns away after the spawning embrace. The male will guard the nest alone.*

Below: *A breeding pair of 'Kribs' (Pelvicachromis pulcher) proudly guard their free-swimming fry. Spawning takes place in rocky caves and is often unseen by the hobbyist.*

Part Two
Popular Aquarium Fishes

Today's modern aquarium shop provides a fantastic array of fishes and the newcomer to fishkeeping may find it totally bewildering, when trying to choose the initial stock for the aquarium. Despite their various shapes, sizes and colours there is some order to be found but the fishes must be chosen for their suitability for the size of aquarium you have. You will also need to ensure that the fishes you choose are suitable companions for the other species you intend to keep in the aquarium.

This part of the book divides the fishes into the general groups familiar to hobbyists, although there are some species from separate families that do not quite fit this convenient arrangement. Egglaying fishes form the major proportion of this section and most of the species described will breed in the aquarium providing, of course, that conditions are suitable and that you have

Above: *The fine marbled Angelfish.*
Below: *A Congo Tetra from Zaire.*

fishes of both sexes in your collection. Coverage of live-bearing species has been limited to the popular highly coloured cultivated fishes, Guppies, Swordtails, Platys and Mollies. Wild-caught species of other genera are described fully in a later section. The fishes described are fairly representative of their family groups and may be regarded, generally, as compatible with other peaceful aquarium species. Where only one species is described you may assume that other members of the genus share the same habits and aquarium requirements. Providing that you observe the common-sense rule of avoiding extremes of size in the same aquarium, a carefully chosen selection of fishes that inhabit differing waters levels will provide you with an aquarium full of life and colour, and the promise of a rewarding hobby in years to come.

Above: *A male Firemouth Cichlid deters intruders with its red throat.*
Below: *The Cardinal Tetra's colours will brighten any aquarium.*

Below: *Mosaic Gouramies explore the tank using elongated pelvic fins.*

BARBS

The active and colourful barb group of fishes is part of the very large cyprinidae family, which includes many hundreds of species. It is not surprising, therefore, to find that barbs range in size from the very small to the very large and this ensures that every hobbyists's taste, as well as every size of aquarium, can be catered for.

Usually omnivorous, barbs are not difficult to feed but, as some species may nibble at soft-leaved plants, it is a good idea to supplement their diet with some vegetable matter in the aquarium. They will take their food from all parts of the water, although the barbels around the mouth (which give these fishes their popular name) are especially adapted to locate food on the aquarium substrate. They have no teeth in the mouth but grind up food using pharyngeal 'teeth' situated in the throat. In the wild, barbs live in relatively still waters and will generally be happy with normal aquarium conditions. However, they will not be offended by water currents set up by efficient filter systems, which may be necessary to keep the water clear from suspended material churned up by their constant foraging activities. Barbs are egg-scattering fishes and have, occasionally, an unfortunate tendency to eat their own eggs. You will need to set up some method of preventing this if you are contemplating breeding your fishes (see *Breeding*, pages 74-5).

Family: CYPRINIDAE

Barbus arulius
Arulius Barb

- **Distribution:** Southern and southeastern India.
- **Length:** Up to 120mm(4.7in).
- **Tank length:** 90cm(36in).
- **Diet:** Worms, crustaceans, insects, plant matter, dried food.
- **Water temperature:** 23-26°C (73-79°F).
- **Compatibility:** May be too active for smaller varieties.

As a young fish, the Arulius Barb is attractively coloured, with a silvery green iridescent sheen on its body. Three dark bars cross the body vertically; one starting level with the dorsal fin, one across the rear end of the caudal peduncle, and

the third between these two. Other smaller patches may occur on the flanks or on the top of the body. Anal and caudal fins are reddish yellow with a red border. A green iridescent area covers the operculum.

Although these colours may not be clearly visible on the fish in the dealer's tanks, it will soon display its natural beauty once it has settled down in a large, well-planted aquarium with six or so companions of the same species. The fish has a pair of fairly long barbels on the upper jaw. Sexing the fish is uncomplicated as the male develops long extended rays from the dorsal fin in maturity. This characteristic is shared by *Barbus filamentosus*. Unfortunately, these very active fishes are prone to nibble soft-leaved plants. Furnish the aquarium with tougher-leaved plants to prevent damage occurring and supplement the fishes' diet with greenfoods.

This species also tends to disturb the substrate with its foraging activities so you will need to have an efficient filtration system. Water conditions are not critical for general maintenance but softer water could be an advantage to ensure the best results from spawning attempts. These fishes are avid egg eaters, so take precautions.

Left and top: **Barbus arulius**
This barb is not very prolific in the aquarium; a brood of 100 young would be a good result.

Family: CYPRINIDAE

Barbus conchonius

Rosy Barb
- **Distribution:** Northeastern India.
- **Length:** 75mm(3in).
- **Tank length:** 60cm(24in).
- **Diet:** Worms, crustaceans, insects, plant matter, dried foods.
- **Water temperature:** 22-25°C (72-77°F).
- **Compatibility:** This constantly active fish may be too boisterous for smaller, decorative characins.

The Rosy Barb has been an extremely popular aquarium fish for about 80 years. It is hardy, colourful and quite undemanding in its aquarium requirements. Perhaps the only criticism that has been levelled against it is that it does not attain the same size in captivity as it does in the wild, where fishes up to 150mm are not uncommon. The back of the fish is olive green and the flanks silvery, with the merest suggestion of pink. A dark spot, outlined with yellow, is visible just forward of the caudal peduncle. Males can be easily

Above: **Barbus conchonius**
Like many aquarium favourites, the Rosy Barb has become the subject of selective breeding.

distinguished from females by their fins, which are reddish, the dark tip to their dorsal fin, and by the darker coloration of their pelvic fins. At breeding time the male becomes brilliant coppery red. Like most egg-scattering fishes, the female is deeper in the body and rounds out more when viewed from above. Although the Rosy Barb is a prolific spawner (and an ideal fish for the beginner), it has an appetite for its own eggs, so you will need to take precautions to safeguard the eggs from the parents. There are several measures you can take to prevent such behaviour: furnish the breeding tank with dense bunches of fine-leaved plants and remove the parents immediately after spawning is complete, or spawn the fishes above a grid or net, through which the eggs fall – another well-used method.

Family: CYPRINIDAE

Barbus cumingi
Cuming's barb

● **Distribution:** Sri Lanka.
● **Length:** 50mm(2in).
● **Tank length:** 45cm(18in).
● **Diet:** Worms, crustaceans, insects, plant matter, dried foods.
● **Water temperature:** 25-27°C (77-81°F).
● **Compatibility:** A peaceful species for the small community.

The body of this species is golden; its iridescences are accentuated by dark-edged scales. Two dark patches are apparent, one immediately behind the gill cover, the other on the caudal peduncle. Fins are red or yellow (the colour varies depending on where the fish is captured) and those of the male are more intensely coloured. The female is deeper in the body and may often be slightly larger than the male. Cuming's Barb is not critical of water conditions but softer water is best for breeding.

Above: **Barbus cumingi**
A lively and attractive fish from Sri Lankan rivers, where two different fin-colour varieties exist.

Family: CYPRINIDAE

Barbus everetti

Clown Barb; Everett's Barb

- **Distribution:** Singapore and Borneo.
- **Length:** Up to 150mm(6in).
- **Tank length:** 90cm(36in).
- **Diet:** Worms, crustaceans, insects, plant matter, dried foods.
- **Water temperature:** 25-27°C (77-81°F).
- **Compatibility:** May be quarrelsome with smaller species.

This hardy Asiatic barb has two pairs of barbels. The overall body colour is a golden reddish brown, which pales towards the belly. Five dark blotches appear almost equidistantly along the flanks, beginning above the eye and ending on the caudal peduncle. The fins are red and the body shape is more elongated than in other species. Females are stouter, but less brightly coloured.

Below: **Barbus everetti**
A relatively large fish for the aquarium, this species has two pairs of barbels and thrives best when kept in a small shoal. It will nibble any soft-leaved tank plants.

The Clown Barb is an active fish, which will need plenty of swimming room, so, ideally, place aquarium plants out of the way around the tank edges. Stout-leaved plants are best as this fish will nibble at the more delicate bushy leaved types. Avoid using fine-particled substrate material in the tank; this will pack down easily and is not suitable for this species, which likes to forage around in the base covering.

Breeding the Clown Barb is less straightforward than breeding other barbs. To ensure that a pair are in prime breeding condition, separate them for three weeks and feed on copious amounts of livefoods, supplemented with greenfoods, before putting them together for spawning. Use plenty of densely bunched plants to help minimize egg eating. Softer water, too, will assist the chances of a positive result to spawning attempts. Even the weather appears to exert an influence, as spawning usually occurs on brighter days. Position the breeding tank so that it receives the morning sunshine, or at least some natural sunlight.

Family: CYPRINIDAE

Barbus fasciatus

Striped Barb

- **Distribution:** Malaya, Sumatra, and Borneo.
- **Length:** Up to 60mm(2.4in).
- **Tank length:** 60cm(24in).
- **Diet:** Worms, crustaceans, insects, plant matter, dried foods.
- **Water temperature:** 22-26°C (72-79°F).
- **Compatibility:** Keep only with species that will tolerate such an active tankmate.

Many barbs have black markings or stripes that contrast strongly with their basic body coloration. The Stiped Barb (or Zebra Barb, to give it its alternative popular name) is a very attractive barb with four or five dark stripes, running along, rather than vertically across, its pale yellow-gold flanks. In young fishes, the body is marked with what appears to be a collection of dots, but with increasing age these join up to form complete bands. Two pairs of barbels are present. The dorsal and anal fins are reddish or yellow and the remaining fins are colourless.

Above: **Barbus fasciatus**
This is an active barb that thrives in an aquarium. It needs plenty of open water for swimming.

Females are heavier in build than males. Like the preceding species, this fish requires ample swimming space, so furnish the aquarium to provide maximum room. Its activities around the aquarium are very much like those of the Clown Barb as it, too, likes to burrow down into the substrate in search of food. Many attempts have been made to breed this species without much reported success.

There is some confusion between this species and the almost identical Lined Barb, *B. lineatus*, which, in fact, can be distinguished by its lack of barbels. Ironically, it has been reported that the Lined Barb will breed without problems in the aquarium. It is possible, therefore, that incorrect identification may account for any contradictory reports on breeding *Barbus fasciatus*; the information may be a genuine report of successful breeding, but of a misidentified species.

85

Above: **Barbus gelius**
This is an excellent barb for a beginner or for anyone without sufficient space for a large tank. The markings on the flanks are rather variable between individuals.

Family: CYPRINIDAE

Barbus gelius
Golden Dwarf Barb
● **Distribution:** India, Bengal, and Assam.
● **Length:** Up to 40mm(1.6in).
● **Tank length:** 45cm(18in).
● **Diet:** Small crustaceans and insects and dried foods.
● **Water temperature:** 20-22°C (68-72°F).
● **Compatibility:** A peaceful fish if kept with similar-sized and equally peaceful tankmates.

The pale gold colour of the body of this barb, which often gives the impression of transparency, is offset by some irregular dark patches. This shoaling species likes shady, well-planted tanks, which simulate its natural habitat of aquatic vegetation under riverbanks. Despite being an infrequent import, this fish is ideal for a small tank and will tolerate temperatures that are slightly lower than usual very well. It is also fairly easy to breed. The parents are not egg eaters but you should, nevertheless, remove them after spawning activity has ended. Take care not to overfeed the tiny fry.

Right: **Barbus lateristriga**
Half-grown specimens are more suitable; the pattern fades with age.

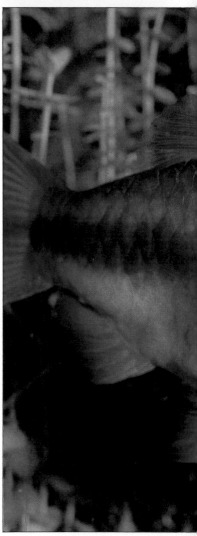

Family: CYPRINIDAE

Barbus lateristriga
Spanner Barb

● **Distribution:** Thailand, Malaysia and Indonesia.
● **Length:** Up to 180mm(7in).
● **Tank length:** 90cm(36in).
● **Diet:** Worms, crustaceans, insects, plant matter, dried foods.
● **Water temperature:** 19-25°C (66-77°F).
● **Compatibility:** The large size and constant activity of this fish may intimidate smaller species.

The popular name of this fish (T Barb is another) refers to the markings on its flanks, which are said to resemble a wrench, or adjustable spanner. As the fish ages, these markings become less distinct and the fish appears quite coarse looking, with the body deepening and the back becoming more arched. Young specimens are best suited to a medium-sized aquarium but they are fast growing. Breeding is not difficult and egg eating is not too prevalent.

Family: CYPRINIDAE
Barbus nigrofasciatus
Purple- or Ruby-headed Barb
- **Distribution:** Sri Lanka.
- **Length:** 60mm(2.4in), larger in the wild.
- **Tank length:** 90cm(36in).
- **Diet:** Worms, crustaceans, insects, plant matter, dried foods.
- **Water temperature:** 22-24°C (72-75°F).
- **Compatibility:** Tank size often affects behaviour; a larger tank usually results in less aggression. Suitable for a community.

The general appearance is of a light gold-brown body crossed vertically by three broad bars, with a fourth through the eye. The fins of the male are dusky black, the female has less black coloration on the body and fins. Although these fishes can be sexed in this way at any time, at breeding time there is no doubt at all – the male turns a rich ruby colour around the head, his body becomes dark red and the bars are almost obliterated.

This barb is a good indicator of the health of the aquarium, often being the first to show signs of White Spot disease. Fortunately, it responds to treatment very well. A raise in temperature usually stimulates spawning, which follows the typical egg-scattering pattern. The usual precautions are necessary to prevent egg eating.

Below: **Barbus 'odessa'**
Mystery surrounds the origins of the most attractive Odessa Barb, a newcomer to the aquarium.

Right: **Barbus nigrofasciatus**
These distinctive barbs can be spawned in the aquarium but remember: they are egg eaters.

Family: CYPRINIDAE
Barbus 'odessa'
Odessa Barb
- **Distribution:** Unknown.
- **Length:** 60mm(2.4in).
- **Tank length:** 60cm(24in).
- **Diet:** Worms, crustaceans, insects, plant matter, dried foods.
- **Water temperature:** 21-30°C (70-86°F).
- **Compatibility:** Suitable for the community aquarium.

The Odessa Barb, a relatively recent introduction to the hobby, is instantly recognizable by the broad band of brilliant red along its flanks. Each scale has a dark base, giving a net-like effect to the body. There are speckles in the dorsal, anal and ventral fins. Closer inspection has fuelled speculation that its ancestry owes something to *Barbus ticto*, *Barbus cumingi*, *Barbus conchonius* or even *Barbus stoliczkae*. This is an active fish, which may turn to fin-nipping, according to some authors. Keeping a shoal of these fishes may do much to alleviate boredom or mischievousness. Reports appear to differ on its readiness to breed, but it has been known to spawn even in the close confines of an exhibition tank at fish shows. The popular name appears to refer to the fish's first aquarium appearance, in the Ukrainian town of the same name.

Above: **Barbus oligolepis**
This attractive barb is best kept in a shoal. It is easy to breed.

Family: CYPRINIDAE

Barbus oligolepis
Checker Barb; Island Barb
● **Distribution:** Sumatra.
● **Length:** 45mm(1.8in).
● **Tank length:** 45cm(18in).
● **Diet:** Worms, crustaceans, insects, plant matter, dried foods.
● **Water temperature:** 22-25°C (72-77°F).
● **Compatibility:** A peaceful fish if kept with similar-sized, equally peaceful tankmates.

Both the popular names of this species are accurate: originally, this fish was found only on the island of Sumatra, but as hobbyists are generally disinclined to favour such geographically inspired names, the alternative name of Checker Barb seems to have taken preference. The reason for this is quite obvious: each scale has a dark edge and a bluish spot at its base, giving the fish a checkerboard effect. Fins are reddish, and outlined in black in the males, and more yellowish, lacking the distinct edging, in females. Apart from differences in fin coloration, the female is stouter and deeper in the body. Like the slightly smaller *Barbus gelius*, this fish can be housed in relatively small aquariums with other peaceful, non-boisterous fishes of a similar size. Males may quarrel with each other, especially at breeding times and so most fishkeepers will keep one male with two or three females. Breeding follows the typical egg-scattering pattern of the barb family. A slight increase in temperature, soft water and plenty of plants to catch the eggs in the breeding tank should ensure successful spawnings.

Family: CYPRINIDAE

Barbus schwanenfeldi

Schwanenfeld's Barb; Tinfoil Barb
● **Distribution:** Thailand, Malaysia and Indonesia.
● **Length:** Up to 350mm(14in).
● **Tank length:** 90cm(36in).
● **Diet:** Worms, crustaceans, insects, plant matter, dried foods.
● **Water temperature:** 20-25°C (68-77°F).
● **Compatibility:** Keep with larger species only.

The Tinfoil Barb is very attractive when young, and many hobbyists buy it without realising quite how large it will grow. The adult fish is even more magnificent; the large rhomboid-shaped body which has highly polished scales, which show off its red fins to perfection. The dorsal fin has a black section, tipped with white, and the deeply cleft caudal fin has black borders to upper and lower lobes. No external sexual differences are visible. These fishes have a healthy appetite for green matter, which must be satisfied in order to keep them in good health and safeguard the aquarium plants. Feed them with lettuce, spinach, *Riccia* or even Duckweed (*Lemna*) to keep them in good condition. The Tinfoil Barb is a very active fish and will need plenty of swimming space. It will inevitably, if accidentally, buffet other fishes around in its constant movement through the aquarium. For this reason, and because of its large size, the Tinfoil Barb is better suited to the public aquarium. However, if you can give it the space, it will certainly prove to be a worthy specimen in your aquatic collection. It is a very popular fish for exhibiting, where it needs to be in top condition – scale damage is very easily seen on a fish of this size – and at maximum size to take the prize. There are no reports of it having been bred in the aquarium.

Below: **Barbus schwanenfeldi**
Small specimens of this barb are suitable for the home aquarium. It needs a good supply of plant food to prevent it from eating the tank vegetation. It grows very rapidly.

Family: CYPRINIDAE

Barbus 'Schuberti'

Golden Barb; Schubert's Barb
- **Distribution:** Unknown.
- **Length:** Up to 70mm(2.8in).
- **Tank length:** 45cm(18in).
- **Diet:** Worms, crustaceans, insects, plant matter, dried foods.
- **Water temperature:** 20-25°C (68-77°F)
- **Compatibility:** A peaceful fish, well suited to a community.

Like the Odessa Barb, Schubert's Barb has a mysterious ancestry. Because of its similarity to *Barbus semifasciolatus* – the Green, or Half-banded Barb – it has been assumed that Schubert's Barb is descended from a gold 'sport' (or colour variant) bred from that natural species. The specific name is said to refer to an American fishkeeper, Tom Schubert, but this species has no scientific recognition. *Barbus 'Schuberti'* has also been related to *B. sachsi*, a very similar-looking species.

Right: Barbus 'Schuberti'
Although of unclear origin, this fish is a perfect aquarium subject.

Whatever its true origins, the fish is very colourful, the reddish fins complementing the gold body very well. A dark black or dark green mark appears across the rear of the caudal peduncle and there are several similarly coloured marks scattered horizontally along the upper part of the body. Females are stouter than males. This fish may be prone to blood-red spots, which appear at the base of the fins and usually indicate inadequate aquarium conditions. Breeding Schubert's Barb presents no problems; they are very willing spawners. The male is an active driver of the female and the fishes will need a reasonably large breeding tank with plenty of bushy plants to ensure good results. Having said this, it is not unknown for a pair of Schubertis to spawn in a bare tank during a fish show!

Family: CYPRINIDAE

Barbus tetrazona tetrazona

Sumatran Barb; Tiger Barb
- **Distribution:** Sumatra and Borneo.
- **Length:** Up to 60mm(2.4in).
- **Tank length:** 60cm(24in).
- **Diet:** Worms, small crustaceans, plant matter and dried foods.
- **Water temperature:** 20-25°C (68-77°F).
- **Compatibility:** May be quarrelsome with other community species; a larger tank often reduces the aggression.

The Tiger Barb is a very distinctive species, with four black bands crossing its golden-brown body. The first band crosses the eye, the next two bracket the dorsal fin, and the last crosses the very rear of the caudal peduncle. The dorsal and anal fins are black based with red edging; and the caudal, pectoral and pelvic fins are red. The male fish has a more intense

Right:
Barbus tetrazona tetrazona
This is the most widespread of the barbs with dark vertical bars.

coloration than the female and his snout is bright red. There are no barbels around the mouth. However, this all-time aquarium favourite has a reputation as a fin-nipper of slower-moving fishes. This may be deliberately malicious or may be caused simply by boredom. The Tiger Barb is naturally a shoaling fish and this perverse behaviour may occur if there are only one or two specimens in the community tank. Keeping these fishes in small shoals will give them something else to think about. Tiger Barbs are seen at their best in a well-planted aquarium where their bright colours show up well against the green background. They are very active fishes, and spend much of their time in midwater levels. Breeding is not difficult, but take precautions to prevent egg eating.

Family: CYPRINIDAE
Barbus ticto stoliczkae
Stoliczka's Barb
- **Distribution:** Southern Burma in the lower Irrawaddy River.
- **Length:** Up to 60mm(2.4in).
- **Tank length:** 60cm(24in).
- **Diet:** Worms, crustaceans, insects, plant matter, dried foods.
- **Water temperature:** 20-25°C (68-77°F).
- **Compatibility:** A beautiful fish for a community collection.

This is, in fact, a sub-species (indicated by its two specific names). *B. ticto stoliczkae* is also known as *B. stoliczkanus*, and is often confused with *B. ticto ticto* and even *B. phutunio*. All these fishes have iridescent sides adorned with two dark blotches, and red, black-speckled dorsal fins. The male has more colour in the fins than the female. Like all barbs, this is naturally a shoaling fish and should be kept in reasonable numbers. It is an easy fish to spawn.

Right: **Barbus ticto stoliczkae**
In this popular aquarium fish the mouth faces slightly upward. It differs from Barbus ticto ticto *in the arrangement of the scales on the flanks. It is easy to breed.*

Family: CYPRINIDAE
Barbus titteya
Cherry Barb
- **Distribution:** Sri Lanka.
- **Length:** Up to 50mm(2in).
- **Tank length:** 45cm(18in).
- **Diet:** Worms, small crustaceans, plant matter and dried foods.
- **Water temperature:** 23-27°C (73-81°F).
- **Compatibility:** A peaceful fish, kept with similar-sized species in a small community.

The Cherry Barb is similar in shape to the Checker Barb, although a little more elongate. The scales are well defined with the middle two rows having dark patches on them, which form a line from snout to caudal fin. Under certain lighting conditions a bluish iridescent

sheen is visible along the upper part of the body. There is one pair of barbels on the upper jaw. The male fish is red and his colour becomes highly intensified at breeding time. The female is brown. Provide areas of shelter for this shy species with floating vegetation or plants with surface-floating leaves. The Cherry Barb will breed fairly easily.

Right: **Barbus titteya**
This is a beautiful but shy barb. During spawning the parent fishes can be fed on white worms.

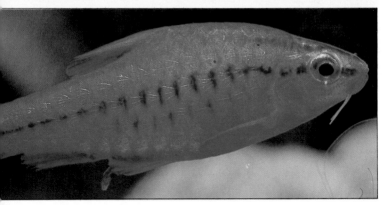

DANIOS

Danios, which are related to barbs, are very active, slim-bodied fishes inhabiting fast-flowing waters. Their upturned mouths indicate that they are naturally surface feeders, although in the aquarium they will take food from any convenient level. These shoaling fishes are ready breeders but, like barbs, will not hesitate to eat their own eggs.

Family: CYPRINIDAE

Brachydanio albolineatus
Pearl Danio

● **Distribution:** Southeast Asia.
● **Length:** 60mm(2.4in).
● **Tank length:** 45cm(18in).
● **Diet:** Worms, small crustaceans and dried foods.
● **Water temperature:** 21-25°C (70-77°F).
● **Compatibility:** Adds activity to the small community aquarium.

The pearly sides of this fish change to a violet or bluish sheen behind the emergence of the pelvic fins when seen under favourable lighting conditions. Two reddish gold lines run from this area to the caudal fin. Fins may be tinged with red but definite, strong colours are not a characteristic of this species, so that accurate description is

difficult. This fish loves bright sunlight and is usually found just below the surface of the water. It is also very active and an expert jumper so cover the tank securely. Spawning is a hectic affair with much driving of the females.

Family: CYPRINIDAE

Brachydanio rerio
Zebra Danio

● **Distribution:** Eastern India and Bangladesh.
● **Length:** 50mm(2in).
● **Tank length:** 45cm(18in).
● **Diet:** Worms, small crustaceans and dried foods.
● **Water temperature:** 18-25°C (64-77°F).
● **Compatibility:** Adds activity to the small community aquarium.

This gold-bodied fish has a pattern of deep-blue horizontal stripes, which is repeated in its fins, with the exception of the pectoral and pelvic fins. The male fish has more fin patterning than the female, and the extra plumpness of the female

Below: **Brachydanio albolineatus**
The streamlined flanks are marked by lines which catch the light.

Above: **Brachydanio rerio**
These fishes can be spawned in pre-conditioned pairs or as a shoal.

gives a distinct curve to the stripes along her flanks. This is an ideal fish for the newcomer to fish breeding.

Family: CYPRINIDAE
Danio aequipinnatus
Giant Danio
● **Distribution:** Sri Lanka and the west coast of India.
● **Length:** 120mm(4.7in).
● **Tank length:** 90cm(36in).
● **Diet:** Worms, crustaceans, insects and dried foods.
● **Water temperature:** 20-24°C (68-75°F).
● **Compatibility:** This very active fish may disturb other fishes.

Although not a very large fish, the Giant Danio is the largest of the Danio group of fishes. Its flanks are bluish green and its belly slightly pink. Its blue body is crossed vertically by three or four thin alternating bands of blue and gold and the fins, with the exception of the pectorals, are pinkish blue. The Giant Danio can be sexed by body shape – the female is stouter – and by the blue body band, which in the male is straight and in the female turns up slightly at the caudal fin. Females often lack the male's more definite coloration. These danios are prolific breeders.

Below: **Danio aequipinnatus**
These fishes need an aquarium with plenty of swimming space.

RASBORAS

The genus *Rasbora* is another large group of fishes within the cyprinid family. Like barbs, rasboras range in size from the very small to the relatively large. Some are slim, like danios, while others have a deeper body shape. All make good aquarium fishes. Being active, most are egg-scatterers, although *R. hengeli* and *R. heteromorpha* deposit eggs on the underside of broad-leaved plants. To simulate the conditions of their native waters and show them off to advantage, house them in a well-planted aquarium with a dark-coloured substrate.

Family: CYPRINIDAE

Rasbora borapetensis

Red-tailed Rasbora
- **Distribution:** Thailand.
- **Length:** 50mm(2in).
- **Tank length:** 45cm(18in).
- **Diet:** Worms, crustaceans, insects and dried foods.
- **Water temperature:** 20-26°C (68-79°F).
- **Compatibility:** Ideal for the small community aquarium.

This is a smart, slim fish with well-developed fins. The mouth is turned slightly upwards, showing that the fish naturally inhabits the middle and upper levels of the water. A dark line, surmounted by gold, runs from immediately behind the eye to the end of the caudal peduncle and another, thinner, one crosses the base of

Below: **Rasbora borapetensis**
These fishes, like the danios, bring welcome activity to the aquarium.

the anal fin. The dorsal and caudal fins are reddish but all other fins are colourless. Sexes can be distinguished by the female's slightly more robust build.

Maintain the water in the slightly acid conditions required by this fish by including some peat in the filter box. Breeding is straight-forward but use thick bunches of plants to trap the eggs and thus protect them from the adult fishes.

Family: CYPRINIDAE

Rasbora heteromorpha

Harlequin Fish
- **Distribution:** Malaysia and Thailand.
- **Length:** 45mm(1.8in).
- **Tank length:** 45cm(18in).
- **Diet:** Worms, crustaceans, insects and dried foods.
- **Water temperature:** 22-25°C (72-77°F).
- **Compatibility:** Ideal for the small community aquarium.

Above: **Rasbora heteromorpha**
A shoal of these silvery fishes will brighten the community aquarium.

This very popular aquarium fish is easily identified by the dark triangle on the flanks of its sharply tapering body. The male's triangle is more clearly defined than the female's, which fades away towards the belly region. The dorsal and caudal fins are marked with red. A related species *R. hengeli*, is similarly marked but slimmer. A shoaling fish, the Harlequin thrives and is seen to advantage when kept in a reasonable number. You should ensure that there are plenty of plants in the aquarium, particularly stout-leaved varieties, such as *Cryptocoryne*, as, unlike most cyprinids, this species is not an egg-scatterer, but deposits its eggs on the underside of leaves to hatch in 26 to 30 hours. However, breeding these fishes is not without problems and success is not always immediate.

Family: CYPRINIDAE

Rasbora maculata

Spotted Rasbora

● **Distribution:** The Malayan Archipelago and Sumatra.
● **Length:** 25mm(1in).
● **Tank length:** 45cm(18in).
● **Diet:** Worms, small crustaceans, and dried foods.
● **Water temperature:** 21-25°C (70-77°F).
● **Compatibility:** Best kept in a species tank, as it is difficult to find other fishes small enough to accompany it safely.

This is the pygmy of the *Rasbora* genus and, indeed, one of the smallest of all aquarium species. The basic body colour is brick red and the belly is yellowish. Because of its size, it is sometimes quite difficult to see clearly the body spots and the black markings on the dorsal and anal fins. The shape is quite squat with the rear part very narrow, the eye is relatively large. Keeping this fish requires some careful planning due to its small size – even Neon Tetras look large beside it! However, although a species tank arrangement is perhaps the best option, smaller species of *Corydoras* will complement it nicely. Breeding, although possible, may be a

Above: **Rasbora maculata**
The colours of this fish appear vivid against a dark substrate.

protracted affair and, of course, the fry are hard to see at first and will need the very tiniest of foods.

Family: CYPRINIDAE
Rasbora trilineata
Scissor Tail
● **Distribution:** The Malayan Archipelago, Sumatra, Borneo.
● **Length:** Up to 150mm(6in).
● **Tank length:** 90cm(36in).
● **Diet:** Worms, crustaceans, insects and dried food.
● **Water temperature:** 19-25°C (66-77°F).
● **Compatibility:** Suitable for a large community aquarium.

From one of the smallest members of the genus, we turn to one of the largest. The Scissor Tail is aptly named; the smartly marked lobes of its caudal fins are never still, opening and shutting continuously, like a pair of tailor's scissors. The fish's specific name refers to the two black caudal fin markings and the dark, yellow-topped longitudinal stripe, which runs three-quarters of the length of the body. With the exception of the caudal fin, all the fins are unmarked. This fish is seen to advantage with a little side lighting, when it takes on a multicoloured iridescence. Females have stouter bodies than males. There is another similar species, *Rasbora caudimaculata*, which has orange markings in the caudal fin instead of black. The Scissor Tail is a very active fish, constantly on the move in the mid- and upper water levels, and you should furnish the aquarium accordingly. Plants create areas of seclusion for the fish but the Scissor Tail does need plenty of swimming space too. The water should be slightly acidic – filtration through peat will help. However, this popular aquarium subject is quite hardy and will thrive in ordinary domestic water.

The male drives the female vigorously when spawning. Bunched plants may help to trap the eggs, which are not very buoyant. Remove the parents as soon as spawning activity ceases.

Below: **Rasbora trilineata**
This is an active fish that needs soft water for breeding. Water should be low on infusorians.

OTHER CYPRINIDS

Since the cyprinid family is found almost worldwide (the major exceptions are South America and Australia), there is an enormous range of such fishes. Apart from the previously mentioned groups, there are others whose colours and shapes make them ideal for the aquarium.

Above:
Epalzeorhynchus kallopterus
This hardy fish browses on algae and flatworms on the tank glass.

Family: CYPRINIDAE
Epalzeorhynchus kallopterus
Flying Fox
● **Distribution:** Sumatra, Borneo.
● **Length:** Up to 140mm(5.5in).
● **Tank length:** 60cm(24in).
● **Diet:** Worms, crustaceans, insects, plant matter, dried food.
● **Water temperature:** 22-27°C (72-81°F).
● **Compatibility:** May be aggressive towards its own kind.

The Flying Fox is a very smart fish with a dark stripe running from snout to caudal fin, accentuated by the pale belly colour beneath it and gold line surmounting it. The dark anal and pectoral and large dorsal fin have white tips. This fish generally keeps to the bottom of the aquarium but will often be seen propped up on its pelvic fins, resting on a broad-leaved plant or sunken log. Sex differences are not known and there are no reports of it being bred in captivity. The Flying Fox may become quite possessive over a patch of territory and harass other fishes.

Family: CYPRINIDAE
Labeo bicolor
Red-tailed Black Shark; Red-tailed Labeo
● **Distribution:** Thailand.
● **Length:** Up to 120mm(4.7in).
● **Tank length:** 60cm(24in).
● **Diet:** Worms, crustaceans, insects, plant matter, dried food.
● **Water temperature:** 22-26°C (72-79°F).
● **Compatibility:** May be aggressive towards intruders into its chosen territory.

Probably because of its common name and striking coloration, this fish is a popular aquarium subject. The large dorsal fin resembles that of the marine shark but there is no scientific relationship between the two. This species appreciates hiding places in the aquarium but may become territorial. It has been rarely bred in captivity.

Family: CYPRINIDAE
Tanichthys albonubes
White Cloud Mountain Minnow; Poor Man's Neon
● **Distribution:** Southeast Asia.
● **Length:** 45mm(1.8in).
● **Tank length:** 45cm(18in).
● **Diet:** Worms, small crustaceans and dried foods.
● **Water temperature:** 16-22°C (61-72°F).
● **Compatibility:** Suitable for the small community aquarium.

Above: **Tanichthys albonubes**
This undemanding fish is often known as the 'Poor Man's Neon'.

This colourful fish was discovered by a Chinese Boy Scout, Tan, (*Tanichthys* means Tan's Fish) in 1930. A red, gold and blue line runs from behind the eye to the caudal peduncle, where it terminates in a dark spot, and dorsal, pelvic and anal fins are tipped with yellow and blue. This hardy fish can be kept outdoors in unheated pools in summer. Breeding is uncomplicated and, unlike many other species in this family, the parents will ignore the newly fertilized eggs.

Below: **Labeo bicolor**
The striking black colour of this species will pale significantly in unsuitable conditions.

Tetras, most of which come from South America, are reknowned for their brilliant colours and sparkling iridescences. However, despite their beauty, they have sharp teeth in the jaws, which, together with an extra, small fin (the adipose) between the dorsal and caudal fins, helps to distinguish these fishes from others in the characidae family. Mostly omnivorous, with a few 'vegetarians', tetras and small characins make excellent aquarium fishes, especially if kept in shoals in a well-planted tank, with plenty of bushy plants to act as receptacles for scattered eggs. Soft, slightly acidic water is preferable, especially for breeding, although most species will adapt quickly to domestic tapwater.

Family: CHARACIDAE

Aphyocharax anisitsi

Bloodfin

● **Distribution:** South America: Rio Parana, Argentina.
● **Length:** Up to 55mm(2.2in).
● **Tank length:** 45cm(18in).
● **Diet:** Worms, small insects and crustaceans and dried foods.
● **Water temperature:** 22-28°C (72-83°F).
● **Compatibility:** Suitable for the small community aquarium but needs plenty of swimming space.

The Bloodfin may be seen as the characoid equivalent of cyprinid species such as the danios, for it spends most of its time swimming in the middle and upper water levels. In the wild it takes much of its food from the water surface. A slender, silver fish, its somewhat plain appearance is offset by its blood-red fins and the delicate blue sheen, which appears when it is seen in reflected light. The anal fin of the male has tiny hooks, used during spawning, which are prone to damage when netting, so handle this fish gently. The Bloodfin is an active egg eater.

Below: **Aphyocharax anisitsi**
This attractive shoaling fish is easy to breed in the aquarium. A fine mesh netting just above the bottom will safeguard the eggs.

Family: CHARACIDAE

Astyanax mexicanus

Blind Cave Characin

● **Distribution:** North and Central America, from Texas to Panama.
● **Length:** Up to 90mm(3.5in).
● **Tank length:** 60cm(24in).
● **Diet:** Insects, crustaceans, worms and dried food.
● **Water temperature:** 19-25°C (66-77°F).
● **Compatibility:** Can cope very well with community life, but a species tank might suit it better.

At first glance, this fish seems to have little to recommend it; it is a plain silvery pink fish with few distinguishing features. Its popularity with fishkeepers, however, lies in its individuality. The most noticeably different thing about this fish is that it has no

Above: **Astyanax mexicanus**
This blind form, from underground waters, shows an uncanny ability to navigate without functional eyes.

eyes, and yet can navigate faultlessly around the most crowded, or densely furnished, aquarium, apparently unaffected by this handicap. In its natural, central American habitat, it inhabits underground caves and although the young have rudimentary eyes these soon fade away, as they are redundant in the pitch-black waters. The fish finds its way around using its lateral-line system – vibrations in the water are reflected back from stationary obstacles or passing fishes and detected by the nervous system, which begins at the row of perforated scales along the flanks.

Family: CHARACIDAE
Cheirodon axelrodi
Cardinal Tetra
● **Distribution:** The tributaries of the Orinoco and Rio Negro in South America.
● **Length:** 45mm(1.8in).
● **Tank length:** 45cm(18in).
● **Diet:** Worms, small crustaceans and dried foods.
● **Water temperature:** 23-26°C (73-79°F).
● **Compatibility:** Ideal for the decorative community tank.

It is not hard to see why this is one of the all-time aquarium favourites. The Cardinal has a vivid electric-blue stripe running from snout to caudal peduncle and a broad band of brilliant scarlet, which, unlike the stripe in its relative, the Neon Tetra, extends along its total length. There is a small white area on the underparts of the fish. Females may be slightly larger and deeper in the body, and the male fish has tiny platelets on the underside of the caudal peduncle. This beautiful coloration is best seen when the fishes are shoaling in a well-furnished aquarium with a dark substrate, under lighting that is not too strong. Spawning is not

Below: **Gymnocorymbus ternetzi**
A good all-round fish, tolerant of others and generally easy to breed.

Above: **Cheirodon axelrodi**
A shoal of these attractive fishes provides a magnificent spectacle.

too difficult; the best results come from using soft, acid water in the aquarium. The tiny fry, which will be clearly visible after three or four days, are free-swimming, but need the smallest foods and so may be difficult to rear.

Family: CHARACIDAE
Gymnocorymbus ternetzi
Black Widow
● **Distribution:** South America: Mato Grosso area of Rio Paraguay and Rio Negro.
● **Length:** 60mm(2.4in).
● **Tank length:** 45cm(18in).

● **Diet:** Worms, small crustaceans, insects and dried food.
● **Water temperature:** 23-26°C (73-79°F).
● **Compatibility:** Community tank.

The jet black rear half of the body and anal fin of this attractive fish have provided the alternative popular names of Petticoat Fish and Blackamoor. Two dark vertical bands cross the otherwise silver part of the body immediately ahead of the dorsal fin. Other varieties have been developed, including a long-finned version, which retains the dark coloration and, more recently, a gold variety. Both are the results of selective breeding. Females are usually deeper bodied and have a slightly more rounded body cavity. The male's caudal fin may have white spots. Spawning is quite eventful with the male dancing around the female before eggs are released and fertilized. Remove the parents immediately after spawning.

Family: CHARACIDAE
Hemigrammus caudovittatus
Buenos Aires Tetra
● **Distribution:** South America, in the Rio de la Plata Basin.
● **Length:** Up to 70mm(2.8in).
● **Tank length:** 45cm(18in).

Above:
Hemigrammus caudovittatus
This fish is a reliable, hardy species, ideal for the beginner.

● **Diet:** Worms, crustaceans, insects, plant matter, dried food.
● **Water temperature:** 18-28°C (64-83°F).
● **Compatibility:** Community tank.

An aquarium favourite for around 60 years, the Buenos Aires Tetra is a very hardy fish, eminently suitable for the beginner. The most noticeable marking is the dark streak on the caudal peduncle, which reaches into the caudal fin, where it is bordered top and bottom by a yellowish white area. There is also a small dark comma-shaped mark just behind the gill cover, but this may be visible only in reflected light. The male fish has a more distinct coloration than the female, and his dorsal, adipose, anal, ventrals and lobes of the caudal fin are red or yellowish red. Females may be deeper bodied.
While the fish makes a good community member, it may nibble soft-leaved plants. Furnish the tank with tougher-leaved specimens and include some vegetable matter in the fish's diet to prevent such tendencies. Spawning this fish is easy and the fry hatch quickly and thrive on a diet of small livefoods.

Family: CHARACIDAE

Hemigrammus erythrozonus
Glowlight Tetra
● **Distribution:** Northeastern South America.
● **Length:** 45mm(1.8in).
● **Tank length:** 45cm(18in).
● **Diet:** Worms, small crustaceans, plant matter and dried foods.
● **Water temperature:** 24-28°C (75-83°F).
● **Compatibility:** Suitable for the community tank.

This fish has subtle coloration, with a horizontal line running the length of the body, ending in a red spot

Above:
Hemigrammus erythrozonus
Despite its lack of bright coloration, the Glowlight Tetra is a favourite.

on the caudal fin. The front of the dorsal fin is red, remaining fins are pinkish or translucent. The female is plumper than the male. The Glowlight is a bottom dweller and appreciates a densely planted aquarium. The water should be soft and acidic for spawning; use lime-free substrate and filter water

Below: **Hemigrammus ocellifer**
Note the bright red eye, which almost matches the tail spot.

through peat. These fishes are egg eaters so remove the parents after spawning activity has ended.

Family: CHARACIDAE
Hemigrammus ocellifer
Beacon Fish
● **Distribution:** Northern South America.
● **Length:** 45mm(1.8in).
● **Tank length:** 45cm(18in).
● **Diet:** Worms, small crustaceans, plant matter and dried foods.
● **Water temperature:** 22-27°C (72-81°F).
● **Compatibility:** Suitable for the community tank.

This fish is also known as the Head- and Tail-light Fish (or even, more fancifully, the Motorist Fish) because of the two bright parts of its coloration – the red top half of the eye and the red-gold patch on the top of the caudal peduncle. An indistinct thin dark line may be seen on the flanks, beginning level with the dorsal fin and ending in the black area on the caudal fin. A black marking surrounded by gold appears behind the gill cover and the caudal fin has red in each lobe. A similar species, *H. ocellifer falsus*, has slightly different coloration and has the honour of having been known as an aquarium fish for some 50 years longer. Sexing and breeding are similar to that of the Buenos Aires Tetra (see page 107).

Family: CHARACIDAE
Hemigrammus rhodostomus
Rummy-nosed Tetra; Red-nosed Tetra
● **Distribution:** South America.
● **Length:** 55mm(2.2in).
● **Tank length:** 45cm(18in).
● **Diet:** Worms, small crustaceans, plant matter and dried foods.
● **Water temperature:** 24-26°C (75-79°F).
● **Compatibility:** Suitable for the community tank.

The head of this strikingly coloured fish is covered with bright red, while the caudal fin is black with four white horizontal stripes. A thin line spreads from the middle of the body to the central dark bar on the caudal fin and is topped by gold as it crosses the caudal peduncle. The female is stouter than the male.

This can be a somewhat shy species and may also be sensitive to changing water quality. Breeding, though possible, is not always straightforward. A similarly marked species is the False Rummy-nose, (*Petitella georgiae*), from Peru and Venezuela.

Below:
Hemigrammus rhodostomus
This fish needs to be in good health for its colours to be really vivid. In common with most tetras, it thrives in soft water.

Above:
Hyphessobrycon erythrostigma
This fish is hardy, living up to four years, but not easy to breed.

Family: CHARACIDAE
Hyphessobrycon erythrostigma
Bleeding Heart Tetra
● **Distribution:** Northern South America: Colombia.
● **Length:** Up to 70mm(2.8in).
● **Tank length:** 90cm(36in).
● **Diet:** Worms, crustaceans, plant matter and dried foods.
● **Water temperature:** 23-25°C (73-75°F).
● **Compatibility:** Best kept in a quiet community tank with other peaceful fishes.

The Bleeding Heart Tetra is larger and deeper bodied than most tetras, with excellent coloration and finnage. The distinguishing 'heart-spot' is visible on the purple-pink sides immediately below the front of the dorsal fin. The sickle-shaped dorsal of the male is reddish, with black rays in front and white edging, and in good specimens reaches well over the caudal peduncle. The anal fin is deeply concave with a bluish white area nearer to the body, and dark outer margin. The female

lacks the large dorsal fin and the anal fin appears less concave.

This fish is easily frightened and will dash around the tank when disturbed. Breeding these tetras still presents a challenge.

Family: CHARACIDAE
Hyphessobrycon flammeus
Flame Tetra
● **Distribution:** South America: Rio de Janeiro, Brazil.
● **Length:** 45mm(1.8in).
● **Tank length:** 45cm(18in).
● **Diet:** Worms, small crustaceans, plant matter and dried foods.
● **Water temperature:** 20-25°C (68-77°F).
● **Compatibility:** Community tank.

Another old aquarium favourite, the Flame Tetra (or Red Tetra) from Rio is a hardy fish, tolerant of varying water conditions. The rear half of the body is flame red while the silvery area in front of the dorsal fin is crossed by two dark bars. All fins are red, except the pectoral fins, which are colourless. The male's anal fin has a black border. The female is plumper than the male and her fins have less red coloration. A shoaling fish, the Flame Tetra is easy to spawn and will breed happily in hard water.

Below:
Hyphessobrycon flammeus
Ideal for the beginner, this peaceful characin will brighten a community tank with its red markings.

Above:
Hyphessobrycon heterorhabdus
This is a delicate characin and not easy to breed successfully.

Family: CHARACIDAE

Hyphessobrycon heterorhabdus

Belgian Flag Tetra

● **Distribution:** South America: Rio Tocantins, lower Amazon.
● **Length:** 45mm(1.8in).
● **Tank length:** 30cm(12in).
● **Diet:** Worms, crustaceans, plant matter and dried food.
● **Water temperature:** 23-25°C (73-77°F).
● **Compatibility:** Best kept in an uncrowded community tank.

The longitudinal band running from the head to the caudal fin is of three colours – red, gold and black – which has given rise to the popular name of Belgian Flag Tetra. The upper half of the eye is bright red. Females are more robust than males. Keeping this species is not always easy; it is more than a little prone to diseases. It should be kept in well-planted, uncrowded tanks, but in shoals of sufficient numbers, so that it can gain confidence from its fellows. It will take dried food but does much better on livefoods. Breeding is not easy; soft acid (peat-filtered) water is vital.

Family: CHARACIDAE

Hyphessobrycon pulchripinnis

Lemon Tetra

● **Distribution:** South America, the precise area is unknown.
● **Length:** Up to 40mm(1.6in).
● **Tank length:** 30cm(12in).
● **Diet:** Worms, crustaceans, plant matter and dried food.
● **Water temperature:** 23-25°C (73-77°F).
● **Compatibility:** Community tank.

The overall body colour of this fish is a delicate lemon colour, which is offset by the stronger yellow and black of the anal fin and dorsal fins. Another contrasting colour is found in the eye, the top half being bright red. In recent years, an albino variety has been developed but, of course, this does not occur in the fish's natural water. The female does not have so much black in her fins and the anal fin may not be quite so concave. Like all decorative tetras, the Lemon Tetra is seen at its best in a suitably furnished tank with plenty of dense plants, some driftwood and a dark substrate. Breeding is variable, according to reports.

Below:
Hyphessobrycon pulchripinnis
A small colourful characin.

Family: CHARACIDAE

Megalamphodus megalopterus

Black Phantom Tetra

● **Distribution:** South America: Rio Guapore on the border between Bolivia and Brazil.
● **Length:** 45mm(1.8in).
● **Tank length:** 45cm(18in).
● **Diet:** Worms, small insects, crustaceans and dried foods.
● **Water temperature:** 23-26°C (73-79°F).
● **Compatibility:** Community tank.

The Black Phantom Tetra is one of two very similar species in the genus, the only difference between the two being colour. The body of the Black Phantom is dusky greyish pink, the fins jet black. A vertical shoulder patch appears on a bluish patch midway between the gill cover and dorsal fin. The male has a pronounced dorsal fin and the anal fin is broad and sharply concave; the female has a shorter, more rounded dorsal fin, reddish anal and ventral fins and more pink coloration to the front half of the body, whereas the male favours grey. A well-planted tank with shady areas and a dark substrate show this fish off to perfection. Spawning is possible (use soft water) but not all males are co-operative.

Below:
Megalamphodus megalopterus
The male uses his large dorsal fin to impress females or deter rivals.

Above: **Micralestes interruptus**
The male's ornate fins develop fully only in a spacious tank offering plenty of swimming room.

Family: CHARACIDAE

Micralestes (Phenacogrammus) interruptus

Congo Tetra; Congo Salmon
● **Distribution:** Central Africa, Zaire region.
● **Length:** 80mm(3.2in).
● **Tank length:** 60cm(24in).
● **Diet:** Worms, insects, crustaceans, and dried foods.
● **Water temperature:** 24-26°C (75-79°F).
● **Compatibility:** Community tank with plenty of swimming room.

This medium-sized characin from Africa has large iridescent scales and flowing fins. The male fish is brilliantly coloured; a wide band of gold runs along the top half of the body and changes to an electric blue-green below the middle line. The dorsal, anal, ventral and caudal fins develop extensions with maturity and all have a white edging which shows up clearly in a tank furnished with dark driftwood, dark green plants and a dark substrate. The female also has large scales but is a more golden brown colour, her caudal fin is square cut and she does not develop fin extensions. As befits an active shoaling fish, spawning entails some hard driving of the female. The fertilized eggs sink to the bottom, where they develop a hard shell before they hatch.

Family: CHARACIDAE
Moenkhausia pittieri
Diamond Tetra
● **Distribution:** Northern South America: Lake Valencia in Venezuela.
● **Length:** 60mm(2.4in).
● **Tank length:** 45cm(18in).
● **Diet:** Worms, insects, crustaceans and dried foods.
● **Water temperature:** 22-27°C (72-81°F).
● **Compatibility:** Community tank.

At first glance this fish seems nothing out of the ordinary, but see it under the correct lighting conditions and you will change your mind immediately. A little sidelighting, such as the morning sunshine coming through the front glass, will show up all the iridescences of the fish's scales, sparkling like clusters of diamonds. The male's fins, although relatively colourless, are edged with blue-white and well formed. The dorsal is sickle shaped and extends well over the caudal peduncle. Females are less sparkling and do not develop a long dorsal fin.

The aquarium should be furnished as for the Congo Tetra, so that the fish's fins can be seen to best advantage. Spawning (in soft, peat-filtered water) is not difficult; the fish is prolific and the free-swimming fry grow quickly.

Above: **Moenkhausia pittieri**
This fish gained its popular name of Diamond Tetra from the sparkling display of its iridescent body.

Family: CHARACIDAE
Moenkhausia sanctaefilomenae
Red-eye Tetra
● **Distribution:** South America: Rio Paraguay and Rio Parnaiba.
● **Length:** Up to 60mm(2.4in).
● **Tank length:** 60cm(24in).
● **Diet:** Worms, crustaceans, insects, plant matter, dried food.
● **Water temperature:** 21-26°C (70-79°F).
● **Compatibility:** Spacious community tank.

Like its larger lookalike relative, *M. oligolepis*, the Red-eye Tetra has a blue-grey body with sharply defined scales, particularly those on the upper part of the deep body. The eye is almost completely red and there is a yellow vertical bar across the rear end of the caudal peduncle. The base of the caudal fin is black with a white area immediately behind it. Dorsal and anal fins may be tipped with white. The straight lateral line is exceptionally prominent, from just in front of the dorsal to the yellow patch on the caudal peduncle. The female is noticeably

plumper than the male, especially at breeding time.

Unless offered supplementary greenfoods, such as lettuce or spinach leaves, the Red-eye Tetra will turn its attention to the soft-leaved plants. There is no difficulty in spawning this species in soft to medium-hard water.

Above:
Moenkhausia sanctaefilomenae
This is one of the best shoaling charcins, but needs space to show off its best points. It behaves peacefully in a community tank and breeds easily. It is ideal for a beginner and a better proposition than the larger M. oligolepis.

Family: CHARACIDAE

Nematobrycon palmeri

Emperor Tetra

- ● **Distribution:** Northern South America: Colombia.
- ● **Length:** Up to 55mm(2.2in).
- ● **Tank length:** 45cm(18in).
- ● **Diet:** Worms, crustaceans, finely chopped meat and dried food.
- ● **Water temperature:** 23-26°C (73-79°F).
- ● **Compatibility:** Community tank.

The Emperor Tetra came into the hobby relatively recently and immediately became a favourite. The violet-purple top part of the body surmounts a blue-black band running the whole length of the fish. The eyes are iridescent blue-green. Like most tetras, the male fish has better fins; the dorsal fin being sickle shaped with extension rays from its tip, the caudal fin is crescent shaped, again having

Above: **Nematobrycon palmeri**
The Emperor Tetra rivals any tropical fish, with its impressive range of body colours and blue-green eye.

extending rays from its tips and from its centre. The long-based anal fin is bright yellow with a thin dark band just inside the margin. Apart from the finnage differences (the female does not develop the ray extensions) there is a variation in the colour of the eyes between male and female – those of the female are more green than blue – but it takes a practised eye to detect the subtle difference.

A shady, well-planted tank will allow the fish to settle down and show of its best. Although soft water is often advocated, hard water is also accepted, even for spawning. Breeding is quite possible and this is a rewarding species to keep.

Family: CHARACIDAE

Paracheirodon innesi

Neon Tetra

● **Distribution:** Northern South America: Upper Amazon.
● **Length:** Up to 40mm(1.6in).
● **Tank length:** 30cm(12in).
● **Diet:** Worms, small insects and crustaceans, plant matter and dried food.
● **Water temperature:** 21-26°C (70-79°F).
● **Compatibility:** Ideal for the smaller community aquarium but not with larger fishes.

Until the Cardinal Tetra came along, the Neon Tetra reigned supreme as the most colourful small tetra. It is said to have been banned from competitive shows after its introduction to the hobby in the 1930s because it was felt it had an unfair advantage over all the rest of the exhibits. A more up-to-date story is that so many of these fishes are being bred commercially in the Far East that they are becoming better known as Hong Kong Tetras. The main colour difference between the Neon and the Cardinal is that the red area of the former does not cover the entire body length, stopping halfway along. The female Neon is plumper than the male and this is often easily noticed by the bending effect it has in the iridescent blue line along the body. The mouth is fitted with a good set of teeth, a reminder of the family relationship between this aquarium jewel and the Piranha.

A hardy fish, it occupies the middle and lower levels and can easily be acclimatized to many types of water. Needless to say, a shoal of Neons in a well-furnished aquarium is an unforgettable sight, but giving them cichlids as tankmates might be tempting providence too much. Soft water is preferred for breeding. Furnish the relatively small tank with a bushy plant to catch the eggs.

Below: **Paracheirodon innesi**
Universally popular, this species is active, colourful, and hardy, and breeds readily in soft water.

Family: CHARACIDAE

Pristella maxillaris

X-ray Fish; Water Goldfish
- **Distribution:** Northern South America and Lower Amazon.
- **Length:** Up to 45mm(1.8in).
- **Tank length:** 45cm(18in).
- **Diet:** Worms, small crustaceans and dried food.
- **Water temperature:** 21-26°C (70-79°F).
- **Compatibility:** Community tank.

Formerly known as *P. riddlei*, the X-ray Fish has a translucent body, although there are other species with a more justifiable claim to transparency. There are few markings on the body, just a small dark blotch behind the gill cover, but the dorsal, anal and ventral fins

Above: **Pristella maxillaris**
This lively fish should be kept in a shoal in subdued light. Breeding success needs a compatible pair.

are attractively marked in yellow, black and white. The female is deeper bodied than the male.

A shoaling species, it should be kept in a shady aquarium with a dark substrate. Breeding is possible, but pairs do not always perform with reliability. Once 'paired' successfully, however, two fishes seem to continue without any difficulty. An albino form has been introduced recently.

Below: **Thayeria boehlkei**
The dark stripe accentuates this fish's oblique swimming position.

Family: CHARACIDAE

Thayeria boehlkei
Boehlke's Penguin Fish
- **Distribution:** South America: Amazon Basin.
- **Length:** Up to 60mm(2.4in).
- **Tank length:** 60cm(24in).
- **Diet:** Worms, small insects and crustaceans and dried food.
- **Water temperature:** 23-25°C (73-77°F).
- **Compatibility:** Community tank.

The black line running from behind the gill cover to the lower edge of the caudal fin appears to be weighing the fish down, making it 'tail-heavy'; this is an optical illusion for the fish swims naturally at an oblique 'head-up' angle near to the surface of the water. Fins are colourless except for the yellowish tinge to the anal fin and the lower edge of the caudal fin. There is some similarity between this species and others in the genus, but recognition is aided by checking the size and location of the black line on the body. Females are stouter in the body. Livefoods are favourite but dried foods will be accepted as an occasional substitute or variation. Breeding is uncomplicated, usually taking place in the evening. Large numbers of eggs are laid following a vigorous driving chase into bushy plants.

OTHER CHARACIN-LIKE FISHES

While not strictly classified within the characidae family, the following species are generally associated with characins by hobbyists. Most of these fishes have adipose fins and most share the same water requirements in the aquarium if not the same natural habitat. You should be able to assess the compatibility of different species by comparing their sizes and natural tendencies; keeping a piranha with smaller fishes may be asking for problems, for example, while large active swimmers may upset shy 'headstanding' species. Some of the larger predatory species also have a tendency to devour aquarium plants, and you should take this into consideration when furnishing a new aquarium, or selecting fishes.

Family: ANOSTOMIDAE

Anostomus anostomus
Striped Anostomus
- **Distribution:** South America: Amazon Basin.
- **Length:** Up to 60mm(2.4in).
- **Tank length:** 60cm(24in).
- **Diet:** Worms, small insects, crustaceans, greenfood, dried food.
- **Water temperature:** 23-26°C (73-79°F).
- **Compatibility:** Community tank with sufficient retreats. May become territorially aggressive.

The Striped Anostomus is a very attractive fish, with a yellow torpedo-shaped body, decorated by three broad zig-zag-edged dark stripes, which run from snout to caudal fins. Dorsal and caudal fins are marked with bright red, but these markings may turn a dull red-brown with increasing age. Females are generally deeper bodied than the males, but there are few other external differences between the sexes. The mouth is small and upturned, a seemingly unusual feature on a fish that spends it time swimming in a 'head-downward' attitude. However, research has shown that the fish browses on the undersides of aquatic leaves and root systems. When feeding from the aquarium floor, the fish has to turn over almost on to its back. The fish remains at an angle when at rest, the stripes camouflaging it perfectly among the plant stems.

Keeping six or eight together seems to reduce any unsocial behaviour. They make excellent aquarium subjects, and settle down well in a tank furnished with plenty of hiding places and tangled root decorations. Ideally, water conditions should be soft and slightly acid. The only drawback with these beautiful fishes is that, so far, no reports have been recorded of any successful aquarium spawnings.

121

Above: **Anostomus anostomus**
This handsome fish feeds with the head pointing downward, often with the body held vertically. It has not been bred in an aquarium.

Below: **Chilodus punctatus**
The characteristic oblique swimming position adopted by the headstanders may help them to hide among vegetation.

Family: CURIMATIDAE
Chilodus punctatus
Spotted Headstander
- **Distribution:** South America: Amazon, Guyana.
- **Length:** Up to 100mm(4in).
- **Tank length:** 60cm(24in).
- **Diet:** Worms, crustaceans, insects, plant matter, dried food.
- **Water temperature:** 21-28°C (70-83°F).
- **Compatibility:** Community tank, furnished with plenty of retreats.

The Spotted Headstander is easy to recognize; the body is covered with well-defined, dark-based scales, which give the spotted effect. A dark line runs from the snout to just into the caudal fin. The large square dorsal fin is spotted, the remaining fins clear. The eye is red. This fish adopts a pronounced 'head-down' position, both for swimming and when at rest. Provide a well-furnished tank with some root decoration. Spawning occurs near to the bottom and the fertilized eggs swell up considerably. Hatching takes two to three days but bear in mind that the young may be problematical to rear.

Family: LEBIASINIDAE
Copella arnoldi
Spraying Characin
- **Distribution:** South America: lower Amazon and Rio Paru.
- **Length:** Male up to 80mm (3.2in), female up to 60mm (2.4in).
- **Tank length:** 45cm(18in).
- **Diet:** Worms, insects, crustaceans and dried food.
- **Water temperature:** 23-27°C (73-81°F).
- **Compatibility:** Community tank.

The golden-brown body has dark-edged scales and the dorsal fin is red, marked with black and white. The upper lobe of the caudal fin is larger than the lower. The male's colours darken with excitement or when spawning. This fish has a remarkable spawning action. In the wild, eggs are laid out of water on the underside of overhanging plant leaves (in the aquarium the cover glass may be used) and the male uses his large caudal fin to splash the eggs to prevent them drying out while they hatch.

Below: **Copella arnoldi**
A pair of Spraying Characins spawn on an overhanging leaf.

Family: GASTEROPELECIDAE

Carnegiella strigata
Marbled Hatchetfish
- **Distribution:** South America: Amazon, Guyana.
- **Length:** 45mm(1.8in).
- **Tank length:** 60cm(24in).
- **Diet:** Crustaceans, insects and dried food.
- **Water temperature:** 24-29°C (75-84°F).
- **Compatibility:** Community tanks, with the proviso that only middle or lower level swimming tankmates are chosen.

Hatchetfishes are small surface-swimming species, a fact borne out by their straight dorsal surface, which allows them to hang just below the water surface lying in wait for insects to alight. Their deep bodies accommodate powerful pectoral muscles that 'flap' the pectoral fins enabling them to 'fly' considerable distances across the surface. *Carnegiella*, the smaller of the two genera in the gasteropelecidae family, can be distinguished from *Gasteropelecus* by the absence of an adipose fin. The Marbled Hatchetfish has attractive marbling below a gleaming gold line running from the eye to the caudal fin. The

Above: **Carnegiella strigata**
A peaceful, surface-dwelling fish that thrives in shady conditions.

caudal fin has a dark base with two small white marks above and below. Although these shoaling fishes can be kept in small well-covered tanks, longer tanks suit their requirements better. Reports of spawnings are few, but indicate that spawning occurs under roots of floating plants in the evening. Eggs are adhesive and stick to the plants. The fry can be raised successfully on small livefoods.

Family: GASTEROPELECIDAE

Gasteropelecus levis

Silver Hatchetfish

● **Distribution:** South America: lower Amazon.
● **Length:** Up to 60mm(2.4in).
● **Tank length:** 60cm(24in).
● **Diet:** Worms, crustaceans, insects and dried food.
● **Water temperature:** 24-30°C (75-86°F).
● **Compatibility:** Community tanks, with only middle or lower level swimming tankmates.

Like the previous species, the Silver Hatchetfish is also well equipped to fly across the water surface – either in pursuit of food or as a means of escape from would-be predators. It can be distinguished from the related genus by the presence of an adipose fin. Although a rather plain fish, the silver sides can appear almost burnished under a little sidelighting. There is a dark line, bordered by a lighter one on each side, running from behind the gill cover to the caudal fin, and this is crossed by a dark bar on the rear of the caudal peduncle. The dorsal fin has a black area on its base. Conditions required are as for the Marbled Hatchetfish. Cover tanks securely as these fishes are expert jumpers. There are no reports of successful aquarium breeding.

Below: **Gasteropelecus levis**
Sometimes rather delicate in an aquarium, this is a lively 'jumper'.

Family: CITHARINIDAE

Nannaethiops unitaeniatus

One-striped African Characin
- **Distribution:** Tropical West Africa to the White Nile.
- **Length:** Up to 65mm(2.6in).
- **Tank length:** 60cm(24in).
- **Diet:** Worms, crustaceans, insects, dried food.
- **Water temperature:** 23-26°C (73-79°F).
- **Compatibility:** Community tank.

The body shape of this characin is elongate with a distinct two-colour pattern. Above a gold-topped dark longitudinal line the back is brown with well-defined scales (another African species characteristic); below, the colour is pale yellow-silver. The fins are pale green-yellow but at spawning time the black front edge of the male's dorsal fin turns red, as does the upper lobe of the caudal fin. The adipose fin is quite large. Females grow larger than males but do not have as much colour.

This peaceful fish is quite suited to a community aquarium, but it does need room in which to swim. Water conditions should be on the soft acidic side. Locate the breeding tank where it receives some morning sunlight. This prolific fish scatters its eggs throughout the tank. Again, egg eating may be a problem.

Above:
Nannaethiops unitaeniatus
This smart, prolific species is often overlooked by hobbyists.

Family: LEBIASINIDAE

Nannostomus beckfordi

Golden Pencilfish
- **Distribution:** South America: Guyana to Rio Negro.
- **Length:** Up to 65mm(2.6in).
- **Tank length:** 30cm(12in).
- **Diet:** Worms, crustaceans, insects and dried food.
- **Water temperature:** 24-27°C (75-81°F).
- **Compatibility:** Community tank.

As with all pencilfishes, the body of this fish is slim and torpedo shaped. Because of its wide distribution, any colour description may not necessarily fit all individuals, and there have been several sub-species classified. The most commonly imported species has a brown body with a gold-topped dark longitudinal line. The dorsal and anal fins are set exactly opposite each other; there is no adipose fin. When excited or in breeding condition, the flanks and bases of all the fins (with the exception of the pectoral fins) become bright red in the male. Tips of the ventral fins are bluish white. Females are less colourful. A shoal of pencilfishes make spectacular viewing, the male fishes constantly show off.

Family: LEBIASINIDAE

Nannostomus marginatus

Dwarf Pencilfish

● **Distribution:** South America: Guyana and the lower reaches of the Amazon.
● **Length:** 40mm(1.6in).
● **Tank length:** 30cm(12in).
● **Diet:** Worms, crustaceans, insects and dried foods.
● **Water temperature:** 24-27°C (75-81°F).
● **Compatibility:** Community tank.

Although this is the smallest of the pencilfishes, most hobbyists agree that it is the most beautiful. The body is stockier than others in the genus and is marked with three dark longitudinal bands. The conspicuous middle band is separated from the one above it by

Above: **Nannostomus beckfordi**
Spawn this species in a densely-planted aquarium to prevent the adults eating their own eggs.

a bright gold band. The dorsal, anal and ventral fins are marked with bright red, but the caudal fin is colourless. Females are deeper in the body than males. Keep these fishes in a small shoal for best effect. Spawning is straightforward but the fish is not prolific, laying only about three dozen eggs. The eggs swell up after fertilization and may be eaten by the parents, so provide dense, bushy plants in the aquarium to trap the eggs and remove the adults after spawning has ceased.

Below: **Nannostomus marginatus**
The Dwarf Pencilfish is a much sought-after community fish.

Family: LEBIASINIDAE

Nannostomus trifasciatus

Three-lined, or Three-banded Pencilfish
● **Distribution:** South America: Guyana, central Amazon, Rio Negro.
● **Length:** Up to 60mm(2.4in).
● **Tank length:** 30cm(12in).
● **Diet:** Worms, crustaceans, insects and dried food.
● **Water temperature:** 22-26°C (72-79°F).
● **Compatibility:** Community tank.

At first sight, the Three-lined Pencilfish could be mistaken for the previous species, but there are a number of physical differences that make for positive identification. Although it also has three longitudinal bands on the body, this fish is longer and much slimmer; there is a red fleck on the gold band near the fish's shoulder, and the caudal fin has a red patch at the base of each lobe. The adipose fin may be tiny or non-

Above: **Nannostomus trifasciatus**
The three longitudinal bands are replaced at night by broad bars.

existent. Females are deeper bodied and slightly less colourful than the males. Mostly a middle and upper water level swimmer, this shoaling fish appreciates a well-planted tank and plenty of livefoods. Breeding is difficult.

Family: LEBIASINIDAE

Pyrrhulina laeta

Half-banded Pyrrhulina
● **Distribution:** South America: Guyana and Middle Amazon.
● **Length:** Up to 80mm(3.2in).
● **Tank length:** 60cm(24in).
● **Diet:** Worms, crustaceans, insects and dried food.
● **Water temperature:** 21-28°C (70-83°F).
● **Compatibility:** Community tank.

Below: **Pyrrhulina laeta**
Despite appearing to spawn here, no reports of successful breeding of this fish have been received.

The Half-banded Pyrrhulina is a slim fish, similar in build to the pencilfishes. The longitudinal dark line on the body reaches only halfway along the flanks, ending just above the anal fin. Scales are dark edged and well defined. The dorsal fin has a dark mark in the middle. The caudal fin of the male is assymetrical, the upper lobe being the larger. Apart from this distinguishing feature, the female fish is smaller and less colourful. A well-established aquarium with plenty of plants and adequate swimming space will suit this fish very well. It inhabits the middle and upper levels of the water, taking most of its food from the surface, and appreciates a predominance of livefoods in its diet. Spawning has not been reported in captivity.

Family: SERRASALMIDAE
Serrasalmus nattereri
Red Piranha
● **Distribution:** South America: Amazon, Orinoco, Parana.
● **Length:** 300mm(12in).
● **Tank length:** 120cm(48in).
● **Diet:** Insects, worms, fish and meat.
● **Water temperature:** 24-27°C (75-81°F).
● **Compatibility:** Species tank.

Comparing the ferocious Piranha with the diminutive decorative tetras gives little immediate evidence that they are related, but they are (although the Piranha is now classified in a separate family), and both have the same sharp teeth. The Piranha is an aggressive predator and should be kept in its own aquarium stocked with tough plants.

The heavy body is sharply truncated at the front end, with the teeth-filled mouth at its extreme tip. The silver grey body is marked with large dark spots and the throat, chest and anal fin region is coloured bright red. The small dorsal fin is set well back on the body and the long-based anal fin is only separated from the caudal by the caudal peduncle. The caudal fin is wide with a black rear edge. Spawning is reported to have occurred in public aquariums but the hobbyist usually only keeps juveniles, which have not reached sexual maturity. Handle these fishes with extreme care to avoid damage and to protect yourself from their very sharp teeth.

Below: **Serrasalmus nattereri**
Only young specimens are really suitable for the home aquarium.

CICHLIDS

Tropical fishes are not always chosen for their good looks, as examination of some of the following species will reveal! The fishes in the cichlidae family have often attracted the attention of hobbyists (sometimes to the point of obsession) by their behaviour, particularly at breeding time. These fishes not only exercise very good parental care of the eggs and subsequent young, but also exhibit diverse methods of reproduction. Some deposit eggs on open sites, others hide them away secretively in caves, while a third group rely on the female fish to incubate the eggs in her mouth. In some species the parents develop a heavy mucus on their skin on which the newly hatched young fishes feed. Some fishes may become hand-tame and even appear to recognize their owner.

Unfortunately, some cichlids can be quite aggressive and may destroy tank decorations and harass other fishes at spawning times. Many are heavy feeders and will quickly pollute the tank with their waste products, and a good filtration system should be employed in the cichlid aquarium to deal with this problem. Species vary in their requirements and you will need to furnish the tank accordingly. South American species will tolerate planted tanks and soft water, but African Lake species will need rocky caves, algae-covered outcrops and hard water if they are to be seen at their best and not quarrel incessantly with their neighbours.

Family: CICHLIDAE

Aequidens curviceps

Sheepshead Acara; Flag Cichlid
● **Distribution:** South America.
● **Length:** 75mm(3in).
● **Tank length:** 60cm(24in).
● **Diet:** Worms, crustaceans, insects and dried foods.

● **Water temperature:** 22-25°C (72-77°F).
● **Compatibility:** Community tank.

Below: **Aequidens curviceps**
This small shy cichlid, which can be quite a rarity, will breed readily in the community aquarium.

The Sheepshead Acara has a stocky body with a rounded head and long-based dorsal and anal fins. The overall impression is of a silvery blue-green sheen on the body, which has well-defined scales. Blue facial markings and specklings on the larger fins add to the attractiveness of this fish. Two dark blotches, often joined by an indistinct dark line, appear on the body, one behind the gill cover, one above the front of the anal fin. A further blotch appears in the centre of the dorsal fin, which has a greenish gold coloration, often with a red tip. The mature male fish develops more pointed dorsal and anal fins than the female. Spawning occurs in open water.

Above: **Aequidens maronii**
This very undemanding cichlid has even bred in a community tank.

Family: CICHLIDAE

Aequidens maronii
Keyhole Cichlid

- **Distribution:** Guyana, Surinam.
- **Length:** Up to 100mm(4in).
- **Tank length:** 90cm(36in).
- **Diet:** Worms, crustaceans and insects.
- **Water temperature:** 22-25°C (72-77°F).
- **Compatibility:** Quiet community or species tank.

The Keyhole Cichlid is a somewhat shy fish, which prefers a quiet tank and will generally ignore its tankmates. Its mottled golden-brown body has rows of sometimes vague, longitudinal markings. A dark band passes from the forehead through the eye and there may be occasional dark areas displayed on the flanks. The intensity of markings may depend on the mood of the fish. This cichlid takes its popular name from the dark blotch midway along the body, the shape of which resembles a keyhole. The fins are green-blue, with the dorsal and anal fins having whitish tips. The anal and dorsal fins of the male fish develop long points and extend well past the caudal peduncle. The Keyhole Cichlid is tolerant of varying water conditions. It breeds on flat surfaces and the young may remain with the parent fishes.

Family: CICHLIDAE

Aequidens pulcher

Blue Acara

● **Distribution:** Central and northern South America.
● **Length:** 160mm(6.3in).
● **Tank length:** 90cm(36in).
● **Diet:** Worms, crustaceans and insects.
● **Water temperature:** 22-26°C (72-79°F).
● **Compatibility:** Community tank of robust fishes or species tank.

Referred to as *A. latifrons*, the Blue Acara is a longstanding aquarium favourite. The body is covered with blue speckling and the face with blue wavy lines. A number of vertical dark bars appear on the flanks of the fish and these vary in intensity depending on the mood of the fish. The dorsal and anal fins extend well back over the caudal peduncle, the male's fins being more pointed than the female's.

It is a pugnacious fish, when the mood takes it, and you would be well advised to avoid keeping it with smaller fishes, such as a shoal of Neon Tetras. It is a very willing spawner; eggs are laid and fertilized on a flat surface in open water and the parents will keep their chosen territory clear of other fishes with some vigour!

Family: CICHLIDAE

Apistogramma agassizi

Agassiz's Dwarf Cichlid

● **Distribution:** Brazil and Bolivia.
● **Length:** 80mm(3.2in).
● **Tank length:** 60cm(24in).
● **Diet:** Worms, crustaceans, insects and dried food.
● **Water temperature:** 23-25°C (72-77°F).
● **Compatibility:** Community tank.

Species within the genus *Apistogramma* combine brilliant colours with all the family care generally practised by cichlids. Most are of modest size, can be accommodated in relatively small tanks, and are sociable community inhabitants. Agassiz' Dwarf Cichlid is a typical example of the genus. The most distinguishing feature of

this species is the spade-shaped caudal fin with a white line just inside its edges. Its iridescent blue scales are especially vivid under sidelighting. The anal fin and long-based dorsal fin have red edges. Females of the genus, generally smaller than males, are very similar to each other – plain golden brown with a diagonal dark stripe through the eye, which makes identificatio of isolated females difficult.

A well-planted tank containing overturned flowerpots or coconut shells is ideal for this fish. Spawning occurs away from the direct gaze of the hobbyist within the safety of such retreats.

Above: **Aequidens pulcher**
Beneath this spawning pair eggs can be seen on a flat rock that the fishes have cleaned.

Below: **Apistogramma agassizi**
The male of this species is easily identified by his blue scales and spade-shaped caudal fin.

Family: CICHLIDAE

Astronotus ocellatus
Oscar

● **Distribution:** South America: Orinoco to Rio Paraguay.
● **Length:** Up to 350mm(14in).
● **Tank length:** 120cm(48in).
● **Diet:** Worms, crustaceans, insects, chopped meat, dried food.
● **Water temperature:** 22-26°C (72-79°F).
● **Compatibility:** A species tank or very large community with other robust fishes of a similar size.

Comparing the adult fish with juvenile forms is not a very productive exercise, for there is a vast difference between them. The young fishes are prettily marked with a silver and black marbling effect, while the adult fishes, shown here, can hardly be so described. Adult fishes have dark sides marked with rusty red areas. At the base of the caudal fin is a red-ringed black spot – the ocellatus of the specific name. There is also a considerable difference in size between juveniles and adults; the pleasantly marked 2-5cm(1-2in) youngster will very rapidly grow into a large bulky individual of up to 35cm(14in). Its alternative names of Velvet Cichlid and Peacock-eyed Cichlid may be more literally descriptive of this fish, but the name 'Oscar' does indicate that the fish has a personality. Once established in its own tank, Oscar, the family pet, often becomes hand tame, frequently allowing its owner to hand feed, and even stroke, it. Caring for this fish is not difficult; it requires plenty of meaty foods and consequently produces a large amount of waste products. The Oscar will need an efficient filtration system and frequent water changes to keep the water quality within healthy limits. Use only tough, well-rooted plants (or just rocks) in the aquarium. Eggs are laid on a flat surface and number thousands. The Oscar has several aquarium forms, the Red and the Tiger, in addition to the natural coloration shown here.

Above: **Astronotus ocellatus**
The size of the adult Oscar belies

its peaceable disposition, both
with other large fishes and with its
owner. It needs lots of meaty foods
and a large, well-filtered tank.

Family: CICHLIDAE

Etroplus maculatus

Orange Chromide

● **Distribution:** India and Sri Lanka.
● **Length:** Up to 80mm(3.2in).
● **Tank length:** 60cm(24in).
● **Diet:** Worms, crustaceans, insects, fish, plant matter and dried food.
● **Water temperature:** 22-28°C (72-83°F).
● **Compatibility:** Quiet community aquarium.

The two or three species in the *Etroplus* genus are the only cichlids found in the continent of Asia. The body shape of this cichlid is oval and the general colour yellow-orange. Each scale has a red centre dot. Three dark patches of variable intensity appear on the upper flanks, the centre one being the most prominent. The dorsal and caudal fins are yellow with red edges, the anal fin, also yellow, is black-edged. Out of the breeding period colours are less intense.

Furnish the aquarium with plenty of retreats and add some aquarium salt to the water, as pure freshwater appears to render the fish susceptible to fungal disease. The eggs are laid on firm surfaces and the fry attach themselves to the sides of the parents until they reach the free-swimming stage.

Family: CICHLIDAE

Heros (Thorichthys) meeki

Firemouth Cichlid

● **Distribution:** Central America.
● **Length:** 150mm(6in).
● **Tank length:** 90cm(36in).
● **Diet:** Worms, crustceans, insects and dried food.
● **Water temperature:** 20-25°C (68-77°F).
● **Compatibility:** Community tank.

The belligerent appearance of the red Firemouth Cichlid (formerly known as *Cichlasoma meeki*) belies its behaviour in the aquarium; it is quite peaceful towards other fishes, although it may occasionally pick a quarrel with smaller members of its own kind. The head is pointed with a sharply rising forehead. The long-based dorsal fin starts far forward, above the edge of the gill cover. A number of dark vertical bars cross the blue-grey body but the main feature is the red area beneath the throat, which extends backwards along the belly into the anal fin. The bright red coloration intensifies in the male at spawning time, and a typical threat posture involves the extension of brilliant gill covers. One bright-edged blotch appears on the gill cover, another midway along the body. Females do not develop such pointed fins as males.

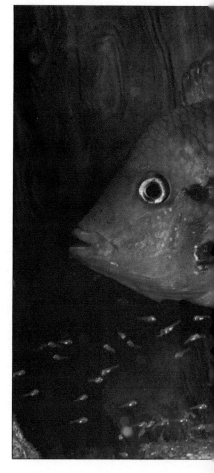

Above: **Etroplus maculatus**
One of the few cichlids from Asia, this species lays brightly coloured eggs. Add some aquarium salt to the water for these fishes.

Below:
Heros (Thorichthys) meeki
This male is guarding a large shoal of young fry. The Firemouth is one of the most striking cichlids.

Family: CICHLIDAE
Julidochromis ornatus
Golden Julie
- **Distribution:**
- **Length:** 70mm(2.8in).
- **Tank length:** 60mm(24in).
- **Diet:** Worms, crustaceans, insects, plant matter, dried foods.
- **Water temperature:** 22-25°C (72-77°F).
- **Compatibility:** Best kept in a rocky furnished cichlid tank.

One of the first exports of new fishes from the African Lakes, the Golden Julie has striking coloration of black and golden yellow horizontal stripes above the central line of the spindle-shaped body. The underparts and fins are plain yellow, and the major single fins have dark edges. Like all African Lake fishes, this species requires hard water and a rocky environment. Being a territorial species, this fish should have numerous retreats available in its tank among built-up rocky terraces so that quarrelling does not occur. The female, smaller than the male, lays eggs inside caves and the male tends the young.

Below: **Julidochromis ornatus**
Easily identified by its bold stripes, this is an interesting hard-water cichlid from Lake Tanganyika.

Family: CICHLIDAE

Labeotropheus fuelleborni

Fuelleborn's Cichlid

● **Distribution:** East Africa, in Lake Malawi.
● **Length:** Up to 120mm(4.7in).
● **Tank length:** 90cm(36in).
● **Diet:** Worms, crustaceans, insects, plant matter, dried food.
● **Water temperature:** 22-25°C (72-77°F).
● **Compatibility:** Best kept in a cichlid community aquarium furnished with plenty of rocks.

The cichlids that inhabit Lake Malawi (formerly Lake Nyassa) are known by the collective names of Mbuna or Chindongo. All these fishes graze on algae from the rocky shore in the shallower areas of the lake. The main identifying feature of these fishes is the characteristic protrusion of the top lip over the bottom; the chisel-shaped teeth have developed to facilitate algae-grazing.

Fuelleborn's Cichlid has 'colour morphs', that is different colour

Above: **Labeotropheus fuelleborni**
This active cichlid needs plenty of swimming space and rocks.

strains exist quite naturally. The normally coloured male is blue with reddish extremities to the fins; mottled yellow and also red-yellow males also occur. Females are a dappled yellow colour. The aquarium must have rocks and a bright light will encourage algal growth on these. Supplement this beneficial green element of the fishes' diet with lettuce or spinach, as well as algae scrapings from other tanks. Most Lake cichlids are active, territorial and quarrelsome, so spacious tanks are obligatory.

A number of yellow egg spots appear on the male's anal fin and play an important part in the spawning sequence; they attract the female as she picks up the previously laid eggs and she simultaneously takes the male's sperm into her mouth where fertilization occurs. The female incubates the eggs in her throat cavity. This spawning method is known as 'mouthbrooding.'

Family: CICHLIDAE

Lamprologus brichardi

● **Distribution:** East Africa: Lake Tanganyika.
● **Length:** 110mm(4.5in).
● **Tank length:** 60cm(24in).
● **Diet:** Worms, crustaceans, insects and dried food.
● **Water temperature:** 22-25°C (72-75°F).
● **Compatibility:** Community tank or larger species tank. The latter is preferable if you have several – it will allow territory independence.

This rather plain grey-chocolate brown fish has blue-white edges to all its fins. There is a horizontal dark bar running from the snout through the eye to a gold-surrounded dark patch on the gill cover. The eye is bright blue and there are additional blue markings on the face. The dorsal and anal fins are quite pointed and the caudal fin is lyre shaped. Although there may be hardly any external clues to aid sexing, the female may be slightly heavier and have shorter fins. To see this fish at its best, create a rocky environment

with plenty of caves; dark coloured rocks (slate is good) will show up the fishes' fins particularly well. If the tank is sufficiently large, several pairs (or even several males with their associated 'harems') can co-habit peacefully, setting up their territories independently of each other. In the more modestly sized community tank, however, you will be restricted to perhaps only one pair. Spawning is done secretively in caves and the young may be regarded as slow growers; they remain with the adults for several months even when subsequent spawnings occur.

Family: CICHLIDAE

Mesonauta festivus
Festive Cichlid
● **Distribution:** South America.
● **Length:** 150mm(6in).
● **Tank length:** 90cm(36in).
● **Diet:** Worms, crustaceans, insects, plant matter, dried food.
● **Water temperature:** 20-26°C (68-79°F).
● **Compatibility:** Community tank of similar-sized fishes.

Left: **Mesonauta festivus**
Once established, a pair of these fishes will continue to breed. This species is peaceful enough to be kept with Angelfishes.

Above: **Lamprologus brichardi**
Although territorial, this species is peaceful if given enough space in a suitably furnished aquarium.

The Festive Cichlid is a rivermate of the Angelfish in the wild, and there is a physical resemblance, too, in the ventral fins, which are bony and filamentous in both species. The grey-green body has but one main decoration; a line passing diagonally upwards from the snout to the tip of the dorsal fin. There is also a small black patch on the top of the caudal peduncle. Above the diagonal line the body is yellow-green, below it silvery. When the fish is excited or under stress, numerous vertical dark bars can be seen crossing the body. Sexual differences are again not too obvious; longer dorsal fins may indicate a male and observation of the breeding tube may also be constructive.

This shy, non-aggressive species will thrive in a well-planted aquarium but it may be prudent to exclude small fishes from its tank when it is fully grown. It is best to employ the usual method of putting several fishes together and letting them choose their own partners. Festive Cichlids are open water spawners and make good parents. This species was formerly known as *Cichlasoma festivum*.

Family: CICHLIDAE

Microgeophagus ramirezi

The Ram

● **Distribution:** Bolivia and Venezuela.
● **Length:** 50mm(2in).
● **Tank length:** 60cm(24in).
● **Diet:** Worms, crustaceans, insects and dried foods.
● **Water temperature:** 25-28°C (75-83°F).
● **Compatibility:** Quiet community tank with decorative tetras, etc.

The Ram (a shortened form of its specific name) is also known to continental European hobbyists as the Butterfly Dwarf Cichlid, a much more descriptive name. The body colours are particularly iridescent – violet-red with sparkling blue-green spots. The first few rays of the red-edged, long-based dorsal fin are jet black and the second or third rays are much elongated in males. A black vertical bar crosses the eye and there is a dark blotch midway along the body. Females develop a bright violet ventral area. There is also an aquarium-bred golden strain, which has brilliant violet iridescences to the flanks.

   The Ram can be acclimatized to harder water over a period of months with gradual partial water changes of harder water, or using a calcium-rich substrate, which will naturally harden the aquarium's soft water. Eggs are laid in a depression dug in the substrate or on a flat stone. This species was formerly known as *Apistogramma ramirezi* and *Papiliochromis ramirezi*.

Family: CICHLIDAE

Nannacara anomala

Golden-eyed Dwarf Cichlid

● **Distribution:** Guyana.
● **Length:** Up to 80mm(3.2in).
● **Tank length:** 60cm(24in).
● **Diet:** Worms, crustaceans and insects.
● **Water temperature:** 22-28°C (72-83°F).
● **Compatibility:** Suitable for a quiet community aquarium.

Above: **Nannacara anomala**
This fish has an exceptionally well developed dorsal fin.

Right: **Microgeophagus ramirezi**
The Ram is a popular, if rather delicate, dwarf cichlid.

The body of this cichlid appears rounded at both ends, the caudal peduncle being very much shortened. The basic colour varies, depending on lighting and how the fish feels; colours range from golden brown through iridescent green to a darker criss-cross latticed pattern when the fish is excited or frightened. Each scale has a dark centre giving a regularly patterned effect to the body. The eye is quite large and golden. The dorsal and anal fins reach back over the caudal fin, the dorsal fin has blue, white and red edging.

   This fish inhabits the lower levels of the water. Provide flowerpots or coconut shells for this species to use both as retreats and spawning receptacles. The female becomes very aggressive while guarding the fertilized eggs and may harass the male.

Family: CICHLIDAE

Pelvicachromis pulcher
Kribensis

- **Distribution:** West Africa, in southern Nigeria.
- **Length:** Up to 100mm(4in).
- **Tank length:** 60cm(24in).
- **Diet:** Worms, crustaceans, insects and dried food.
- **Water temperature:** 24-28°C (75-83°F).
- **Compatibility:** Community tank with plenty of hideaways.

The modestly sized 'Krib' is a well-established aquarium favourite and hard to confuse with any other species. The caudal fin, which has a few 'eye-spots' in the upper lobes, is spade-shaped in the male and rounded, without pattern, in the female. The male's dorsal fin is long, trailing over the caudal fin. A feature of the female's coloration is the plum-coloured ventral area, which becomes intensified when spawning; this, coupled with a general highlighting of colours and

Above: **Pelvicachromis pulcher**
Cichlids are usually excellent parents. This male is taking his turn at guarding the offspring. Members of the Pelvicachromis *genus are secretive spawners, often surprising the fishkeeper with an unexpected brood. Be sure to provide rocks and some dense vegetation for shelter.*

a considerable darkening of the ventral fins in the female, serves to assist parent recognition by the young fishes. Like most dwarf cichlids, these fishes are secretive spawners. Parent fishes guard the eggs, which hatch in two or three days. The fry are free-swimming about four days later.

Right: **Pseudotropheus auratus**
In the wild this very active cichlid lives in the rocky areas of Lake Malawi. The juvenile's coloration is similar to that of the adult female (bottom). This species is suitable only for the experienced aquarist.

Family: CICHLIDAE

Pseudotropheus auratus

Malawi Golden Cichlid

● **Distribution:** East Africa, in Lake Malawi.
● **Length:** Males up to 110mm (4.3in), females to 90mm (3.5in).
● **Tank length:** 90cm(36in).
● **Diet:** Worms, crustaceans, insects, plant matter, dried food.
● **Water temperature:** 22-25°C (72-77°F).
● **Compatibility:** Best kept in cichlid community aquarium, furnished with rocks.

The juvenile fish slightly resembles *Julidochromis ornatus* in coloration but the body is much stockier. The adult male is a dark, blue-black fish with two gold stripes along the top of the body, and with a turquoise dorsal fin. The female retains the juvenile coloration of a yellow body with two dark stripes along the top of the body, a black, yellow-edged dorsal and black-speckled caudal fin. This African Lake cichlid needs hard water and the usual rocky furnishings. These cichlids are mouthbrooders – the female incubates the fertilized eggs in her throat until hatching.

Family: CICHLIDAE

Pterophyllum scalare

Angelfish

● **Distribution:** South America: Amazon and some tributaries.
● **Length:** Up to 150mm(6in).
● **Tank length:** 60cm(24in).
● **Diet:** Worms, crustaceans, insects, plant matter, dried food.
● **Water temperature:** 22-30°C (72-86°F).
● **Compatibility:** A community tank but not with small fishes.

The tall elegant lines of the Angelfish make it easy to distinguish. Several aquarium-developed colour varieties have become available since the discovery of the original black-striped silver fish. The body shape is not typically cichlid shaped; it is

Above: **Pterophyllum scalare**
This elegant favourite is now available in many different forms.

strongly compressed laterally, which allows the fish easy access among the water plant stems. The tall dorsal and anal fins are carried stiffly away from the body, and the ventral fins are thin bony structures. There are few external characteristics to determine sex. However, at breeding time, this egg-depositing species extends a small tube from the vent through which eggs and sperm pass in the respective sexes and the female's tube is broader and blunter than the male's. Eggs are laid on near-vertical surfaces, such as plant leaves, and are guarded until the fry are free-swimming.

Family: CICHLIDAE

Symphysodon aequifasciata axelrodi

Brown Discus

● **Distribution:** South America: Amazon (near Belem).
● **Length:** Up to 120mm(4.7in).
● **Tank length:** 100cm(39in).
● **Diet:** Worms, crustaceans, insects and plant matter.
● **Water temperature:** 25-30°C (77-86°F).
● **Compatibility:** Species tank in groups of six or more.

Considered by many hobbyists to be the ultimate in aquarium fishes, the Discus requires specialist care; bacteria-free, very soft water and a quiet spacious tank shared with a few fellow species. The disc-shaped body has long-based dorsal and anal fins, which almost form one continuous fin with the caudal fin, being interrupted only by the caudal peduncle. Several dark stripes – often indistinct – cross the brown body vertically, with a bold stripe passing through the eye. Sexing is very difficult and hobbyists usually allow the fishes to select their own partners. The young, when hatched from deposited eggs, find their first food in the mucus on their parents' bodies. This means that artificial hatching remotely from the parents is not so practicable as with other cichlid species. The Brown Discus is a challenging species.

Below: **Symphysodon aequifasciata axelrodi**
Like other discus fishes, this one needs soft, bacteria-free water.

LABYRINTH FISHES, GOURAMIES, SIAMESE FIGHTING FISHES
Although from different families, these fishes are linked by their possession of an extra breathing organ (situated in the head immediately behind the gills), which stores moist atmospheric air from the water surface. This enables the fish to survive where dissolved oxygen levels are low. Gouramies are slow-swimming, graceful fishes, Siamese fighting fishes live up to their name if two males share a tank, and African species are very predatory. Although some species are mouthbrooders, most are bubblenest breeders, guarding the fertilized eggs under a nest made from bubbles, which they blow at the water surface. Provide plenty of plants in the tank to give the female areas of retreat during breeding.

Family: BELONTIIDAE

Betta splendens

Siamese Fighting Fish
● **Distribution:** Southeast Asia.
● **Length:** 60mm(2.4in).
● **Tank length:** 45cm(18in).
● **Diet:** Worms, crustaceans, insects and dried foods.
● **Water temperature:** 25-28°C (77-83°F).
● **Compatibility:** Best kept in a species tank.

The Siamese Fighting Fish familiar to hobbyists bears little resemblance to the drab-coloured, short-finned fish found in the wild. Selective breeding has produced the many brightly coloured varieties available today. The body is elongate, with the wide flowing dorsal, anal and caudal fins of the male fish adding extra dimensions. The ventral fins are long and sabre shaped. The presence of the auxiliary breathing organ enables the fish to be kept in relatively small aquariums. The male fish is pugnacious towards any other male – a fact borne out both by its popular name and the culture in Thailand of staged fights between these fishes for betting purposes. Keep only one male in a community tank, along with one or two females. Spawning involves

the building of a bubblenest by the male, under which eggs are expelled by the female in a nuptial embrace. After spawning, leave the male to guard the nest and fry.

Above and below:
Betta splendens
These striking Siamese Fighting Fishes show two of the colour forms available. Keep males apart.

Family: BELONTIIDAE

Colisa chuna
Honey Gourami
● **Distribution:** Northeastern India, Bangladesh.
● **Length:** 45mm(1.8in).
● **Tank length:** 45cm(18in).
● **Diet:** Worms, small crustaceans, insects and dried foods.
● **Water temperature:** 24-26°C (75-79°F).
● **Compatibility:** Community tank with similar-sized fishes, or species tank.

The Honey Gourami is the smallest of the *Colisa* genus. The oval-shaped body is golden yellow in the male and light brown in the female. Dorsal and anal fins are about two-thirds of the body length and the ventral fins are limited to single filaments. These 'feelers' are equipped with taste cells at their tips so that the fish can locate food in murky waters.

Above: **Colisa chuna**
This male is startling in colour compared to the drab female.

At breeding time the male's colours intensify to a brilliant yellow and he develops a turquoise area beneath the throat, which extends to cover most of the anal fin. The female has a dark longitudinal line along her flanks. The bubblenest fry are very small but present few problems.

Family: BELONTIIDAE

Colisa lalia
Dwarf Gourami
● **Distribution:** Northeastern India, Assam, Bangladesh.
● **Length:** Up to 50mm(2in).
● **Tank length:** 30cm(12in).
● **Diet:** Worms, crustaceans, insects and dried food.
● **Water temperature:** 20-26°C (68-79°F).
● **Compatibility:** Community tank.

The blue-green body has red diagonal stripes. Iridescent specklings extend into the red-edged fins; ventral fins are red-yellow. The plumper females have much less colour. The male constructs a bubblenest from saliva and plant materials. He guards the nest and fry vigorously. Provide a well-planted tank and remove the female after spawning.

Below: **Colisa lalia**
A popular dwarf species.

Family: ANABANTIDAE

Ctenopoma oxyrhynchus

Sharp-nosed Ctenopoma; Marbled Climbing Perch
- **Distribution:** Central Africa, Zaire.
- **Length:** 100mm(4in).
- **Tank length:** 60cm(24in).
- **Diet:** Insect larvae and smaller fishes in the regular diet.
- **Water temperature:** 25-30°C (77-85°F).
- **Compatibility:** Species tank or in a community with large fishes.

The main difference between the labyrinth fishes of Asia and those of Africa lies in the fishes' disposition towards others: Asian fishes are generally peaceful (but highly defensive of their bubblenests at breeding time), while those of Africa are essentially predatory. The *Ctenopoma* genus contains many species with cryptic or mottled markings; this coloration provides excellent camouflage as the fish lies in wait for prey. In this respect the fish behaves similarly to the South American Leaf-fish, *Monocirrhus polyacanthus* (page 184). Body colour is a variable red-brown; a dark blotch in the centre of the flanks seen in juveniles fades with age. In very young fish, the rear half of the body is very dark. The dorsal and anal fins may become more pointed in male fishes, but other sexual differences are unknown. Furnish the tank with plenty of plants and submerged root systems to provide shelter.

Family: HELOSTOMATIDAE

Helostoma temmincki

Kissing Gourami
- **Distribution:** Southeast Asia, Thailand, Malaysia, Sumatra, Java, Borneo.
- **Length:** 300mm(12in).
- **Tank length:** 90cm(36in).
- **Diet:** Worms, crustaceans, insects, plant matter, dried foods.
- **Water temperature:** 24-28°C (75-83°F).
- **Compatibility:** Community tank.

There are two colour forms: the natural form is silvery green, with rows of longitudinal dots. The more normal aquarium form is totally pink. At one time this was believed to be a separate species, *H. rudolfi*. The lips, which are almost prehensile, are equipped with a rasping surface for removing algae from rocks and other surfaces. There are no externally visible sexual differences. This fish grows much larger in the wild than in the domestic aquarium, and is also sought after as food. In captivity it needs a reasonable amount of space and the inclusion of vegetable matter in its diet. Only use tough plants to furnish the aquarium. This fish has the quaint habit of kissing other members of the same species. Occasionally it will harrass other fishes by kissing their sides, so keep this species with fishes more of its own size. Spawning is said to occur at evening, with masses of floating eggs being produced. Incidentally, there is no social significance in the kissing action.

Above: **Ctenopoma oxyrhynchus**
Unlike its peaceable Asian relatives, this African labyrinth fish is extremely predatory. It is best kept in a species tank away from smaller fishes.

Below: **Helostoma temmincki**
This medium-sized fish grows much larger in the wild and is very prolific – up to 1000 eggs can be produced at each spawning. The young are ignored by the parents.

Family: BELONTIIDAE

Macropodus opercularis
Paradisefish

- **Distribution:** Korea, China, Vietnam, Taiwan.
- **Length:** Up to 90mm(3.5in).
- **Tank length:** 60cm(24in).
- **Diet:** Worms, crustaceans, insects, plant matter, dried food.
- **Water temperature:** 15-24°C (59-75°F).
- **Compatibility:** Keep in a species tank, or with robust fishes, capable of looking after themselves.

It is thought that this species was introduced into Europe in about 1869. However, there is some speculation that it was this fish, and not the humble coldwater Goldfish, which was referred to by the diarist, Samuel Pepys, as early as 1665. Coming as it does from the Far East, and latitudes further away from the equator than most other tropical species, it can tolerate lower temperatures with comfort, the maximum being the normal tropical temperature of 24°C(75°F). With such a long pedigree, it is not surprising that several subspecies have evolved, or been discovered. *M. chinensis*, the Roundtail Paradisefish, *M. cupanus cupanus,* the Spike-tailed Paradisefish, *M. cupanus dayi*, the Striped or Red Spike-tailed Paradisefish, and *M. opercularis concolor*, the Black Paradisefish, have all been reported, in addition to *M. opercularis*. Body coloration is variable, but the sides are adorned with alternate red and blue-green vertical bars. A typical feature of the species is the long extension that develops on the upper and lower lobes of the caudal fin. The dorsal and anal fins are patterned and progressively turn red towards the tips; the ventral fins are red. Females are less colourful, but still have red bars on the sides. The Paradisefish does not enjoy the reputation of a good community fish, being quite intolerant most of the time and becoming violently aggressive during spawning periods. It is best

Above and right:
Macropodus opercularis
Two males of this colourful, but potentially aggressive species.

kept in a well-planted species tank, where it can display its beautiful colours and spawning behaviour at no other fish's expense. It will willingly accept a variety of foods, including dried and other prepared foods, in addition to livefoods. Spawning occurs under a bubblenest and you should take precautions to protect the female (see *Colisa lalia*, pages 150-1). This species is reasonably prolific and the fry are not difficult to raise. They become free swimming after three to five days. Feed them infusorians.

Family: BELONTIIDAE

Trichogaster leeri

Pearl Gourami

- **Distribution:** Thailand, Malaysia, Sumatra, Borneo.
- **Length:** Up to 110mm(4.3in).
- **Tank length:** 60cm(24in).
- **Diet:** Worms, crustaceans, insects and dried food.
- **Water temperature:** 24-30°C (75-86°F).
- **Compatibility:** Community tank.

The Pearl Gourami is one of the most graceful fishes for the aquarium; its slow, unhurried movements around the tank are reminiscent of the Angelfish (*Pterophyllum sp.*). These two species also share the same characteristic filamentous ventral fins. In this species they are very long and can be moved around in any direction. Those of the cichlid cannot be moved around with such deftness, neither do they have taste cells at their tips. The dorsal fin of the male Pearl Gourami extends well over the caudal peduncle and, like the anal fin, has trailing filaments. The body is silver and covered overall with a dark lacelike pattern which accounts for yet another of this species' popular names: the Lace

Above: **Trichogaster leeri**
At spawning time the breast and belly of the male become blood-red in colour. This species is also known as the Mosaic Gourami.

Gourami. The patterning extends into the dorsal, anal and caudal fins. A dark line runs from the snout along the body, merging with the patterning just before the

caudal peduncle. At breeding time the male's throat, chest, ventral fins and front part of the anal fin become bright red-orange. The female has shorter fins and less colour, although she shares the same lacelike body patterning. These external sexual characteristics do not occur until the fish has almost reached its full size. Spawning follows the typical bubblenest pattern.

Family: BELONTIIDAE
Trichogaster trichopterus
Three-spot Gourami
● **Distribution:** Thailand, Malaysia, Java, Sumatra, Borneo.
● **Length:** Up to 150mm(6in).
● **Tank length:** 60cm(24in).
● **Diet:** Worms, crustaceans, insects and dried food.
● **Water temperature:** 24-29°C (75-84°F).
● **Compatibility:** Community tank, but may harass smaller species.

The popular name is not quite accurate, for the third 'spot' is not a coloured mark on the body at all, but the eye. The body shape is elongate and similar to (although somewhat stockier than) the

previous species. The markings on the body (or lack of them) account for the different varieties of this species. The basic species is silvery blue-grey and, in addition to the two dark spots on the body – one midway below the dorsal fin and one on the rear of the caudal peduncle – there are a number of diagonal transverse darker bars (often somewhat indistinct) over the entire body. Blue-white speckling patterns appear in the single fins. The ventral fins are blue and, as in most gouramies, filamentous. The male develops slightly more pointed fins than the female; she is also somewhat plumper. This species is a more active gourami for the community tank, and has a reputation for eating the aquatic coelenterate, *Hydra*. Spawning in this very prolific species follows the family pattern. The aquarium trade has not been slow to market various colour forms of the species, with popular names such as Marbled, Cosby, Golden Gourami, Blue Gourami and Silver Gourami.

Below: **Trichogaster trichopterus**
This is a very prolific species. The fry must be sorted into size groups to prevent cannibalism.

EGGLAYING TOOTHCARPS (KILLIFISHES)
The fishes in the cyprinodontidae family combine brilliant colours and
generally small size with fascinating breeding methods. Many species live
in waters that dry up completely every year and the fertilized eggs are
deposited in mud to lie dormant throughout the dry season until rain refills
the streambed and stimulates hatching of the eggs. Other fishes lay eggs
among bushy plants in the wild (small nylon mops, easy to make, will be
readily accepted in the aquarium). The fertilized eggs of some species
can be simply floated in shallow containers to hatch within a few days.
With other species, you may need to store the eggs in a semi-dry
atmosphere for a few weeks, or even months, before hatching occurs.
The ability of the eggs of such species to remain for so long in a dry
condition has made it possible for hobbyists in different parts of the world
to exchange eggs by post, thus increasing the availability of these fishes.

Because of their small size (and often predatory nature) these surface-
swimming fishes are often kept in small, well-planted species tanks.
Despite their tropical origins, it is not always necessary to keep the water
at 24°C(75°F); they are quite content with a few degrees lower. Water
conditions should be acidic, and killifishes are often kept in water in
which peat has been allowed to soak for long periods.

Family: CYPRINODONTIDAE
Aphyosemion australe
Lyretail
● **Distribution:** West Africa:
Gabon, Cameroon, Congo.
● **Length:** Up to 55mm(2.2in).
● **Tank length:** 30cm(12in).
● **Diet:** Worms, crustaceans,
insects and dried food.
● **Water temperature:** 23-28°C
(73-83°F).
● **Compatibility:** Species tank.

The genus *Aphyosemion* is found
in West Africa, below the Sahara
and north of the equator. The
fishes inhabit shallow pools and
streams where, due to the intense
and prolonged heat of the day, the
water temperatures may become
quite high; conversely, the
temperature falls quickly after
nightfall. As a result, the fishes
have become tolerant to changing
water conditions and will live
happily at 'normal' tropical
temperatures, around 24°C(75°F).
Despite their fairly localized
distribution, a number of colour
variants of some species do exist,
each coming from a separate
location. The Lyretail has the
generic spindle-shaped body: the
dorsal surface flattened and the
mouth upturned – both
characteristics of a surface-
feeding fish. The body colour of

the male is yellowish brown to brownish orange, and a light area of metallic blue-green occurs immediately behind the eye, spreading back as far as the dorsal fin. Red facial markings and bright red dots on the flanks add even more decoration. The centre of the caudal fin continues the body ground colour, with some red patterning. The outer edges are red and yellow, and the white tips extend to form the characteristic lyre shape. White-tipped dorsal and anal fins have red and yellow

Below: **Aphyosemion australe**
Sometimes known as the Cape Lopez Lyretail, this toothcarp is fairly hardy kept in soft water.

areas separated by a thin blue line.

A densely planted tank with a dark substrate and subdued lighting makes a good environment for this species, which is best kept in isolation from other fishes. The genus includes species that spawn in two different ways, according to their native habitat: egg-hangers or egg-buriers. Egg-hangers inhabit waters that do not evaporate completely in the hot season, while the egg-buriers lay their eggs in the mud so that they will survive total drying out until the onset of the rainy season stimulates hatching of the fry. The Lyretail is an egg-hanger, scattering its eggs among the aquarium plants. Hatching takes about 10-12 days.

Family: CYPRINODONTIDAE

Aplocheilus dayi
Ceylon Killifish
- **Distribution:** Sri Lanka.
- **Length:** Up to 70mm(2.8in).
- **Tank length:** 30cm(12in).
- **Diet:** Worms, crustaceans, insects, fish and dried food.
- **Water temperature:** 21-25°C (70-77°F).
- **Compatibility:** Community tank, but with larger species only.

The body of the Ceylon Killifish is not quite so spindle shaped, having slightly flattened sides. The main colour feature is the blue-green iridescent sheen of the sides of the body, which are marked with a few dark flecks. The top of the body is golden brown, the belly pale blue. The major unpaired fins are yellowish green, with similar dark fleckings. The dorsal fin is short and the anal fin is long based, that of the male being more pointed than that of the female. The female is less colourful and there may be some dark transverse bars on the rear body.

These fishes are excellent jumpers, so whether they occupy a species tank or share a tank with larger fishes, provide a tight-fitting cover for it. Spawning occurs over a period of one or two weeks near the bottom of the tank among plants or roots; egg-laden plants can be removed to a separate tank for hatching, within 12-14 days.

Family: CYPRINODONTIDAE

Aplocheilus panchax
Blue Panchax
- **Distribution:** India to Malaysia.
- **Length:** Up to 80mm(3.2in).
- **Tank length:** 30cm(12in).
- **Diet:** Worms, crustaceans, insects, fish and dried food.
- **Water temperature:** 21-25°C (70-77°F).
- **Compatibility:** Keep with larger species only.

The Blue Panchax, known to the hobby since 1899, continues to be popular. The basic body colour is golden brown, shading down to a paler colour on the belly. The

popular name refers to the dark-edged iridescent blue scales. The dorsal fin has a yellow-edged black spot and a white top. The red-speckled caudal fin has white top and bottom edges, while the similarly speckled, long-based anal fin has a red and black margin.

This overall colour pattern can only be used as a guide; due to the widespread distribution of this species, many localized colour variants occur. Females are generally paler in colour with more rounded fins. The Blue Panchax is predatory towards smaller fishes.

Above: **Aplocheilus dayi**
The growing fry should be sorted into sizes to prevent cannibalism.

Below: **Aplocheilus panchax**
An established aquarium favourite since 1899. It spawns among plants over a period of days.

Family: CYPRINODONTIDAE

Cynolebias bellotti
Argentine Pearlfish
- **Distribution:** South America, in Rio de la Plata.
- **Length:** Male up to 70mm(2.8in), female slightly smaller.
- **Tank length:** 45cm(18in).
- **Diet:** Worms, crustaceans, insects and dried food.
- **Water temperature:** 19-30°C (66-86°F).
- **Compatibility:** Species tank.

The South American Argentine Pearlfish is a true 'annual' fish, for each season its natural habitats dry up completely. The male's body colour ranges from grey to dark blue covered with bluish white dots extending to the head and all single fins. A dark diagonal band runs through the eye. The female is pale brown-yellow with irregular dark transverse markings. At spawning time the male turns almost black. Since males are very quarrelsome, keep pairs of fishes in separate small species tanks.

Provide a substrate of peat-fibre several centimetres deep. The fish spawns in a unique manner to ensure the survival of the species. Fertilized eggs may be pushed into the peat, or the fishes may burrow into the peat layer to spawn. Store the peat in semi-dry conditions for several weeks before reimmersion.

Above: **Cynolebias bellotti**
The males quarrel, so this species is best kept as a single pair.

Below: **Epiplatys sexfasciatus**
The eggs of this rather timid fish hatch over a long period and the fry must be sorted according to size to prevent cannibalism.

Family: CYPRINODONTIDAE
Epiplatys sexfasciatus
Six-barred Epiplatys
- **Distribution:** West Africa: Ghana to Gabon.
- **Length:** Up to 100mm(4in).
- **Tank length:** 45cm(18in).
- **Diet:** Worms, crustaceans, insects, fish and dried food.
- **Water temperature:** 22-28°C (72-83°F).
- **Compatibility:** Species tank.

The Six-barred Epiplatys, another long-established favourite, is a rich bronzed green-blue colour with red-dotted scales. The base of the red-speckled dorsal fin is only about half the length of the anal fin, which is yellow with a red edge. The patterning of the body extends slightly into the caudal fin, which has red rays and a red-edged blue outer area. Six, sometimes indistinct, dark vertical bars appear on the lower half of the body. Again, this coloration and patterning may vary from one locality to another as the fish is spread over a very wide area of West Africa. The female is less spectacular, with rounded fins. Peat-filtered water will approximate to that of the fish's natural habitat. Some floating plants in a well-planted tank will make this surface-feeding species feel completely at home.

Family: CYPRINODONTIDAE
Jordanella floridae
American Flagfish
● **Distribution:** North America, Florida, and Mexico.
● **Length:** Up to 60mm(2.4in).
● **Tank length:** 60cm(24in).
● **Diet:** Worms, crustaceans, insects, plant matter, dried food.
● **Water temperature:** 19-22°C (66-72°F).
● **Compatibility:** May be pugnacious in a community tank.

This species from Florida and Mexico has a stocky green-blue body, adorned with rows of bright red spots. In the male these extend into the dorsal and anal fins and there is a blotch midway along the flanks. The female is less colourful, but has a dark blotch on the rear of the dorsal fin. The fish needs vegetable matter in its diet

Above: **Jordanella floridae**
This hardy fish has interesting breeding habits that resemble those of brood-protecting cichlids.

and a tank in a sunny position will encourage soft algal growth. Spawning occurs either in a depression in the substrate (cichlid-fashion), or among bushy plants. The male will harrass the female after spawning, so it is best to remove her at this point. The eggs, easily visible, are guarded by the male and hatch after 10 days.

Family: CYPRINODONTIDAE
Oryzias melastigma
● **Distribution:** India and Sri Lanka.
● **Length:** Up to 50mm(2in).
● **Tank length:** 45cm(18in).
● **Diet:** Worms, crustaceans, insects and dried food.

● **Water temperature:** 23-26°C (73-79°F).
● **Compatibility:** Community tank of similar-sized fishes.

In this species the dorsal region is flat, the snout tip-tilted. Coloration is a delicate blue-grey, especially when seen in reflected light. A thin dark line runs from behind the gill cover to the caudal fin.

This fish will tolerate hard water but may require softer water for spawning, which follows an unusual pattern. Fertilized eggs hang from the female's vent in a grapelike bunch; as she swims, they dislodge, stick to the aquarium plants, and hatch after about two weeks.

Below left: **Oryzias melastigma**
This fish inhabits flooded rice paddy fields in its native regions.

Family: CYPRINODONTIDAE
Pachypanchax playfairi
Playfair's Panchax
● **Distribution:** Seychelles, Zanzibar.
● **Length:** 90mm(3.5in).
● **Tank length:** 45cm(18in).
● **Diet:** Worms, crustaceans, insects and dried food.
● **Water temperature:** 22-25°C (72-77°F).
● **Compatibility:** Community tank, but not with very small fishes.

The typically cylindrical-shaped body is golden brown with an emerald-green sheen highlighted with rows of red dots. The red speckling extends into all the single fins, which have red edges. The female of this species is more uniformly coloured than the male, and has colourless fins, but she can be easily identified by the black marking in the dorsal fin. The main physical characteristic of the species is the tendency – especially around breeding time – for the scales to stand out from the body, very much in the manner of a fish suffering from dropsy (see pages 67 and 68), although in this case there is nothing to be alarmed about. These fishes can be aggressive and should be kept only with tankmates of a similar size. Fry may be regularly found among the tank's floating plants, the result of spontaneous spawning action that occurs over a period of one to two weeks. About 100-150 eggs may be laid.

Below: **Pachypanchax playfairi**
This killifish should be kept in an aquarium with similar-sized fishes.

CATFISHES

Catfishes have an enthusiastic following in fishkeeping circles and some hobbyists even specialize in these fishes to the exclusion of other species. The proven popularity of catfishes is a far cry from the mistaken belief that they are generally kept only as scavengers to survive on the leftovers of other fishes. Most catfishes dwell on the substrate and use their sensitive barbels to locate food, but some larger species can be very predatory. Many are nocturnal by nature, hiding away during the daytime, so furnish the catfish aquarium to provide plenty of hiding places.

Family: CALLICHTHYIDAE

Callichthys callichthys
Armoured Catfish
● **Distribution:** South America: eastern Brazil to La Plata.
● **Length:** 180mm(7in).
● **Tank length:** 60cm(24in).
● **Diet:** Fish, insects, plant matter and dried food.
● **Water temperature:** 20-26°C (68-79°F).
● **Compatibility:** Community tank.

This species – the only one in the genus – is one of the larger bottom-dwelling members of the Armoured Catfish family, to which it gives its name. Its body is dull brown, with a blue sheen covered by two rows of overlapping bony scutes. There are two pairs of barbels. The male's dorsal, pectoral and adipose fins have thick front rays, those of the pectoral fins are red. Females may be larger but lack the strong fin spines and red coloration of males.

Keep this species in well-filtered water to prevent sediment stirred up by the fish's foraging activities from settling on fine-leaved plants. For spawning, a bubblenest is built among surface plants. The male fish, which grunts during courtship, guards the nest until hatching.

Family: CALLICHTHYIDAE

Corydoras aeneus
Bronze Corydoras
● **Distribution:** South America: Trinidad, Venezuela, La Plata.
● **Length:** Up to 70mm(2.8in).
● **Tank length:** 45cm(18in).
● **Diet:** Worms, crustaceans, insects, plant matter, dried food.
● **Water temperature:** 19-26°C (66-79°F).
● **Compatibility:** Community tank.

The Bronze Corydoras is among the most frequently imported species of tropical fishes and is a common sight in dealers' tanks. The body shape is arched, with the forehead rising quite steeply from a down-turned mouth, around which are three pairs of barbels. The flanks are bronze coloured with a darker area immediately behind the gill cover which tapers to a point level with the rear end of the dorsal fin. These fishes are most easily sexed from above; the female broadens out *behind* the pectoral fins whereas the male is

fatter at their insertion points.

Keep this gregarious fish with a number of its own species, not in isolation. Spawning activity is often brought on by a slight lowering of temperature. The female carries fertilized eggs between her ventral fins to a pre-selected spawning site. The fry are easy to raise.

Above: **Callichthys callichthys**
It is quite normal for this species to swallow air at the surface for intestinal respiration. The male grunts while guarding the eggs.

Below: **Corydoras aeneus**
This is another fish that scavenges for waste food in the aquarium.

Family: CALLICHTHYIDAE

Corydoras melanistius
Black-spotted Corydoras
● **Distribution:** South America: Guyana, in the Essequibo River.
● **Length:** Up to 60mm(2.4in).
● **Tank length:** 45cm(18in).
● **Diet:** Worms, crustaceans, insects, plant matter, dried food.
● **Water temperature:** 19-26°C (66-79°F).
● **Compatibility:** Community tank.

This smartly patterned *Corydoras* is a very popular member of the genus. The grey-yellow body is covered with dark speckles; a dark bar runs obliquely through the eye

Above: **Corydoras melanistius**
This small, well-camouflaged catfish with short barbels swims near the bottom of the aquarium, scavenging for scraps of food.

and a dark blotch in the dorsal fin spreads on to the body, covering a wedge-shaped area from the base of the dorsal fin to the intersection of the two rows of scutes. The caudal and anal fins are speckled. Sexing is as for *C. aeneus* (see pages 166-7) and spawning, too, follows the usual *Corydoras* pattern. A subspecies, *C. m. brevirostris,* has vertical dark bars in the caudal fin.

Family: CALLICHTHYIDAE

Corydoras paleatus
Peppered Corydoras
● **Distribution:** South America in southeastern Brazil and the La Plata Basin.
● **Length:** Up to 70mm(2.8in).
● **Tank length:** 45cm(18in).
● **Diet:** Worms, crustaceans, insects, plant matter, dried food.
● **Water temperature:** 19-26°C (66-79°F).
● **Compatibility:** Community tank.

The patterning of this hardy and widespread species gives more of a marbled effect than one of distinct spots. The dorsal surface has large irregular dark blotches, which spread partially down the flanks, and the rest of the body is 'peppered' with dark flecks. Some patterning appears in the dorsal, anal and caudal fins. The dorsal fin is tall and pointed and the upper caudal lobe is relatively large.

Although a native of South America, like many of the most popular aquarium fishes, the Peppered Catfish is farmed commercially in Florida, such is the demand for it.

Below left: **Corydoras paleatus**
This is the easiest to breed of all the Corydoras catfishes. It is ideal for a beginner, being hardy, undemanding and long-lived.

Family: CALLICHTHYIDAE

Dianema urostriata
Striped-tailed Catfish; Flag-tailed Catfish
● **Distribution:** South America.
● **Length:** 150mm(6in).
● **Tank length:** 90cm(36in).
● **Diet:** Omnivorous.
● **Water temperature:** 22-26°C (72-79°F).
● **Compatibility:** Community tank.

Undoubtedly, the main attraction of this fish is the black and white horizontal stripes on the caudal fin. In addition, the fish has an elegantly streamlined body and dark speckles on the head and back with a number of larger, well-spaced dark spots along the flanks. The barbels are long and usually held out stiffly in front.

This catfish spends a lot of its time in midwater and so appreciates a large aquarium with plenty of swimming space. Like many catfishes, this shoaling fish is nocturnal. The related *Dianema longibarbis* has been observed making a bubblenest but, to date, there have been no reports of this species breeding in captivity.

Below: **Dianema urostriata**
This usually shy fish is showing off its boldy striped caudal fin; the reason for the popularity of this elegant species with fishkeepers.

Family: LORICARIIDAE

Hypostomus plecostomus

Sucker Catfish

- **Distribution:** South America.
- **Length:** 200mm(8in).
- **Tank length:** 90cm(36in).
- **Diet:** Plant matter, fruits, algae, crustaceans and invertebrates.
- **Water temperature:** 19-26°C (66-79°F).
- **Compatibility:** May be intolerant with its own kind but is usually peaceful with other fishes.

Suckermouth, or Mailed, Catfishes have much to offer – excellent coloration, a peaceful disposition and an appetite for algae second to none. The body of this catfish is covered (with the exception of the belly) with bony platelets, which give it protection. The flat ventral surface and disc-shaped mouth, which it uses to suck on to surfaces, prevents the fish being swept away by water currents. The lips have teeth, which assist grazing of algae from firm surfaces, although the removal of algae from broad leaves is done with equal damage-free efficiency. A characteristic of the family is the ability to protect the eye against excessive light by enlarging a lobe over the iris. Sexing is difficult but the male is usually smaller and may develop spines on pectoral fins and bristles on the cheeks.

This is a very hardy species and given sufficient room and a diet with added greenfood, it will live for many years. It has not yet bred in the aquarium.

Above: **Hypostomus plecostomus**
This hardy and peaceful catfish is active mainly during the night. It is popular with hobbyists for its efficient algae-consuming services.

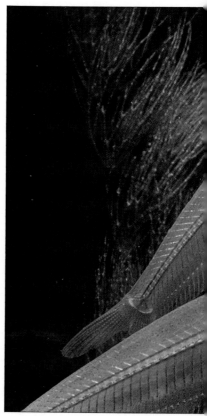

Family: SILURIDAE

Kryptopterus bicirrhus

Glass Catfish

- **Distribution:** Thailand, Java, Sumatra and Borneo.
- **Length:** 100mm(4in).
- **Tank length:** 60cm(24in).
- **Diet:** Worms, crustaceans, insects and dried foods.
- **Water temperature:** 21-26°C (71-79°F)
- **Compatibility:** Community or species tank.

Below: **Kryptopterus bicirrhus**
*These fishes are often kept for
their unusual form and transparent
body. Keep several together;
single specimens tend to pine.*

This is another species which may
be kept purely for its novelty effect.
The body is quite transparent
(except for an opaque silver sac
containing the vital organs) but
takes on different hues according
to the direction of the light striking
it. A pair of long barbels are carried
stiffly in front of the fish. The dorsal
fin consists of a single ray but the
anal fin runs almost the entire
length of the body. There are no
obvious sexual differences.

Glass Catfishes are sensitive
shoaling fishes; a well-planted tank
will provide them with a sense of
security. They congregate together
among the plants, usually near to
the surface, constantly undulating
their bodies to and fro while
hanging obliquely in the water.
Unlike most catfishes, this species
is active during daylight hours.
They have not yet bred in captivity.

Family: LORICARIIDAE
Otocinclus vestitus
Pygmy Suckermouth
● **Distribution:** South America: around Rio de Janeiro in Brazil.
● **Length:** Up to 40mm(1.6in).
● **Tank length:** 45cm(18in).
● **Diet:** Worms, plant matter and dried food.
● **Water temperature:** 19-25°C (66-77°F).
● **Compatibility:** Community tank.

This miniature member of the loricariid family performs a useful service clearing up soft green algae in the aquarium; it can often be seen clinging to the front glass. The body is elongate and flat bottomed, the mouth underslung for efficient grazing. The dorsal surface is dark brown-green with a broad dark stripe running from the snout to the caudal peduncle, where it ends on the base of the caudal fin as a broad blotch. The caudal fin has a further black band just inside its edge. The underside of the body is yellowish. Males are more slender than females.

This species, incorrectly referred to as *O. affinis,* is usually peaceful but may cling to the sides of other fishes. Discourage this semi-parasitic behaviour by supplementing its diet with vegetable matter, such as lettuce, spinach or green peas. Reports of

Above: **Otocinclus vestitus**
This small, mainly nocturnal catfish is not very easy to breed.

breeding indicate that eggs are laid on plant leaves and that some degree of parental care is shown.

Family: LORICARIIDAE
Rineloricaria lanceolata
Whiptail Catfish
● **Distribution:** South America: Brazil.
● **Length:** 150mm(6in).
● **Tank length:** 60cm(24in).
● **Diet:** Algae, greenfoods, small crustaceans, pellets.
● **Water temperature:** 19-25°C (66-77°F).
● **Compatibility:** Community tank.

The filamentous extensions to the caudal fin, itself at the end of a very long spindly body, resemble the end of a whip. The remaining fins are set well forward on the body, and the dorsal fin is particularly tall. The fish's coloration and its substrate-hugging contours make excellent camouflage. Seen from above, the male fish is slimmer than the female, displaying bristles on the cheeks when sexually mature. Spawning takes place in hollow logs in the wild (use PVC pipes in the aquarium) and the male guards the deposited eggs until they hatch. A striking and peaceful fish.

Above:
Rineloricaria lanceolata
A sought-after species because of its distinctive shape and pattern.

Family: MOCHOKIDAE
Synodontis nigriventris
Upside-down Catfish
● **Distribution:** Africa: Zaire basin.
● **Length:** 90mm(3.5in).
● **Tank length:** 60cm(24in).
● **Diet:** Insects, crustaceans, plant matter and dried foods.
● **Water temperature:** 23-27°C (73-81°F).
● **Compatibility:** Community or species tank.

The belly of this fish is dark, lightening towards the dorsal surface; the reverse of most fishes. This is to offer a protective camouflage, when seen from above, as it swims in the inverted position (hence the popular name). The body is a mottled brown with patterning extending into all fins. The dorsal fin has strong front spines and the adipose is large – a characteristic of the genus.

Below: **Synodontis nigriventris**
This Upside-down Catfish is in a typical pose. The upturned belly is mottled for protective camouflage.

LOACHES

Like catfishes, loaches forage for food on the aquarium substrate and appreciate plenty of hiding places. Body shapes range from threadlike to flat-bottomed. Some are sensitive to changes in barometric pressure; their erratic behaviour may precede adverse weather conditions.

Family: COBITIDAE

Acanthophthalmus kuhli

- **Distribution:** Southeast Asia.
- **Length:** 110mm(4.3in).
- **Tank length:** 60cm(24in).
- **Diet:** Worms, crustaceans, and sinking foods.
- **Water temperature:** 22-24°C (72-75°F)
- **Compatibility:** Community tank.

The basic colour of the wormlike body is yellow-orange. Three dark bars cross the head vertically and a number of equally spaced dark bars cross the rest of the body, but do not completely encircle it. The ventral regions are unmarked. Three pairs of barbels are present and there is an erectile spine beneath the eye. Dorsal, ventral and anal fins are set well back. There are several similarly marked species, or subspecies, in the genus and close examination of the colour markings is necessary for positive identification.

This gregarious fish spends all its time among the plant roots and is very difficult to net. There are no obvious sexual differences, but females may become stouter. Spawning is said to occur near the water surface.

Above: **Botia horae**
A hardy loach, active during the night. As with all members of the Botia genus, *this species has an erectile spine under the eye.*

Family: COBITIDAE

Botia horae
Hora's Loach
- **Distribution:** Thailand.
- **Length:** Up to 10cm(4in).
- **Tank length:** 45cm(18in).
- **Diet:** Worms, crustaceans, insects, plant matter, dried food.
- **Water temperature:** 26-30°C (79-86°F).
- **Compatibility:** Community tank, but watch it carefully.

The Skunk Botia, to give it its alternative popular name, has a greenish, creamy yellow body. A dark stripe runs along the top of the body from head to caudal peduncle, where it turns down each flank. There may be some thin indistinct vertical bars on the rear of the body. Like all *Botias,* the body is flat bottomed and highly arched. There are no visible sexual differences.

   This peaceful, hardy loach will defend its favourite retreat against other fishes, but does not set up a territorial area like other species in the genus. It is a nocturnal species and often more active when kept in a shoal. Primarily a bottom-feeder, it does venture higher in the water. A recent reclassification has suggested the name *Botia morleti* for this species.

Left: Acanthophthalmus kuhli
This fish adopts a resting pose away from its usual haunt among the aquarium plant roots.

Family: COBITIDAE

Botia lohachata
Pakistani Loach

● **Distribution:** India and Pakistan.
● **Length:** 120mm(4.7in).
● **Tank length:** 60cm(24in).
● **Diet:** Worms, small crustaceans, plant matter and dried foods.
● **Water temperature:** 24-30°C (75-86°F)
● **Compatibility:** Community tank.

The body profile is not quite so arched as in *B. horae,* giving the fish a more elongate appearance. The silvery grey flanks are covered with a series of Y-shaped markings, alternately separated by a short vertical bar rising from the ventral surface. The dorsal and caudal fin are marked with black. Some *Botia* species have a disconcerting habit of lying motionless on their sides for quite a long time (usually after a meal), only darting off the moment you try to net out the 'body'. They can be quite nervous when first introduced into the tank, diving straight down into the substrate and leaving just the rear part of the body and caudal fin waving about. However, given time, they usually emerge safely. The nocturnal Pakistani Loach can be tempted from its resting place by worm foods. Once it associates move-ment outside the tank with food, it appears with increasing frequency.

Above: **Botia lohachata**
The striking colour pattern of this shy fish makes identification easy.

Family: COBITIDAE

Botia macracantha

Clown Loach

● **Distribution:** Sumatra, Borneo.
● **Length:** Up to 30cm(12in).
● **Tank length:** 60cm(24in).
● **Diet:** Worms, crustaceans, plant matter and dried food.
● **Water temperature:** 24-30°C (75-86°F).
● **Compatibility:** Community tank.

This is the most colourfully marked species in the *Botia* genus. The orange-yellow body is crossed by three dark bands: the first, and thinnest, runs through the eye, the second crosses the body between the gill cover and the dorsal fin; the third crosses the body, connecting the rear parts of the dorsal and anal fins. The pectoral, ventral and caudal fins are bright red. The specimens seen in dealers' tanks are relatively small, but given a large tank and plenty of good food the Clown Loach develops slowly into a large, high-backed, sturdy species that makes a stunning exhibit on the show bench. This gregarious fish needs the company of its own kind to thrive in the aquarium. It also appears to strike up associations with other shoaling bottom-dwelling species, such as *Corydoras* catfishes. It is not unusual for this fish to be active during the day. It has not yet been bred in captivity.

Below: **Botia macracantha**
Also known as the Tiger Botia, this is the most colourful loach. There are no external sex differences.

Family: COBITIDAE

Botia modesta

Orange-finned Loach
- **Distribution:** Thailand, Vietnam, Malaysia.
- **Length:** 170mm(6.5in).
- **Tank length:** 60cm(24in).
- **Diet:** Worms, crustaceans, insects and dried food.
- **Water temperature:** 25-30°C (77-86°F).
- **Compatibility:** Species tank.

The very small scales of this species give the body a velvety smooth appearance. The highly arched body is blue-grey, sometimes with a violet tinge under certain lighting conditions. There is a dark, often indistinct, mark across the rear of the caudal peduncle. Fins are a contrasting bright orange-red or greyish yellow. There is some confusion between this species and the related *B. lecontei;* the fin colours may be red or yellowish in both species. However, *B. lecontei* does not grow to the same size and

Left: **Botia modesta**
*Active at night, this species, like
other loaches, uses its barbels to
detect food in the substrate.*

there may be a difference in the
curve of the ventral region. The
usual spine occurs beneath the
eye and there are three pairs of
barbels. This species likes to dig in
the substrate, but this activity may
be the result of boredom, rather
than a natural instinct. Keep a few
of the same species together to
help prevent this habit, which
quickly upsets the aquascape. Like
members of the callichthyidae
family, loaches can utilize
atmospheric air and can often be
seen dashing to the surface for a
quick gulp; oxygen is extracted in
the rear part of the intestine and
the surplus air is passed out of the
anus. Despite the fishes' ability to
survive in oxygen-depleted waters,
you should not use this as an
excuse to neglect the water
conditions in the aquarium; clean
water and aeration are essential.

Family: COBITIDAE

Botia sidthimunki

Dwarf Loach; Chained Loach
● **Distribution:** Thailand.
● **Length:** Up to 35mm(1.4in).
● **Tank length:** 45cm(18in).
● **Diet:** Worms, crustaceans,
insects, plant matter, dried food.
● **Water temperature:** 25-30°C
(77-86°F).
● **Compatibility:** Species tank or
with similar-sized fishes.

The body is elongate and the basic
colour is a metallic light gold. A
series of dark chain-like markings
runs along the top of the body
from snout to caudal fin and
extends about midway down the
flanks, where the 'links' may join
together to form a continuous line
along the body. Below this line the
belly and ventral area are more
silvery than gold. The fins are
colourless, although, in more
mature fishes, some dark patches
may appear in the lobes of the
caudal fin. There are no obvious
sexual differences.

   This delightful small species is
not as timid or retiring as others in
the genus and can be very active,
even by day. Contrary, also, to
other members of the family, it
does not confine its activity to the
floor of the aquarium but swims a
great deal in midwater, where it
rests perched up on its ventral fins
on a broad-leaved plant or
submerged log. This species is
best kept in a shoal and the tank
should have plenty of hiding
places. It is not particular about
food requirements and will accept
most foods but, like its relatives, it
relishes worm foods. Maintain
water conditions at their optimum
level with regular water changes.
This is a very fast-swimming fish,
especially when chased by a net.
Take care not to damage the spine
beneath the eye when handling the
fish; a strategically placed plastic
bag may be a better and less
injurious, means of capturing it.

Left: **Botia sidthimunki**
*This attractive species is an active
fish and best kept in a shoal.*

OTHER EGGLAYING SPECIES

With the huge selection available, not all popular fishes fall neatly into convenient classified groups. Many fish families are 'mono-specific' (that is, having only one species) and it is well worth considering some of these 'oddball' fishes for inclusion in your aquatic collection.

Family: NANDIDAE
Badis badis
Badis
- **Distribution:** India.
- **Length:** Up to 80mm(3.2in).
- **Tank length:** 30cm(12in).
- **Diet:** Worms, crustaceans, insects and dried food.
- **Water temperature:** 26-28°C (79-83°F).
- **Compatibility:** Community tank.

This fish can easily be mistaken for a Dwarf Cichlid. The body is yellowish, greenish and brown and covered with rows of alternate red, yellow and black scales. Another name for the fish is Dwarf Chameleon Fish, which refers to the very changeable colour pattern of the species; it is able to change its colours to match that of the substrate over which it swims. A dark bar runs from the snout diagonally upward through the eye. Fins are dark blue or green, the

Right: **Badis badis**
This is the most peaceful member of an otherwise aggressive family.

dorsal being marked with red or green longitudinal stripes. The male's colours intensify when spawning, or when threatening other males. Females are similarly, but not so intensely, coloured. This peaceful, shy, bottom-dwelling species needs plenty of hiding places. Eggs are laid in flowerpots or in other secluded areas.

Family: ATHERINIDAE
Bedotia geayi
Madagascar Rainbowfish
- **Distribution:** Madagascar.
- **Length:** Up to 150mm(6in).
- **Tank length:** 60cm(24in).
- **Diet:** Worms, crustaceans, insects, plant matter, dried food.
- **Water temperature:** 23-25°C (73-77°F).
- **Compatibility:** Community tank.

Two dark bands run along the flanks of the brassy yellow cylindrical body. The broader upper band has iridescent scales scattered along its length. There are two dorsal fins, the first usually held flat against the body. The anal fin is very long based. The second dorsal, ventral and anal fins are orange yellow, the larger dorsal and anal fins having a dark edge.

The male's caudal fin has a black inner edge with red outside it. The female is less brightly coloured. Livefoods are essential for this active, upper-level swimming fish. It spawns in plants or nylon mops over a period of days.

Below: **Bedotia geayi**
Like its relatives, the Madagascar Rainbowfish has two dorsal fins.

Family: MELANOTAENIIDAE

Melanotaenia maccullochi

Dwarf Rainbowfish

- **Distribution:** Northern Australia.
- **Length:** Up to 70mm(2.8in).
- **Tank length:** 60cm(24in).
- **Diet:** Worms, crustaceans, insects and dried food.
- **Water temperature:** 20-25°C (68-77°F).
- **Compatibility:** Community tank.

This well-established aquarium favourite is easily recognizable by its two dorsal fins and the rows of dark brown-red spots along the green-yellow flanks. The male's first dorsal fin is more pointed than the female's. The blue-green gill cover has a bright red spot in the centre. The female is less brightly coloured. This hardy species limits its activity to the upper levels of the aquarium; keep it in a shoal in water that is not too soft. Adding some salt to the water will have a

Below: **Melanotaenia maccullochi**
This peaceful fish can be kept as a small shoal in a community tank.

Above: **Monodactylus argenteus**
This fish should be kept in a shoal.

beneficial effect, as the natural habitats of these fishes are coastal waters or rivers, which receive seawater from time to time. Spawning occurs in bushy plants or nylon mops over a period of days, although most eggs are laid on the first day. Hatching takes around 7-10 days and at first the young require small livefoods. Growth is relatively slow, but increases rapidly once the fish attains a body size of 1cm(0.4in).

Family: MONODACTYLIDAE
Monodactylus argenteus
Fingerfish
● **Distribution:** Coastal areas; the Red Sea to Australia.
● **Length:** Up to 230mm(9in).
● **Tank length:** 90cm(36in).
● **Diet:** Worms, crustaceans, insects, plant matter, dried food.
● **Water temperature:** 24-27°C (75-81°F).
● **Compatibility:** Brackish water species tank. Adult fishes require full-strength seawater.

The Malayan Angel, to give this species its alternative popular name, has a body shape and coloration not unlike the South American Angelfish, but the fins are not so well developed. A black bar crosses the head vertically through the eye, and there is a second vertical thin dark bar immediately behind the gill cover. The dorsal fin is yellow and its base, like that of the anal fin, almost reaches the caudal fin. The anal fin is silver and has a faint yellow area immediately behind its dark front edge. The caudal fin has only a hint of yellow. Ventral fins are restricted almost to mere stumps, more in keeping with those of some marine fishes. This very active, and easily frightened, fish is found in large shoals in coastal waters. While juveniles can be kept in fresh water, it does better kept in brackish water. It has not yet been bred in captivity.

183

Family: NANDIDAE

Monocirrhus polyacanthus

South American Leaf-fish
● **Distribution:** South America: Amazon, Rio Negro, Guyana.
● **Length:** Up to 80mm(3.2in).
● **Tank length:** 30cm(12in).
● **Diet:** Fish.
● **Water temperature:** 24-28°C (75-83°F).
● **Compatibility:** Only with larger fishes; best kept in a species tank.

Its popular name describes this species exactly: the mottled, marbled coloration of the body resembles a decaying, dead leaf. The fish uses this camouflage to great advantage, hanging apparently lifeless, head-down in the water, waiting for unsuspecting prey to pass by. The mouth is then suddenly extended and the inrush of water also carries in the victim. Obviously, you should not keep this fish with any fishes less than half its size, and it is best kept in a tank specially set up for it. Furnish the tank with plenty of plants or root stems in which the fish can lurk. Provide plenty of livefoods (including young livebearers). The fish spawns by depositing eggs on the underside of a spawning site.

Above:
Monocirrhus polyacanthus
The female should be removed from the tank after spawning, leaving the male to tend the brood.

Since the young fishes grow at differing rates, it is best to sort them into groups of similar size to prevent cannibalism.

Family: MELANOTAENIIDAE

Melanotaenia nigrans

Red-tailed Rainbowfish
● **Distribution:** Eastern Australia, south to Sydney.
● **Length:** Up to 100mm(4in).
● **Tank length:** 90cm(36in).
● **Diet:** Worms, crustaceans, insects and dried food.
● **Water temperature:** 18-16°C (64-79°F).
● **Compatibility:** Community tank.

Like other members of the *Atherinoidei* suborder, these fishes are generally recognizable by their two separate dorsal fins; these are genuine ray-supported fins, and should not be confused with the adipose fin found in some species. The scales are quite large and dark at the front edge, but red at the rear edge; this gives the fish a netted appearance. The flanks are iridescent blue-green and there are a number of longitudinal stripes separated by lighter zones. When these are lit from the side, the effect is dazzling. The male's dorsal, anal and caudal fins are red with a yellow iridescent patterning and a black edge. The female's fins lack this dark edging. This active fish requires plenty of swimming space and is quite tolerant of hard water; the addition of a little aquarium salt to the water is beneficial. The scattered eggs take several days to hatch. The young are not difficult to rear. With the increase of information about this genus (sometimes also known as *Nematocentris*), there is some confusion as to identification. The true *M. nigrans* has a dark longitudinal line along its length. This species may be more correctly known as *M. splendida inornata* or *M. splendida fluviatilis*.

Below: **Melanotaenia nigrans**
This active species is recognizable by its two separate dorsal fins.

Family: PANTODONTIDAE

Pantodon buchholzi

Butterflyfish

● **Distribution:** Africa: Niger Cameroon, Zaire.
● **Length:** 100mm(4in).
● **Tank length:** 60cm(24in).
● **Diet:** Crustaceans, insects, fish.
● **Water temperature:** 24-29°C (75-84°F).
● **Compatibility:** Community tank, but not with small fishes.

The Butterflyfish is an unusual fish, and the only representative of its genus. Totally dissimilar – and entirely unrelated – to the marine Butterfyfishes, it takes its name from the shape of its large pectoral fins which, when viewed from above, do resemble butterfly wings. The long, almost tissueless rays of the ventral fins are also reminiscent of the Butterfly's anntenae. The mouth is large and this predatory fish lurks

Above: **Pantodon buchholzi**
Although it takes most of its food from the surface, this fish can also leap out to catch flying insects.

immediately below the water surface waiting for insects to alight. Camouflaged by its mottled coloration, it can hide in floating plants waiting for any small, unsuspecting fish to pass by. The large pectoral fins enable the fish to leap above the water surface and glide across it, much in the manner of the South American Hatchetfishes, but it does not 'flap' these large fins to the same extent. Keep these fishes in a tank furnished with floating plants and secure the cover firmly. Spawning has been recorded but the fry may be difficult to rear.

Right: **Telmatherina ladigesi**
After a slow start, this fish is sexually mature in seven months.

Family: ATHERINIDAE

Telmatherina ladigesi
Celebes Rainbowfish

- **Distribution:** Southeast Asia: Celebes only.
- **Length:** Up to 70mm(2.8in).
- **Tank length:** 60cm(24in).
- **Diet:** Worms, crustaceans, insects and dried food.
- **Water temperature:** 20-25°C (68-77°F).
- **Compatibility:** Community tank.

The coloration of this species is quite subtle, but very beautiful. The symmetrically contoured, slightly elongate body is yellowish, with a delicate iridescent blue sheen. A bright blue-green line runs from behind the gill cover to the caudal peduncle. These colours are best seen when the morning sunshine comes through the front glass of the aquarium. The two dorsal fins and the anal fin have sooty black first rays. The second dorsal and anal fins of the male are large; the first few rays grow very long and give the fish a slightly ragged appearance. The female does not develop these extensions to the dorsal and anal fins, instead they remain rounded. The ventral fins are yellow. The caudal fin has black streaks on the upper and lower edges. Coming from fast-flowing waters, this species requires a roomy tank with well-oxygenated, well-filtered water, which should be moderately hard. The spawning period may extend over several weeks; eggs are laid among bushy plants over several days and hatch 12-14 days later.

LIVEBEARING FISHES

Who could fail to be attracted by these fascinating multicoloured fishes that breed readily in captivity! Fertilization occurs internally, as does the development of the eggs, so that the female gives birth to free-swimming young. This provides excellent material for selective breeding, as is proved by the large number of colour and finnage strains that have been developed in the aquarium. Broods are produced at approximately one month intervals and several can occur without re-mating being necessary. Females are best isolated in small, separate, densely planted tanks to deliver their young. Because of their readiness to breed, you should exercise close control if you are to maintain pure strains; the breeding programme can soon be spoiled by inadvertent cross-breeding. Guppies, Swordtails, Mollies and Platys are established aquarium favourites, all requiring well-planted tanks and a regular supply of essential vegetable matter in their diet. They also appreciate livefoods.

Family: POECILIIDAE
Poecilia latipinna
Sailfin Molly
● **Distribution:** Mexico, Texas, Florida, the Carolinas to Virginia.
● **Length:** Males 110mm(4.3in), females larger.
● **Tank length:** 60cm(24in).
● **Diet:** Worms, crustaceans, insects, plant matter, dried food.
● **Water temperature:** 20-24°C (68-75°F).
● **Compatibility:** Community tank.

The natural form of this large attractive Molly is a silvery blue-green fish with many bright speckles along the sides. In addition to the gold form shown here, black and albino colour strains have been developed in the aquarium. The mouth is scooplike

Above: **Poecilia latipinna**
Note the male's taller dorsal fin and modified anal fin.

and upturned. The major feature is the male's very tall, long-based dorsal fin, which is frequently erected. The male's anal fin is modified into a rodlike structure, the *gonopodium*, and is used as a spawning aid. The female's anal fin is the normal fan shape.

These fishes require ample swimming space – males may quarrel if kept together in too small a space – and plenty of greenfood, if they are to reach their maximum size and develop all their physical features. A large tank that receives some direct sunlight, to encourage some lush algae growth, will be ideal. Provide medium-hard water and add some aquarium salt to it (approximately one teaspoonful per 10 litres/2.5 Imp. gallons). Move gravid (pregnant) females to a well-planted tank, in which to give birth, well before the end of the month-long gestation period.

Family: POECILIIDAE

Poecilia sphenops

Pointed-mouth Molly
- ● **Distribution:** Venezuela, Colombia, Mexico, Texas, Leeward Islands.
- ● **Length:** Males up to 70mm (2.8in); females to 100mm (4in).
- ● **Tank length:** 45cm(18in).
- ● **Diet:** Worms, crustaceans, insects, plant matter, dried food.
- ● **Water temperature:** 23-28°C (73-83°F).
- ● **Compatibility:** Community tank.

This species must be one of the most frequently 'discovered' – according to the literature, it has about 40 synonyms bestowed upon it by ichthyologists over the years. (It was first described in 1845.) This is not necessarily the result of faulty identification, but can be explained by the fact that this species has such a widespread distribution. According to reports, this species was very frequently imported into Europe in the 1920s, with at least ten varieties available from dealers. This species, also popularly known as the Liberty Molly, is the most often seen today (although it is not actually as common as other Molly varieties). The very slender body is bluish green in colour with rows of small orange-red dots. The shorter-based dorsal fin is small, but beautifully marked with black and white, and has a broad red margin immediately inside the dark edge. The caudal fin is also red, streaked with black. The male's gonopodium may be orange-yellow. The female fish is less brightly coloured and does not have the modified anal fin. Follow the advice given for the care of previous species, remembering that space and greenfoods are essential for this fish.

Below: **Poecilia sphenops**
This species probably provided the male parent for the Black Molly.

Family: POECILIIDAE
Poecilia hybrid
Black Molly
● **Distribution:** Central and southern states of the USA, northern South America.
● **Length:** 70mm(2.8in).
● **Tank length:** 60cm(24in).
● **Diet:** Worms, crustaceans, insects, plant matter, dried foods.
● **Water temperature:** 23-28°C (73-83°F).
● **Compatibility:** Community tank.

In the case of many livebearing species, the colours of aquarium specimens may be quite different from the original wild form. The Black Molly, which has become such an aquarium favourite, has no exact wild form. Despite various theories about its 'pedigree', it was probably developed by very selective inbreeding from progressively darker forms of *P. sphenops* only. This 'development' of various strains continues, with Lyretail forms being produced in such diverse colours as Black, White, Blue-green, and Black-and-white Speckled.

Mollies are generally hardy, but do react badly to poor conditions and chilling: ill-health is usually signalled by sluggish movements, clamped fins and 'shimmying' –

Below: **Poecilia hybrid**
The velvet-black colour of the popular Black Molly makes a striking contrast in the aquarium.

sideways undulations of the body without any forward movement. Fungus, too, is easily spotted in the black varieties. Given plenty of greenfood, a little aquarium salt in the water and stable conditions, Mollies readily – and very frequently – produce young. Female fishes are especially susceptible to stress during the gestation period. Move them to a separate 'delivery tank' (*not* a breeding trap) in good time, to prevent premature births.

Family: POECILIIDAE
Poecilia reticulata
Guppy
● **Distribution:** Northern Brazil, Venezuela, Guyana, Barbados, Trinidad.
● **Length:** Males up to 30mm (1.2in); females to 60mm (2.4in).
● **Tank length:** 30cm(12in).
● **Diet:** Worms, crustaceans, insects, plant matter, dried food.
● **Water temperature:** 22-28°C (72-83°F).
● **Compatibility:** Community tank, but fancy fishes may be harassed.

The Guppy is instantly recognizable – its fame has spread outside the aquarium hobby, with the result that even a long-distance cargo plane has been named a Guppy! These adaptable fishes, with their prodigious appetite for mosquito larvae have been used for the biological

Above: **Poecilia reticulata**
*This is a prolific and immensely
popular fish. The females may
produce young every four weeks.*

control of mosquitoes throughout
the tropics. Perhaps the alternative
popular name of Millions Fish is
slightly more apt, but the name of
its 'importer' from Trinidad, the
Reverend Robert John Lechmere
Guppy, will be forever
remembered. It began its scientific
classification with the name
Girardinus guppii, although it was
recognized as a local race of the
Venezuelan species *Girardinus
reticulatus,* first described by
Peters in 1859. Later transferred to
the genus *Lebistes,* it remained
there until 1963, when it was
moved to its present genus,
Poecilia, although the old name is
often included as *Lebistes.*

Males are small, brilliantly
coloured fishes with very
ornamental finnage. Keeping males

together may result in split fins, as
they constantly show off to each
other. The females are plainer, and
larger bodied, with little
decoration, although in recent
years more colour has been
developed in the caudal fin by
selective breeding. Many
cultivated finnage strains – Pintail,
Speartail, Spadetail, Top Sword,
Bottom Sword, Doubletail, Veiltail,
Fantail, Deltatail, etc – are
internationally recognized and
there are just as many colours to
be reckoned with, too. Monitor
different strains closely to prevent
unwanted cross-fertilization.

Right: **Xiphophorus helleri**
The male of this elegant species is easily recognizable by the sword-like extension to the caudal fin.

Family: POECILIIDAE
Xiphophorus helleri
Swordtail
- **Distribution:** Southern Mexico, Guatemala.
- **Length:** Males 100mm(4in), excluding 'sword'; females larger.
- **Tank length:** 60cm(24in).
- **Diet:** Worms, crustaceans, insects, plant matter, dried foods.
- **Water temperature:** 21-26°C (70-79°F).
- **Compatibility:** Community tank, but may harass smaller species.

Despite its appearance, the 'sword' is not used as an offensive weapon, but is merely a development of the caudal fin in the male fish. The body is elongate, the mouth upturned for easy feeding at the water surface. The male has the usual modification to the anal fin for fertilization purposes. The female lacks both the sword and modified anal fin, although in many instances a mature female will develop male characterisics. This 'sex reversal' is quite common in this species. The Swordtail is a hardy fish and adapts well to the community tank. Inter-male rivalry includes rather vigorous displays; backward and forward swimming actions are common, and the fish is quite spectacular when seen at full speed in reverse. These actions may intimidate smaller fishes in the aquarium. Dense planting in the aquarium will allow other species some quieter retreats from all this activity. Like other livebearers, the Swordtail needs plenty of green matter in its diet. Provide hard water, since soft water does not allow the fish to develop properly. Do not keep this fish with Mollies if aquarium salt has been added to the water. Be sure to fix the aquarium cover securely as these fishes are expert leapers.

This prolific species lends itself readily to genetic experimentation and many colour strains have been developed. High-fin and double-sword varieties have occurred fairly regularly and hobbyists appear to have forgotten how colourful the original wild fishes can be. Favourite strains include the Berlin, Tuxedo, Green, Red-eyed Red, Red Jet, Wagtail, Weisbaden and Simpson Hi-Fin.

Family: POECILIIDAE
Xiphophorus maculatus
Platy
- **Distribution:** Originally, southern Mexico, Guatemala, Honduras.
- **Length:** 40mm(1.6in); females slightly larger.
- **Tank length:** 45cm(18in).
- **Diet:** Worms, crustaceans, insects, plant matter, dried foods.
- **Water temperature:** 20-25°C (68-77°F).
- **Compatibility:** Community tank.

The Platy (an abbreviated form of the fish's original scientific name, *Platypoecilus,)* is a shorter, stockier version of the Swordtail, but lacks the ornamental extension to the caudal fin. Like its relative, the species has undergone dramatic colour transformations

since it was introduced into the aquarium in the early 1930s. Popular varieties include the Blue, Comet, Moon, Red, Tuxedo and Bleeding Heart. Another popular one, the Wagtail, has a plain coloured body (with the exception of the black mouth) and black fins. Various other ground colours can be found in the 'Wagtail' configuration.

The aquarium should be well planted and if some direct sunshine encourages the growth of soft green algae, then so much the better. Do not add aquarium salt to the hard water. Spawning follows the generic pattern.

Below: **Xiphophorus maculatus**
The Platy is deeper bodied than its relation, the Swordtail.

Family: POECILIIDAE

Xiphophorus variatus
Variatus Platy

- **Distribution:** Mexico.
- **Length:** Males up to 55mm (2.2in); females to 70mm (2.8in).
- **Tank length:** 30cm(12in).
- **Diet:** Worms, crustaceans, insects, plant matter, dried foods.
- **Water temperature:** 20-24°C (68-75°F).
- **Compatibility:** Community tank.

The body shape is elongate, similar to the related Swordtail but relatively stockier. The extra length is concentrated around the caudal peduncle. There are blackish markings and dots along the body, and scales are often well defined. There is usually a markedly blue iridescence. The early domesticated form retained this coloration, together with a yellow dorsal fin and red caudal fin. Some vertical barring may be visible and the female may have a darker patch around her vent. This tentative description is made all the more difficult because, once again, aquarium varieties differ very much in colour from the original wild specimens. A yellow form with a red caudal peduncle and fin is known as the Marigold Platy; other strains are called

Leopard, Sunset, Tuxedo, Tiger and Delta-Topsail. Close observation is needed to sex the fish as soon as possible. Isolating the sexes and rejecting inferior colours is vital if you are to maintain the purity of the strain.

Above and below:
Xiphophorus variatus
This is an excellent livebearer for a beginner, even though it may be difficult for an aquarist to discover which of the many different varieties he is keeping.

Part Three
Central American Cichlids

Above and below: *Central American cichlids will lay their eggs on hard surfaces, such as rocks or flowerpots.*

The States of Mexico and Texas, together with the 'land bridge' and islands of Central America, are very important areas for fish-keepers, as many aquarium fishes are collected here. In addition to the popular live-bearing species, such as Swordtails, Platies and Mollies, the other main group of fishes found here are cichlids, larger perchlike fishes whose reproductive method may be seen as truly spec-tacular – even if, in its exe-cution, the aquarium may take on the appearance of a shell-shocked war zone. Some of these cichlids are fishes of very large proportions (and preda-tory natures to match), which have a certain intrinsic appeal of their own. These 'Guapotes', as they are known, are only suitable for very large aqua-riums. However, there are many species that can be accommodated in average-sized tanks and which are

relatively tolerant of other fishes. The colours and body patterns of Central American cichlids can rival those of the supposedly more colourful African and South American genera. One common feature of all these cichlids is that size is absolutely no indication of social behaviour; the smallest species, *Neetroplus nematopus,* will defend its territory with as much vigour and determination as the largest Red Devil. The challenge to fishkeepers involves not only providing them with adequate accommodation, a balanced diet and exemplary water conditions, but also acting as a peace-keeping force in some instances! Most Central American cichlids can be spawned in aquariums, and a ready market for the fry has helped to stimulate interest still further. The rewards come from witnessing the extraordinary caring parental behaviour of these fishes.

Above: *A pair of True Texas Cichlids tending their fry.*

Above and below: *Males often take up threatening postures.*

Cichlasoma citrinellum

Red Devil; Midas Cichlid; Lemon Cichlid

- **Habitat:** Crater Lakes of Nicaragua, The Rio San Juan system.
- **Length:** 250mm (10in).
- **Diet:** Shrimp, earthworms, spinach, foodsticks and large flake food.
- **Sex differences:** Sexually mature males develop a distinctive hump on the head – a so-called 'nuchal' hump.
- **Aquarium compatibility:** Aggressive when adult.
- **Aquarium breeding:** Large specimens often clash violently during pre-spawning activity. Jaw locking and chasing are permanent behaviour patterns during this period. In a group of cichlids the pair will usually become territorial and vigorously defend a corner of the aquarium from all-comers. If they are sexually mature and ready to spawn, the two fishes will display breeding tubes – small points between the ventral and anal fins. Sometimes the pair will engage in

Below: **Cichlasoma citrinellum**
This large male displays the head hump (or 'nuchal' hump) that is characteristic of adult Red Devils.

extended cleaning of a rock or piece of bogwood. Alternatively, if the female is not ready, the male will attack her. This is shown by the female 'cowering' or being beaten into submission in the upper corner of the aquarium. In this situation, the female can suffer extensive body and fin damage. If the spawning is successful, several hundred eggs are produced. After 24-48 hours, the infertile eggs show signs of fungus attack; the parents will clean off the debris from unviable eggs, although sometimes the fungus spreads to developing eggs. Once the fry have emerged, the parents will often move them from site to site, picking each one off, one at a time. The fry are usually free swimming on the fifth or sixth day after spawning and will follow the parents around the spawning area as they search for food.

A problem exists relating to the identity of *Cichlasoma citrinellum* and *Cichlasoma labiatum*. The latter is thought of as a large-lipped species, usually displaying some orange-red pigment. *C.citrinellum* is found in yellow or red forms and is a simple-lipped species. The problem is caused by the polymorphism

Above:
Cichlasoma cyanoguttatum
The True Texas Cichlid is ideal for large cichlid community systems. (C. carpinte is the Texas Cichlid known to European hobbyists).

described clearly by Dr Paul Loiselle in commercial literature (following Professor Barlow's work published in 'Investigations of Ichthyofauna of the Nicaraguan Lakes') as the *Cichlasoma labiatum* species complex. Scientists have observed introgressive hybridization between *C.citrinellum* and *C.labiatum* in the smaller lakes, where the lack of suitable partners makes such hybridization the only viable alternative for survival.

Aquarium stock has developed from imports into the USA and Germany during the 1960s and 1970s. Therefore, the original genetic strength of colour, size and shape have become diluted. Nonetheless, *C.citrinellum* has made an indelible mark on the aquarium hobby.

Cichlasoma cyanoguttatum

True Texas cichlid
- **Habitat:** Mexico, in Rio Grande, Rio Pecos, Rio Conchos.
- **Length:** 250mm (10in).
- **Diet:** Shrimp, earthworms, insect larvae, foodsticks, leaf spinach and flake food.
- **Sex differences:** Males develop the frontal, or nuchal, hump and

can be slightly stronger in colour.
- **Aquarium compatibility:** Large individuals can become dominant in a cichlid group and will relentlessly bully subdominant or weaker fish. Spawning pairs undoubtedly require isolation from a community aquarium.
- **Aquarium breeding:** Spawning pairs are dark in the mid- body/caudal region, light from the head back to the centre of the body. The female prepares the spawning site while the male chases off intruders. The parents share responsibility for cleaning the eggs, although the female takes on the major part of the work. The female digs pits in which to place hatching fry and frequently moves them from site to site. Fry growth is dependent on the frequency and amount of feeding. Rearing a proportion of the fry separately ensures that a reasonable number develop.

Cichlasoma friedrichsthalii

Friedrichsthal's Cichlid

- **Habitat:** Widespread throughout Mexico, Guatemala, Honduras, Belize, Costa Rica and Nicaragua.
- **Length:** 250mm (10in).
- **Diet:** Although a fish eater in its natural habitat, young farm- or tank-raised specimens will take almost any prepared food.
- **Sex differences:** Males are larger than females, display a more ornate body speckling and sport elongated dorsal and anal fin rays.
- **Aquarium compatibility:** As with all of the large *Cichlasoma* species, this fish is best kept with similarly sized cichlids, such as *C.synspilum* and *C.maculicauda*. Juveniles are similar in appearance to *C.motaguense* and are also reminiscent of *Petenia* youngsters.
- **Aquarium breeding:** Aquarium spawnings are rarely mentioned in literature, although it is reasonable to assume that this species spawns in much the same way as closely related forms, such as *C. motaguense*.

Above: **Cichlasoma hartwegi**
An adult spawning pair of Tail Bar Cichlids with fry. The male is the upper and noticeably larger fish of the pair. This species, although a relative newcomer to fishkeeping, has proved fairly easy to spawn, which should ensure its continuing availability around the world.

Below: **Cichlasoma friedrichsthalii**
A female specimen displaying the characteristic lines and blotches extending from the eye to the tail.

Cichlasoma friedrichsthalii is frequently confused with *Cichlasoma motaguense*, from which it can be distinguished by the vertical bars on either flank. A series of black blotches blend into this pattern between the base of the caudal fin and the eye. This part of the pattern is shared with *C.motaguense*.

Cichlasoma hartwegi
Tail Bar Cichlid

- **Habitat:** Mexico, in the Rio Grijalva over sand and rock substrate.
- **Length:** 150mm (6in).
- **Diet:** Shrimp, insect larvae, leaf spinach and flake food.
- **Sex differences:** Males in spawning/brood-caring colour are silver with a hint of red speckling; the posterior half of the body has black criss cross markings. The caudal base has a characteristic broad stripe (sometimes extending in an inverted arc from tail to eye), which the author refers to in the suggested common name.

- **Aquarium compatibility:** This is not known to be an aggressive species and would seem ideally suited to small to medium-sized community aquariums.
- **Aquarium breeding:** Successful spawnings have been recorded. It is said to be an easy species to breed, with typical parental care being shown by the breeding pairs. Moderately sized broods are produced; you can expect about 100-200 fry.

This species is similar to *Cichlasoma fenestratum*, which also comes from Mexico and grows to 200mm (8in), with pink to red fin edges and strong pink markings on the head. *C.fenestratum* and *C.hartwegi* have vertical body stripes, seemingly more pronounced in the former species, although the caudal peduncle bar is distinctive in *C.hartwegi*. The Tail Bar Cichlid was described to science in 1980, and so it is a relative newcomer to the list of Central American cichlids entering the fishkeeping hobby.

Cichlasoma labiatum
Large-lipped Cichlid; Red Devil
● **Habitat:** Lakes in Nicaragua.
● **Length:** 200-250mm (8-10in).
● **Diet:** A great deal of research has been made into the feeding patterns of members of the *C.labiatum* group. In lakes and rivers, they are recorded as feeding on snails, organic debris, small fishes, aquatic insects and fish eggs. In aquariums, this can be mirrored with frozen or freeze-dried foods.
● **Sex differences:** Males display pronounced lips and often have long, extended anal and dorsal fin rays.
● **Aquarium compatibility:** Apart from a continual desire to dig into the aquarium substrate, the Red Devil is as compatible within a Central American cichlid community as any comparably sized species.
● **Aquarium breeding:** Aquarium-raised specimens spawn easily, although parental care appears to diminish rapidly within the first week of the fry becoming free swimming. Removing the fry into a rearing tank is essential. Spawning males can prove to be extremely aggressive and excessive jaw locking, tail beating and biting can leave a female very much the worse for wear. Large fishes can produce up to 7500 eggs!

Several colour forms exist, including white, yellow, yellow-orange and red. The large-lipped form with a red body is said to be extremely scarce in nature and correspondingly rare in aquarium circles. Juveniles are grey to green, with several cross bands. Hybridization has occurred between this species and *C. citrinellum* (See pages 198-199 for more about these species.)

Below: **Cichlasoma labiatum**
This colour form is the one most likely to be seen by fishkeepers. Red-bodied specimens are rare.

Cichlasoma maculicauda
Black Belt Cichlid

- **Habitat:** Southern Mexico, Guatemala, Belize, Costa Rica and Panama.
- **Length:** 300mm (12in).
- **Diet:** Only tank-raised fishes are available and these will feed on almost any aquarium prepared food. Mature fishes will relish *Gammarus* shrimp and large earthworms.
- **Sex differences:** Sexing juvenile Black Belt Cichlids can be achieved only with a certain amount of educated guesswork. In groups of semi-adult specimens (about 150mm/6in), the males exhibit early sexual behaviour as they establish a pecking order and display to the females. Adult males are slender in direct comparison to females, often displaying longer anal and dorsal fin rays and showing stronger red in the caudal fin.
- **Aquarium compatibility:** This is a typical *Cichlasoma* species of medium to large size, once much sought after by aquarists. It is ideal for a general community system of cichlids. Its colour

Above: **Cichlasoma maculicauda**
It is easy to see how the popular name of this striking cichlid arose; the black belt-like bar is a very prominent feature of the fish. This male specimen displays the beautiful red patterning that ensures its popularity among cichlid enthusiasts worldwide.

pattern of red cheek and caudal fin will enhance any Central American cichlid display.
- **Aquarium breeding:** Aquarium spawnings have been achieved, although not frequently, as in the case of *C.nicaraguense* and *C.synspilum*. Spawning males darken under the head and forward ventral area whereas females display a white ventral region after spawning. The distinctive colour change in the female helps to attract fry so that the brood can be controlled.

Juveniles rarely show the red patterning, although the distinctive vertical mid-body stripe and lateral caudal peduncle bar make them quite distinguishable from similar species, such as *C.synspilum*, which lacks the mid-body vertical bar pattern of *C. maculicauda*.

Cichlasoma managuense

Jaguar Cichlid; Managua Cichlid

- **Habitat:** Honduras, Nicaragua and Costa Rica. In turbid slow-moving waters, especially in small tributaries of large rivers. Found close to rock substrate in Lake Nicaragua.
- **Length:** 300mm (12in).
- **Diet:** As the fishes available are usually small tank-raised specimens, they will eat virtually any prepared foods, although it is not advisable to feed them totally on a diet of pellets or foodsticks as they will tend to produce a considerable amount of organic debris in the system. A diet of fish, shrimp and earthworms will ensure fast growth.
- **Sex differences:** Adult males appear more ornately patterned than females and usually display extended anal and dorsal fin rays.
- **Aquarium compatibility:** Large specimens can be particularly aggressive among their own kind and to smaller fishes, but youngsters are reasonably compatible with similarly sized fishes in the aquarium.
- **Aquarium breeding:** Successful aquarium spawnings are recorded, usually at the expense of other aquarium occupants, which are relentlessly harassed by the parent fishes in protection of their offspring.

The aquatic hobby confused this species with *Cichlasoma motaguense* for many years. However, the silver background colour in the Managua Cichlid (particularly bright in the colour form known as the Jaguar Cichlid) is not seen in the Motaguense Cichlid, which has a yellow-brown base to its overall colour patterning.

Cichlasoma nicaraguense

Nicaragua Cichlid

- **Habitat:** Nicaragua (Lake Managua) and Costa Rica.
- **Length:** Males 250mm(10in); females 200mm(8in).
- **Diet:** Juveniles and adults accept a wide variety of prepared and frozen food, and particularly relish chopped earthworms and fresh leaf spinach.
- **Sex differences:** This species is fairly easily sexed in maturity; the females are slightly smaller than males and retain a simpler nonetheless bright coloration of yellow and blue-green. A lateral line black body stripe – prominent in juveniles – is retained by the female, but is seen as an indistinct central body spot in the predominantly yellow

Below: **Cichlasoma managuense**
An adult male Jaguar Cichlid in dominant colour form – the highlight of any large cichlid community. An impressive species.

adult male.
- **Aquarium compatibility:** This medium to large species is ideal for a large cichlid community aquarium. It is not one of the most aggressive species of Central American *Cichlasoma* available, but is still capable of causing considerable damage in a small fish community. Ideally, keep this species with *C.synspilum* and *C.maculicauda* until they sex out in size and colour, when surplus fishes may be removed if necessary.
- **Aquarium breeding:** The Nicaragua Cichlid has proved easy to spawn once a compatible pair have formed a lasting bond. A deep pit is dug in the substrate and the eggs placed into it in a clump. Fishkeepers have found it best to leave the parents to raise the fry, as this encourages future breeding success. In one instance, an aquarist removed the eggs to raise them artificially and noticed that the pair became aggressive towards one another.

Egg numbers depend on the maturity of the parents, but reports suggest a spawn of 300-500 eggs is not uncommon, with likely hatching rates between 20 and 50 percent. Immature males will cause a greater number of eggs to be infertile. Therefore, early spawnings can be expected to produce lower hatching rates. The eggs of this species are reported to be non-adhesive, a characteristic unique among Central American cichlids.

Above: **Cichlasoma nicaraguense**
A female Nicaragua Cichlid. These fishes are extremely popular among fishkeepers for their brilliant colours.

This brightly coloured cichlid took European cichlid enthusiasts by storm when it first appeared in 1979/80. The colours on sexually mature pairs – brilliant greens, yellows and blues – rival those of many coral reef fishes. The female displays a blaze of colour normally associated with outstanding males in some cichlid species. The superb adult colour pattern of the Nicaragua Cichlid has undoubtedly caused a great upsurge of interest in keeping Central American cichlids. Juvenile fishes are plain silver with a black lateral stripe and mid-body blotch, and rarely herald the outstanding beauty of the adult.

Cichlasoma nigrofasciatum

Convict Cichlid; Zebra Cichlid
- **Habitat:** Guatemala, El Salvador, Honduras, Nicaragua and Costa Rica.
- **Length:** 100mm (4in).
- **Diet:** The Convict must be the easiest species to accommodate on the dietary front; juveniles and adults will accept every form of tropical fish food. By enhancing the diet with bloodworm, chopped earthworms and frozen shrimp, a pair can be brought easily into spawning condition.
- **Sex differences:** Juvenile Convict Cichlids are difficult to

separate into males and females, although the former tend to be more aggressively active when approaching sexual maturity. Also, adult males display particularly intense black vertical bands. These are less prominent in females, which – especially in breeding dress – are orange-yellow in the ventral region. And males invariably possess larger dorsal and anal fins that usually extend into filaments.

- **Aquarium compatibility:** Few community aquariums have not been plunged into chaos by the introduction of a renegade cichlid by the novice fishkeeper. Most aquarists will encounter cichlids for the first time in this manner and the most likely species to be purchased in ignorance of its aggressive tendencies is undoubtedly the Convict Cichlid. The aggression stems from the cichlid's desire to spawn and protect its progeny. While it may infuriate the irate fishkeeper, who hates to see community fishes victims of serious assault, this behaviour ensures that the fish will be successful in raising its fry, both in the natural habitat and in the aquarium.
- **Aquarium breeding:** This is one of the easiest species of *Cichlasoma* to spawn and raise. A breeding pair will choose a

Below:
Cichlasoma nigrofasciatum
An adult male, showing the normal colour form of the Convict Cichlid.

vertical or horizontal spawning site and defend the area vigorously from all-comers, including cichlids larger than themselves. Commercially bred generations are said to be less protective of free-swimming fry and lose interest in the brood within a week, in some instances. It is wise to remove at least 50 percent of the free-swimming fry to a separate raising system.

The zebra-like banding pattern is highlighted on the spawning male whereas the female develops a yellow underside to attract the brood.

Wild-caught specimens, said to be highly coloured (especially in spawning condition), are rarely encountered. The Convict Cichlid is commercially bred extensively in the Far East and also in the USA, where a gold variety is well established in the hobby.

Cichlasoma octofasciatum
Jack Dempsey Cichlid
- **Habitat:** Mexico (Yucatan), Guatemala and Honduras.
- **Length:** 200mm (8in).
- **Diet:** Commercial or tank-bred specimens will feed on a wide range of foods, although they show a preference for crustaceans, shrimps, snails, etc. Large specimens will greedily take foodsticks, whole shrimps and earthworms. This species will also show interest in green foods, such as leaf spinach or

lettuce, but this should be offered only occasionally.

- **Sex differences:** Sexually mature males are blue-black in colour; females tend to be paler in their markings.
- **Aquarium compatibility:** Of the small to medium-sized cichlids, the Jack Dempsey Cichlid is probably the most pugnacious, hence its common name. It is entirely suited to smaller cichlid communities if kept with Firemouth, Convict and Salvin's Cichlids. (See pages 55, 59, 65.)
- **Aquarium breeding:** Aquarium spawnings are said to have produced broods of up to 800 fry, although aquarium-raised breeding pairs are more likely to produce and raise much smaller broods. As the fry begin to show dark stripes on the body, remove them to a separate raising tank before the parent fishes begin the spawning cycle again and lose interest in protecting the brood.

Known under the name of *Cichlasoma biocellatum* for some time in commercial literature, the Jack Dempsey is a popular species among newcomers to cichlids.

Cichlasoma panamense
Panama Cichlid
- **Habitat:** Small tributaries of the Chagres and Bayano Rivers in Panama.
- **Length:** 100mm (4in).
- **Diet:** A typical cichlid diet should enable the fishkeeper to develop the aquarium-raised specimens of this species that are available

Above:
Cichlasoma octofasciatum
This ebullient cichlid was one of the earliest species made available.

from time to time.
- **Sex differences:** The adult male is larger than the female and, especially in breeding dress, displays a red body hue broken by a dark line of vertical blotches from the caudal base to the mid-point of the body. Brood-caring females display a pale ventral region and a broken vertical line of blotches on the body.
- **Aquarium compatibility:** Ideally suited to the smaller cichlid community system, this tenacious yet unaggressive species is one of the most recent newcomers to the European aquarist market.
- **Aquarium breeding:** Aquarium spawnings have been widely reported. Spawning pairs are said to prefer caves and plant pots as breeding sites. Brooding females display a light and dark body pattern, presumably for fry recognition and protection. This species was originally allied with *Neetroplus* and, from aquarium keeping aspects, can be considered similar to some extent. It appears that the Panama Cichlid does not share the awesome aggression of *Neetroplus* but is capable of producing and raising similarly sized broods in the aquarium.

Juveniles have a uniform grey body, which does little to recommend the species initially,

Above: **Cichlasoma panamense**
An adult, illustrating the stark contrast in patterning when compared to the somewhat plain juvenile.

but its small size and relatively peaceful nature will ensure its popularity as an ideal small community aquarium cichlid.

This species is a relative newcomer in comparison to other well-known forms; it became widely available for aquarium use in 1983 following a scientific survey carried out in the rivers of Panama.

Cichlasoma robertsoni
Metallic Green Cichlid
● **Habitat:** Lakes, lagoons and rivers in Mexico, Guatemala and Honduras.

● **Length:** 200mm (8in).
● **Diet:** Crustaceans, insect larvae and flake food.
● **Sex differences:** Males are larger and display a brighter coloration than females.
● **Aquarium compatibility:** A moderate cichlid by normal *Cichlasoma* standards, this species is suitable for small to medium-sized aquarium communities.
● **Aquarium breeding:** Habitat observations reveal that this cichlid holds territories close to submerged tree trunks and large rocks in river conditions. It is capable of breeding in a cichlid

Below: **Cichlasoma robertsoni**
A handsome new cichlid, but not yet widely available to fishkeepers.

community, even one containing *Neetroplus nematopus*, according to Dr. Paul Loiselle.

The Metallic Green Cichlid is similar in shape and general appearance to the Firemouth Cichlid (*Cichlasoma meeki*), but differs in colour pattern and body spot. It has metallic green scales that catch the light, making it a most beautiful newcomer to the fishkeeping hobby. It is a substrate sifter and tends to dig continually into the aquarium gravel.

Cichlasoma salvini
Salvin's Cichlid; Tricolor Cichlid
- **Habitat:** Mexico, Guatemala, Honduras.
- **Length:** 150mm (6in).
- **Diet:** This cichlid shows a preference for larval or shrimp foods and will retain its good colour if fed regularly on bloodworm and *Gammarus* shrimp.
- **Sex differences:** Sexually mature males only two-thirds grown develop a red blotch in the ventral body/anal fin region, which makes this one of the most attractive of the smaller cichlids.
- **Aquarium compatibility:** A tenacious dwarf Central American cichlid, Salvin's Cichlid

will enhance any community, large or small. In certain community aquariums, however, this beautiful cichlid would be bullied because of its distinctive pattern and smaller size. Breeding pairs can be very aggressive and will bite other aquarium cichlids viciously unless given an aquarium of their own for breeding activites.
- **Aquarium breeding:** This species is said to prefer placing eggs on a sloping or vertical surface. Egg numbers have been recorded at 1000, although half that figure is the accepted norm. Both parents show bright colour patterns, especially while they are protecting the eggs and fry. Other fishes are said to associate the bright colour with aggression and endeavour to avoid them during this period. Fry hatch within three days and will soon take newly hatched brine shrimp and powdered food. Experience shows that it is best to remove fry from the parents and separate

Below: **Cichlasoma salvini**
A striking female specimen that shows clearly why the beautiful Tricolor Cichlid is one of the most popular species available.

the parent fishes to save the female from the somewhat over-enthusiastic attentions of the male in his desire to repeat the spawning cycle *before* the female is ready to start breeding again.

The Tricolor Cichlid is not widely known in fishkeeping circles, but it is an ideal species to consider for a breeding programme. It is well suited to small to medium-sized aquariums because it reaches sexual maturity at the relatively small size of 100mm(4in).

Cichlasoma spilurum
Blue-eyed Cichlid; Jade-eyed Cichlid
● **Habitat:** Guatemala and Belize.
● **Length:** 125mm (5in).
● **Diet:** This species will thrive on much the same fare as other small to medium-sized cichlids, and will particularly relish bloodworm and *Daphnia*.

● **Sex differences:** Males display a yellowish ventral region and are generally longer in the body and in the dorsal and anal fins than females. Brood-caring females have a distinctive series of vertical black bars, not dissimilar to those of the Convict Cichlid, (*C. nigrofasciatum*).

Below: **Cichlasoma spilurum**
A male specimen of the Jade-eye Cichlid. An excellent species to

● **Aquarium compatibility:** Spawning couples – in keeping with the tenacious smaller cichlids – can be difficult; otherwise they are perfectly suited to small systems.
● **Aquarium breeding:** Breeding Jade-eyed Cichlids is relatively easy. Mature pairs will accept an upturned plant pot or rock cluster as a spawning site. Large broods can be expected and free-swimming fry should be removed to separate quarters when they are 14 days old.

The Jade-eyed Cichlid is probably the most underrated of the small Central American species. A spawning pair display warm colours and contrasting patterns that merit greater interest being shown in this species. They prove excellent parents and will successfully raise broods within a community aquarium without too much disruptive behaviour.

Cichlasoma synspilum
Firehead Cichlid; Quetzal
● **Habitat:** Guatemala and Belize.
● **Length:** 300mm (12in).
● **Diet:** Young specimens will take almost any prepared food. Adults can become fussy, preferring

introduce fishkeepers into the fascinating world of Central American cichlids. An easy species to breed.

large prawns, pellets, leaf spinach and earthworms.

● **Sex differences:** Adult males are brighter in colour than females and develop a slight nuchal hump. Juveniles can be sexed at the half-grown stage using the developing males' brighter colour pattern and fin development as a guide.

● **Aquarium compatibility:** This brightly coloured species will enhance any large Central American cichlid community. Together with *C.nicaraguense*, *C. synspilum* must take a good deal of the credit for promoting Central American cichlids to the aquarium hobby. If kept with similarly sized species, Firehead Cichlids will co-exist peacefully, although once a sexually mature pair have formed a bond, greater aggressive behaviour results.

● **Aquarium breeding:** A spawning pair can produce large broods, although the difficulty lies in finding two compatible specimens. Pair bonding can result in continual spawning cycles. Fry rearing is best undertaken by removing 50-75 percent of the brood to a separate aquarium. If some fry are allowed to progress with the parents, there will be a high mortality rate in the period between 7 and 14 days after hatching, but continued parental care and pair bonding will be ensured by taking such action.

Above: **Cichlasoma synspilum**
A female specimen, illustrating how vibrant this widely available species can be. Males display nuchal humps and an even brighter colour than females.

Cichlasoma synspilum is one of the most widespread of the commercially known larger species and is the species most likely be available at your local dealer. To develop a group of *C.synspilum* with the priority of creating a good spawning pair, start by buying between four and six juveniles. If possible, buy half of these from a different source to prevent close inbreeding. Raise the group in a 120×45×30cm (48×18×12in) aquarium or similarly sized system. As the cichlids become sexually active, the dominant male will display to the best female. At this stage, take the balance of the subdominant fishes back to the retailer as surplus to requirements. Although you will lose a good percentage of the original purchase price, you will have secured a compatible pair that should produce reasonably sized broods for you to raise and sell to offset the loss. As with all fishbreeding programmes, your constant aim should be to breed fishes of the best quality. Raising large numbers of fishes of variable quality usually creates more problems than you might imagine, particularly when you come to dispose of them.

Herotilapia multispinosa
Rainbow cichlid
- **Habitat:** Lakes, streams and rivers in Nicaragua and Costa Rica.
- **Length:** 125mm (5in).
- **Diet:** Young specimens will pick at any food which falls to the substrate and show a preference for larval foods, such as bloodworm and gnat larvae, which would be a natural food source in the wild.
- **Sex differences:** Male Rainbow Cichlids are more brightly coloured than females, with areas of yellow, brown and red overlaid with a line of black blotches that begins just behind the eye and extends along the mid lateral line. This is punctuated by a large spot or blotch just beyond the middle of the body and finishes with a blotch at the base of the tail. The female shares the same basic pattern, although drab by comparison, and is shorter overall with shorter fins.
- **Aquarium compatibility:** This is perhaps the most compatible of the small Central American cichlids available to aquarists. It is an excellent small dither fish among large *Cichlasoma* species, which will not feel threatened by its diminutive stature in the aquarium.

Above: **Herotilapia multispinosa**
The Rainbow Cichlid is an ideal species to keep in a small community system. Very easy to breed.

- **Aquarium breeding:** This species is easy to breed and will spawn when only halfway to adult size! Breeding females change from their usual drab pattern to take on a yellow hue, which appears to be for brood recognition. A pair will accept almost any site in the aquarium for spawning, including bogwood, rocks or plant pots.

Aquarium-bred specimens are so far removed from the original wild form that the colour pattern is reduced to a brown body with lateral banding or spots.

Neetroplus nematopus
Pygmy Green-eyed Cichlid
- **Habitat:** Lakes and rivers in Nicaragua and Costa Rica. River populations live in fast-flowing waters above rock-strewn substrates.
- **Length:** 75-100mm (3-4in).
- **Diet:** Lake populations are known to be algae grazers and should be offered fine leaf spinach, lettuce or peas. In addition, *Neetroplus* will accept any larval or shrimp food and will thrive even if fed solely on flake

Above: **Neetroplus nematopus**
One of the smallest yet one of the most aggressive species available.

food. However, a varied diet soon brings sexually mature fishes into breeding condition.

● **Sex differences:** Adult males appear to develop a slight nuchal hump and usually can be identified by their dominant behaviour. Some aquarists suggest that males exhibit slight finnage extensions in comparison with females and this can be a useful guide.

● **Aquarium compatibility:** All aquarium rules are broken by this tiny Central American cichlid. A 75-100mm (3-4in) male can cause havoc in small and large aquariums alike, and it will not show any fear of large fishes, especially if paired and brood protecting. Although ideally suited to small aquariums, these demons would not come unstuck in a busy large cichlid community!

● **Aquarium breeding:** These are cave- or hole-spawning cichlids. In the aquarium, a breeding pair will accept a small plant pot buried in the gravel (leaving an opening only large enough for them to squeeze through) or a narrow space in a rockwork cluster. Once the eggs have been produced, the female reverses her colour pattern. The body darkens from grey to black, and the characteristic black bar becomes white. (This colour change is one of the most extreme to occur among cichlids.) The male also reverses his colour pattern when brood protection begins. Although up to 100 eggs can be produced in one spawning, about 30-40 is the usual number. Brood-protecting parents will not hesitate to attack intruders, but other community fishes tend to recognize the demon pair as potential trouble to be avoided.

Neetroplus nematopus is noted as a 'cleaner' fish to larger cichlids, much in the same way as the Cleaner Wrasse(*Labroides dimidiatus*) attends to its fellow marine fishes.

Below: **Neetroplus nematopus**
A male displaying the fin extensions and slight nuchal hump. These fishes are said to pick parasites off Cichlasoma nicaraguense *in the wild.*

4

Part Four
African and Asian Catfishes

Above: *The One-spot Catfish from Zaire,* Synodontis notatus.

Above: *Young, aquarium-bred Pearl Catfishes* (Mystus armatus), *a recent breeding success.*

Above: *Transparent* Kryptopterus bicirrhus *from Asian rivers.*

At one time catfishes were looked upon as mere scavengers for the aquarium, clearing up the other fishes' leftovers. Very few species were popular apart from the ubiquitous South American *Corydoras.* Today, however, modern fishkeepers are well versed with species from other continents and a wide range of species is available from Africa and Asia. These fishes have diverse forms and come from many different water conditions. In fact, their natural exposure to varying conditions has made them extremely adaptable and able to survive the rigours involved in the long journeys to their eventual aquarium home. Once in captivity, all have proved to be extremely hardy and ideal aquarium subjects, providing that certain precautions are taken. If catfishes (especially the larger species) are relegated to a scavenging existence, it should come as no

suprise if, in hunger, they turn their attention to weaker, smaller fishes. In addition to the obvious attractions of colours, patterns and body shapes, the behaviour of catfishes brings another interest. Not only are many species nocturnal but some also prefer to swim upside-down as a way of life. There is still some confusion on species identification. To many commercial dealers at the 'natural source' end of the chain, the fishes are often looked upon as food fishes, with scant regard for their correct scientific names. However, despite (or perhaps because of) this problem, many hobbyists have become devoted, themselves, to studying catfishes and, through their efforts, much has been done to redress this lack of positive information. African and Asian catfishes provide all the diversity a keen aquarist desires. They are exciting, unpredictable and still fairly unknown.

Above: *This large* Brachysynodontis batensoda *also swims inverted.*

Above: *The large, very predatory* Mystus wykii *from Thailand.*

Above: *The beautiful* Synodontis dhonti *from Lake Tanganyika.*

Family: BAGRIDAE

Members of the *Bagridae* family are divided between Africa and Asia, but the latter are less well documented as their natural habitats are so diverse. These active and voracious fishes, which are generally nocturnal, are caught for two reasons: the larger ones for food, the smaller species for aquariums. The skin is scaleless, and distinctive features include strong-spined dorsal and pectoral fins, and three pairs of barbels.

Auchenoglanis occidentalis

Giraffe-nosed Catfish
- **Habitat:** Rivers and lakes of Africa
- **Length:** 600mm (24in)
- **Diet:** Wide ranging, including shrimp, earthworms and fish
- **Sex differences:** Males are possibly more highly coloured and more slender than females
- **Aquarium compatibility:** Ideally suited to most large-fish communities. Accepts a wide pH range of 6.6-8.1
- **Aquarium breeding:** Not known

Juvenile Giraffe-nosed Catfishes are almost irresistible to fishkeepers with a soft spot for unusual catfishes. In the adults, however, the attractive giraffe blotch pattern pales to a less attractive brownish tone, although when they reach adult size few aquariums could provide enough space to accommodate them. In the wild, these fishes use their long snouts to dig into the river silt for all manner of insect and crustacean foods. In the aquarium, the digging capabilities of large specimens can be extremely

Above:
Auchenoglanis occidentalis
An attractively patterned juvenile with the distinctive snout, which it uses to sift the substrate for food.

disruptive and damaging to filter beds and therefore to the water quality over a period of time.

Leiocassis siamensis

Bumblebee Catfish
- **Habitat:** Rivers and creeks of Thailand
- **Length:** 150mm (6in)
- **Diet:** Shrimp, insect larvae, snails. Will thrive on frozen shrimp and bloodworms, and will adapt to prepared foods
- **Sex differences:** Males are slender by comparison with the deeper bodied females
- **Aquarium compatibility:** Young specimens are relatively safe to keep among general community species, although adult fishes should not be kept with small tetras or livebearing fishes.
- **Aquarium breeding:** Not known

The Asian Bumblebee Catfish is well known among catfish enthusiasts and is often the first 'unusual'

species encountered by fishkeepers. Large specimens are clearly night prowlers, capable of consuming resting diurnal fishes. Take great care, therefore, not to introduce this species into a community of small fishes.

Lophiobagrus cyclurus
Tanganyikan Dwarf Bagrid

- **Habitat:** The shoreline rubble of Lake Tanganyika
- **Length:** 100mm (4in)
- **Diet:** Small shrimp, chopped earthworms, bloodworm and flake food
- **Sex differences:** Females are larger and generally more robust than males
- **Aquarium compatibility:** Excellent for a Tanganyikan cichlid community – keeps very much to itself
- **Aquarium breeding:** A pair dig out a hollow in the sand or gravel

Above: **Leiocassis siamensis**
This sleek and attractive catfish is a favourite species with hobbyists.

underneath rocks or cavework. They spawn in the cave, producing 30-40 eggs which are then cared for until they hatch. Fry can be raised easily on brineshrimp and powdered flake.

Lophiobagrus are said to produce a poisonous body slime that can kill other fishes if kept in a confined space with them. This unproved factor should not detract from the ideal aquarium compatibility and breeding opportunity this species offers. These catfishes have been kept together with Tanganyikan cichlids without any problems.

Below: **Lophiobagrus cyclurus**
An ideal 'scavenger' for an African Rift Valley community aquarium.

Mystus armatus

One-spot Catfish; Pearl Catfish
- **Habitat:** India, Burma, possibly Thailand
- **Length:** 125mm (5in)
- **Diet:** Crustaceans, insect larvae, etc. Will accept suitable aquarium foods
- **Sex differences:** Males are smaller and more slender in the body than females
- **Aquarium compatibility:** Juvenile *Mystus* are fairly peaceful towards community fishes. It is only when they attain more adult proportions that they begin to predate on small fishes. Predation usually occurs at night, when these catfishes are active
- **Aquarium breeding:** The Pearl Catfish was the first *Mystus* species to be spawned in the aquarium. Several females and a single male were introduced into a cool freshwater aquarium containing plants but no substrate. Early the following morning, the females produced several hundred eggs, of which at least one hundred proved fertile. Fry development was quite rapid; within days the youngsters could be seen swimming freely

Despite their predatory tendencies when adult, this species is well suited to larger Asian communities containing large barbs, gouramis and other catfishes, or South American communities containing cichlids, large characins and catfishes. As shoaling fishes they are best kept in small groups of four to six individuals. In a group they will feed across the substrate, taking a broad range of prepared, freeze-dried and frozen foods.

Mystus micracanthus

Two-spot Catfish
- **Habitat:** Sumatra, Java, Borneo and Thailand
- **Length:** 125mm (5in)
- **Diet:** Crustacean foods, shrimps, etc. Will accept aquarium foods
- **Sex differences:** Males are smaller and more slender in the body than females
- **Aquarium compatibility:** Not safe with very small fishes, although they are ideally suited to an Asian-style community aquarium containing barbs and gouramis
- **Aquarium breeding:** As in *Mystus armatus*

The Two-spot Catfish was available in aquarium circles without a scientific name until a connection was made to a description of

Below: **Mystus armatus**
These juveniles, illustrated with an adult, are from the first successful aquarium spawning of this species.

Above: **Mystus micracanthus**
Catfish enthusiasts agree that the Two-spot Catfish is one of the most attractive Mystus *species.*

Mystus micracanthus by the ichthyologist Bleeker, in 1846. The artist's impression at that time showed a catfish without any obvious markings, although another researcher in the early 1940s described it with two body spots.

It is one of the most attractively coloured species within the genus and will thrive in a neutral system.

Mystus vittatus
Pyjama Catfish

- **Habitat:** Creeks and rivers throughout tropical Asia
- **Length:** 125-150mm (5-6in)
- **Diet:** Small aquatic insects, fish fry and larval foods in the wild. Will accept a wide range of aquarium foods
- **Sex differences:** Males are smaller and more slender than females
- **Aquarium compatibility:** Predatory towards smaller fishes, but suitable for larger cichlid/barb communities
- **Aquarium breeding:** Egg scatterers

This is one of the best-known Asian catfishes, although many aquarium books seem to overlook the fact. It was spawned in the aquarium for the first time in 1985 by an East German aquarist, Dr. Hans Franke. Of the several thousand eggs produced, a high percentage hatched after several days.

Below: **Mystus vittatus**
Deep-bodied specimens, as here, are likely to be females.

Family: CHACIDAE
The genus *Chaca,* formerly thought to be monotypic, is found from India to Malaysia. This aquarium oddity is a sedentary predator, attracting prey to within reach of its huge mouth by waving its worm-like barbels.

Chaca chaca

Frogmouth; Angler Catfish

- **Habitat:** Brahmaputra/Ganges drainage basin of India and Bangladesh, in rivers and creeks outside the normal rain forest areas
- **Length:** 180mm (7in)
- **Diet:** Fish and crustaceans
- **Sex differences:** Not known
- **Aquarium compatibility:** Can be kept with large fishes and will eventually feed on prawn pieces, etc. Small specimens will starve unless fed deliberately
- **Aquarium breeding:** Not known

Observations of this nocturnal catfish in its natural habitat make interesting reading. '*Chaca* are inactive most of the time; they rest motionless on the substrate for long periods and when approached by small fish the maxillary barbels are moved in such a way as to be mistaken for a worm – luring its prey. Once an unsuspecting fish is within range, *Chaca* sucks its prey

Above: **Chaca chaca**
Like the true Angler Fish, this predatory catfish attracts its unsuspecting prey by means of worm-like lures, in this case the barbels. A fascinating species.

into the oral cavity. It is the extraordinary *Chaca* mouth that gives away its predatory nature. The spread of vision is assisted by the position of the eyes, which are set well apart almost at the extremities of its wide mouth. Such is the fish's application to remaining concealed on the streambed that it will not move even when prodded. A closer study of its cryptically patterned body will reveal that the caudal fin extends a long way forward over the top of the caudal peduncle. Another species, *Chaca bankanensis,* which occurs only in the rain forest creeks of the Southern Malay Peninsula and Indonesia, has a darker colour pattern than *Chaca chaca.*

Family: CLARIIDAE

This family contains fishes which appear to have little to recommend them! Members of the *Clarias* genus have given rise to some hair-raising myths, which include stories of these fishes leaving local watercourses and attacking dogs and frightening people! Having said this, these cylindrically shaped, well-barbelled fishes are expert escapers and you should therefore ensure that the hood of their tank is firmly secured.

Clarias batrachus
Walking Catfish

- **Habitat:** Widespread in Asian rivers and pools
- **Length:** 450mm (18in)
- **Diet:** Any food accepted
- **Sex differences:** Adult males have thickened pectoral spines.
- **Aquarium compatibility:** Large specimens can be difficult to keep with large community fishes because they are voracious feeders capable of shredding the fins of less robust species
- **Aquarium breeding:** Commercial and scientific experiments have resulted in many spawnings. A large system is required

This species is commercially bred in the Far East by fish farmers and as such is widely available among Singapore shipments in its albino form. Malayan 'wild' forms are

Above: **Clarias batrachus**
The Walking Catfish uses its barbels to probe the substrate for food. Keep large fishes singly.

described as green to dark brown with reddish margins.

In its natural habitat (where some albinoism occurs) eggs are deposited in holes about 250mm (10in) long made in the pond bank below the water surface. It is estimated that between 2000 and 15,000 fry are raised in each nest.

In Florida and several other States of America, the Walking Catfish is banned because of its introduction into native waters. Wild stories of giant specimens attacking pet dogs and confusing car drivers at night by walking across roads are exaggerated. However, the introduction of stock by storm flooding into the Everglades is said to pose a threat to native fishes.

Heteroptneustes fossilis
Stinging or Liver Catfish
- **Habitat:** Widespread across Asia in pools, ditches, rivers and lakes
- **Length:** 300mm (12in)
- **Diet:** Any insect or crustacean foods. Juveniles and adult specimens feed well on pellets, foodsticks and prawns or earthworms
- **Sex differences:** Males are more slender and often more attractively patterned than females, sometimes with yellow lateral stripes
- **Aquarium compatibility:** Suitable for a community of large fishes, but predatory towards small fishes
- **Aquarium breeding:** Aquarium spawnings are known but

Above: **Heteroptneustes fossilis**
Possibly confused with the Walking Catfish but more slender.

unrecorded; habitat accounts are available, however

Available under several common names, including the Liver, Fossil and Stinging Catfish, captive specimens of this species adapt well to life in the aquarium. Large specimens have prominent dorsal and pectoral fin-spines, which are said to be spiked with a mild venom.

These fishes spawn in the rainy season, placing yellowish eggs in depressions, or nests, hollowed out by the pair. Adults show parental care beyond the hatching and free-swimming stage of the fry.

Family: MOCHOKIDAE
The continuing popularity of this African family is due to the genus *Synodontis*, whose many species make ideal aquarium fishes. These nocturnal fishes are tolerant of both varying water conditions and other fishes. Many have fine coloration and finnage and some exhibit the unusual habit of swimming inverted, taking food from the water surface while in this position. The adipose fin is large and fatty, barbels are especially well produced, and large erectile spiny dorsal and pectoral fins foil attempts at capture by hunters, or swallowing by would-be predators.

Brachysynodontis batensoda
Giant Upside-down Catfish
- **Habitat:** Widespread in the basins of the Nile, Niger, Volta and Chad Rivers

- **Length:** 200-250mm (8-10in)
- **Diet:** The gill-filters show this fish to be a plankton feeder. In the aquarium, provide shrimp, insect larvae, chopped earthworms, foodsticks and pellets.
- **Sex differences:** Not obvious,

although deeper bodied fishes are possibly female
● **Aquarium compatibility:** Reasonably peaceful among other catfishes. Ideal in a community system of large fishes
● **Aquarium breeding:** Not known

A large inverting species well known to enthusiasts as the emblem of the Catfish Association of Great Britain. It is recognizable through its large adipose fin and cannot be mistaken for *Hemisynodontis* because it lacks the membraned maxillary barbels characteristic of that species. *Brachysynodontis* has proved extremely hardy and adaptable in the aquarium and will thrive in acidic or alkaline systems. Feeding has not proved a problem; once settled they will take almost any food, especially foodsticks, pellets and shrimps.

Above:
Brachysynodontis batensoda
The largest truly inverting catfish.

Euchilichthys guentheri

False Chiloglanis; False Suckermouth
● **Habitat:** Fast-flowing streams on the Zaire River
● **Length:** 100mm (4in)
● **Diet:** Insect larvae, algae and small crustaceans
● **Sex differences:** Not known
● **Aquarium compatibility:** Non-aggressive, although territorial towards its own kind. An interesting species suitable for most communities
● **Aquarium breeding:** Not known

The first *Euchilichthys* imported from Zaire were mistaken for giant *Chiloglanis*. The False Suckermouth has a longer head, nostrils set close together and a free border to the eye. In the aquarium they tend to suffer from too low a pH (it should be around 7.0), oxygen deficiency and an incorrect diet. Frozen larvae, bloodworm and *Daphnia* will provide a suitably balanced diet.

Left: **Euchilichthys guentheri**
A close relative of Chiloglanis *sp., this catfish enjoys the same bright, well-aerated water conditions.*

Synodontis afrofischeri
Fischer's Catfish
- **Habitat:** Lake Victoria, Nile basin
- **Length:** 125-150mm (5-6in)
- **Diet:** Crustaceans, insect larvae, plant debris and terrestrial insects. Aquarium specimens will accept frozen Gamma shrimp, brineshrimp and *Mysis* shrimp, leaf spinach, chopped earthworms, foodsticks and pellets, frozen or freeze-dried bloodworm, gnat larvae and mosquito larvae.
- **Sex differences:** Not known
- **Aquarium compatibility:** This species will adapt to a wide range of water chemistry (acidic-alkaline systems) and mixes with most aquarium fishes
- **Aquarium breeding:** Not known

A study of this species in Lake Victoria proved the species to be sexually mature at 75mm (3in) and a high percentage of the females to be

Above: **Synodontis afrofischeri**
This river and lake species accepts a wide range of water conditions.

constantly carrying eggs. Spawning occurs in peaks between January and August/September in pre- or post-rainy season surges. It is suggested that the spawning peaks are part of a reproductive strategy that serves to synchronize reproductive activity with increased food and favourable spawning and rearing areas prior to or following the rains, which occur in March-June and October-November.

Adult females produce between 200 and 15,000 eggs. Should an aquarium spawning occur, the lucky fishkeeper would have an incredible number of fry to raise!

Below: **Synodontis alberti**
A young specimen that is distinctly patterned and clearly large-eyed. Both are good recognition points.

Above: **Synodontis angelicus**
One of the best-known Synodontis *species available to fishkeepers and much sought after by enthusiasts.*

Synodontis alberti
Albert's Catfish
- **Habitat:** Zaire River
- **Length:** 150mm (6in)
- **Diet:** Crustaceans, insect larvae, etc. Aquarium specimens will accept flake food, frozen bloodworm, *Daphnia*, gnat and mosquito larvae, brine shrimp, finely chopped earthworms, pellets and foodsticks
- **Sex differences:** Adult male specimens retain a slight giraffe-like body pattern, whereas larger and more robust females lose this pattern as the body finally fades to a light grey
- **Aquarium compatibility:** An excellent community catfish suitable for almost any tropical system
- **Aquarium breeding:** Not known

The large eye and long sweeping maxillary barbel enable this species to be easily recognized. As one of the smaller *Synodontis*, Albert's Catfish can be accommodated in any modest aquarium. Juveniles display a particularly attractive silver body, ornately patterned with large spots, as shown opposite.

Synodontis angelicus
Polka-dot Catfish
- **Habitat:** Rivers on the main Zaire system
- **Length:** 200mm (8in)
- **Diet:** In the wild, this species takes insect larvae, fish fry, terrestrial insects, plant debris and shrimp. In the aquarium, it will accept flake foods, frozen bloodworm, *Mysis* shrimp and brineshrimp, chopped earthworms, and pellets or foodsticks.
- **Sex differences:** Females are larger and more robust in the body, and develop a drab body colour in maturity as the white patterning fades. Males are slightly smaller, slender in the body and retain some of the white spots as adults.
- **Aquarium compatibility:** Semi-adult specimens are territorial. Safe with small community fishes
- **Aquarium breeding:** Unknown

The Polka-dot Catfish was once the most sought after species among fishkeepers. The black body, spotted in yellow or white dots, offers an attractive pattern – often lacking in catfishes. Different populations have distinct patterns. One form with a combination of stripes, bars and spots was originally thought to be a subspecies, *S. angelicus zonatus*.

Synodontis aterrimus

False Nigriventris; Dark Synodontis
- **Habitat:** Zaire rivers
- **Length:** 100mm (4in)
- **Diet:** In the wild, this species lives on insect larvae and terrestrial insects that have fallen into the water. In the aquarium it will accept bloodworm, *Daphnia*, mosquito and gnat larvae (freeze-dried or frozen), and floating foodsticks
- **Sex differences:** Females are larger than males
- **Aquarium compatibility:** An ideal community catfish suitable for small community systems
- **Aquarium breeding:** Not known

This dwarf species is marginally similar to *Synodontis nigriventris*, well known to fishkeepers as the Upside-down Catfish. The latter is slightly smaller and lighter in colour than *Synodontis aterrimus*, however. Both species are true inverting catfish and possess dark ventral surfaces that provide effective camouflage. *Synodontis* species that spend a high percentage of their time swimming upside-down are usually surface feeders on hatching fly larvae.

Synodontis brichardi

Brichard's Catfish
- **Habitat:** Zaire River
- **Length:** 125-150mm (5-6in)
- **Diet:** In the habitat, this fish lives on shrimp, and possibly algae and insect larvae. Aquarium

Above: **Synodontis aterrimus**
A true inverting species ideal for small aquariums. Provide a suitable diet for its surface-feeding habits.

specimens will feed on Gamma shrimp, brineshrimp and *Mysis* shrimp, chopped leaf spinach and foodsticks.
- **Sex differences:** Not known
- **Aquarium compatibility:** Extremely peaceful towards other species. Can sometimes be the target for aggressive species
- **Aquarium breeding:** Not known

A mainstay of Zaire fish exports along with *Synodontis decorus*, the Banded or Brichard's Catfish is extremely popular among enthusiasts. Its streamlined body, unusual in this group, suggests that it is a fast-water fish and will therefore flourish in a bright, fresh system of pH 6.9-7.5 with plenty of aeration. Aquarium specimens will accept shredded leaf spinach, which may indicate a need to provide a 'green base' to their diet.

Synodontis caudalis
Whiptail Synodontis; Whiptail Catfish

- **Habitat:** Zaire River and pools
- **Length:** 200mm (8in)
- **Diet:** Little is known about its natural diet, but it is likely to be typically wide ranging. Aquarium specimens accept shrimp, bloodworm, flake, pellet and foodsticks
- **Sex differences:** Not known
- **Aquarium compatibility:** Fairly peaceful towards other community fishes. Can sometimes be territorial towards other *Synodontis* species
- **Aquarium breeding:** Not known

The Whiptail Catfish is so named by the author because of its characteristic extensions to the tail fin. Its body pattern and shape resemble those of *Synodontis camelopardalis,* an equally rare import from the same region, although the Whiptail grows larger and has a much darker, almost reticulated pattern.

Above: **Synodontis brichardi**
The streamlined shape is a clear adaptation to life in the fast-flowing waters of the Zaire River.

Synodontis decorus
Clown Catfish

- **Habitat:** Zaire rivers and pools
- **Length:** 300mm (12in)
- **Diet:** Crustaceans, algae and insect larvae in the wild, but will accept aquarium foods
- **Sex differences:** Males are more slender than females and have a darker pattern
- **Aquarium compatibility:** Juveniles are peaceful, although semi-adult specimens can be extremely disruptive to smaller community systems
- **Aquarium breeding:** Not known

The Clown Catfish is one of the most popular species of all the African catfishes because of its attractive body and fin patterning, and also because it is often available. Large specimens are known to develop a whiplike extension of the dorsal fin, which sometimes reaches as far back as the caudal fin.

Adults tend to be less active than juveniles and often become very secretive during daylight hours.

Left: **Synodontis caudalis**
Mistaken for Synodontis robertsi *for many years until the latter fish was made available in Zaire fish imports, this species is often confused with* S. camelopardalis.

Synodontis eurystomus (S. polli)

Leopard Catfish
- **Habitat:** The rocky shoreline of Lake Tanganyika
- **Length:** 150mm (6in)
- **Diet:** Crustaceans, snails and algae in the wild; will accept most aquarium foods
- **Sex differences:** Females reach the full stated length of 150mm (6in); males usually reach only 125mm (5in)
- **Aquarium compatibility:** Peaceful except with its own kind or species that most resemble it
- **Aquarium breeding:** Not known; an alkaline system required

The dark leopard markings of this species commend it to catfish enthusiasts. It is collected with the Pygmy Leopard Catfish, *Synodontis petricolor*, which is adult at 100mm (4in) and often confused with it. Both species are specialized snail feeders, although in aquariums they will accept a wide range of frozen and prepared foods.

Above: **Synodontis decorus**
A juvenile of this popular African catfish. Dorsal fin extensions develop in adults of both sexes.

Synodontis flavitaeniatus

Pyjamas Catfish
- **Habitat:** Zaire Rivers and pools
- **Length:** 200mm (8in)
- **Diet:** The natural diet has not been recorded, but is probably typical of *Synodontis*. Juvenile and adult aquarium specimens will accept a wide range of foods, including frozen insect and crustacean foods, flake, pellet and foodsticks, tablet foods and shrimps
- **Sex differences:** Adult females are deeper in the body than males and usually display a plain body
- **Aquarium compatibility:** Peaceful towards most fishes

Below: **Synodontis eurystomus**
A striking species justly popular among enthusiasts. A snail-feeder from Lake Tanganyika.

although it can be territorial to its own kind
● **Aquarium breeding:** Not known

The Pyjamas Catfish has a unique and striking colour pattern of horizontal yellow and brown stripes. It is a much sought after species that still commands a high price.

A public aquarium in Holland boasts a twenty year-old specimen, a pointer to the longevity of many catfishes in captivity.

Synodontis greshoffi

Greshoff's Catfish
● **Habitat:** Zaire Rivers and pools
● **Length:** 200mm (8in)
● **Diet:** This species is a typical opportunist feeder and will

Below: **Synodontis greshoffi**
Although superficially similar to several other Synodontis *species, the large eye, prominent adipose fin and long barbels are characteristic.*

Above: **Synodontis flavitaeniatus**
The golden-yellow body stripes are an outstanding feature of young specimens. They have ensured its popularity among enthusiasts.

accept prepared foods, flake, pellet, foodsticks and tablets. Enhance this 'dried' diet with alternate offerings of frozen insect larvae and crustacean foods
● **Sex differences:** Not known
● **Aquarium compatibility:** An ideal community species
● **Aquarium breeding:** Not known

Greshoff's Catfish is often confused with other *Synodontis* species, although its large eye, deep body and large adipose fin are distinctive characteristics. The long maxillary barbels clearly identify the species, however. When not pointing ahead, these stretch back along the body to reach the ventral fins.

Above: **Synodontis koensis**
A relatively small species with a variable colour pattern and indistinct adipose fin.

Synodontis koensis
Ko River Catfish
- **Habitat:** Rivers, Ivory Coast
- **Length:** 100-150mm (4-6in)
- **Diet:** Insect larvae, terrestrial insects, crustaceans and general plant and organic debris. Suitable aquarium foods can be substituted for this natural diet
- **Sex differences:** Males have a more acutely pointed humeral spine, a darker colour pattern and a larger adipose fin than females
- **Aquarium compatibility:** A small, peaceful species
- **Aquarium breeding:** Not known

This small to medium-sized species is sometimes encountered through West African imports into Europe. The colour pattern is extremely variable, even among population groups and between males and females. It is remarkably similar in appearance to another West African species, *Synodontis tourei*, which the author tentatively suggests is a form of *Synodontis koensis*.

Synodontis multipunctatus
Many-spotted Catfish
- **Habitat:** The rocky and sandy shoreline of Lake Tanganyika
- **Length:** Males 200mm (8in); females 280mm (11in)
- **Diet:** Crustaceans, algae and insect larvae. Will accept suitable aquarium foods

- **Sex differences:** Males may possess longer pectoral spines and tend to be smaller than females
- **Aquarium compatibility:** Perfect for African Rift Valley Lake cichlid community systems. Generally peaceful, but can be territorial towards its own species
- **Aquarium breeding:** A 'cuckoo' relationship is known to exist between this catfish and mouthbrooding cichlids, which has led to some fry being raised in aquariums.

A popular export from the Burundi district of Lake Tanganyika, *Synodontis multipunctatus* is undoubtedly one of the world's most attractive catfishes. It is often confused with *Synodontis petricolor*, which is smaller; *Synodontis eurystomus*, which is also smaller but also has a darker body pattern; and *Synodontis dhonti*, which grows larger and loses the beautiful spots and body stripes as it becomes mature.

Its main diet in Lake Tanganyika is certainly snails (applicable to most of the Rift Valley Lake species mentioned) and this crustacean part of the diet can be made up by frozen foods, such as Gamma shrimp, brineshrimp and *Mysis*.

Synodontis multipunctatus will thrive in an alkaline system (pH 7.5-8.2) with a good rock aquascape alongside Lake Tanganyikan and Lake Malawi cichlids. Two individuals will clash over territorial claims, and so it is wise to keep them singly or in groups of three or

Above:
Synodontis multipunctatus
No two specimens share the same pattern, which makes this one of the most intriguing Synodontis *species.*

more to prevent bullying.

During cichlid spawnings, these catfishes are known to swim between the pair, eating expelled cichlid eggs and replacing some with their own. The mouthbrooding female cichlid is then said to pick up the catfish eggs alongside her own. Although the catfish eggs are less than half the size of the cichlid eggs, which are 3-4mm (0.12-0.16in) across, the female is said to mistake the catfish eggs for her own. Aquarists have suggested the catfish fry hatch in the cichlid's mouth. The catfishes develop faster, hatch and then predate on the later cichlid hatchlings. This assumption arises from the lower fry numbers produced by females known to be raising catfish fry together with their own.

Synodontis nigrita
Dark-spotted Catfish; False Upside-down Catfish
- **Habitat:** Widespread in the rivers of West and Central Africa
- **Length:** 200mm (8in)
- **Diet:** Almost all foods accepted
- **Sex differences:** Males are slender in comparison with females
- **Aquarium compatibility:** Somewhat boisterous as it grows to the semi-adult size; more suited to a medium-sized to large cichlid community
- **Aquarium breeding:** Not known

At 50mm (2in), *Synodontis nigrita* is often sold as the 'Upside-down Catfish', and many fishkeepers would believe they are purchasing the true Upside-down Catfish,

Below: **Synodontis nigrita**
One of the most commonly imported species from Nigeria. It is distinguishable from other closely related forms by its many spots.

Above: **Synodontis notatus**
The spots on the body can vary in number, but this specimen displays the usual one spot on either side.

Synodontis notatus
One-spot Catfish
- **Habitat:** Zaire River
- **Length:** 250mm(10in)
- **Diet:** Aquarium specimens will consume a wide variety of prepared foods. They will thrive if offered standard frozen insect and crustacean foods, chopped leaf spinach, and dried foods
- **Sex differences:** Males are slender, possess longer pectoral spines and longer caudal fin lobes than females
- **Aquarium compatibility:** Juveniles are reasonably peaceful towards community fishes, but semi-adults can be disruptive and boisterous
- **Aquarium breeding:** Not known

The large spot pattern of this species is quite variable; in one survey of 100 specimens, 15 percent displayed extra body spots, usually two and three spots. *Synodontis notatus* was once available in large numbers, but recent Zaire shipments have shown it to be less plentiful.

Synodontis petricolor
Pygmy Leopard Catfish
- **Habitat:** Shoreline of Lake Tanganyika
- **Length:** 100mm(4in)
- **Diet:** Crustaceans
- **Sex differences:** Adult males are probably smaller (75mm/3in) than females
- **Aquarium compatibility:** Ideal for the miniature to large Rift Valley Lake cichlid community
- **Aquarium breeding:** Not known

Synodontis petricolor is perhaps one of the most beautiful species in this large genus. Its colour pattern is confusingly similar to the equally attractive Many-spotted Catfish, *Synodontis multipunctatus*, although the white borders to the fins are absent in the latter species.

The Pygmy Leopard Catfish is the smallest of the Rift Lake species and as such is perfect for most systems, although, sadly, it is very rarely available to fishkeepers.

Right: **Synodontis petricolor**
An excellent dwarf catfish to include as part of a Rift Valley Lake cichlid community. Perhaps one of the most beautiful Synodontis *species, this fish is universally acclaimed for its handsome coloration.*

Synodontis robbianus

Brown-spotted Catfish
- **Habitat:** Niger River
- **Length:** Perhaps this species is a semi-surface feeder in its natural habitat, as it is quick to take floating bloodworm and mosquito larvae when kept in the aquarium. A blend of dried flake and freeze-dried foods, together with frozen shrimp and insect larvae, will ensure this species thrives in captivity
- **Sex differences:** Females are deeper bodied than males of this species

Above: **Synodontis robbianus**
The leaf-brown body sets this fish apart from the grey of Synodontis nigrita; *both share a spotted skin.*

- **Aquarium compatibility:** Good community species, ideal for medium-sized aquariums
- **Aquarium breeding:** Not known

This small *Synodontis* could easily be confused with the more readily available *Synodonits nigrata*. It is much smaller in adult size, however, and has a longer adipose fin and a brown, rather than grey, body.

Family: PANGASIIDAE
Within this Asian family, particularly the genus *Pangasius,* are found some of the largest freshwater fishes, reaching some 2000mm(80in) or more in length. Fortunately, smaller species are available, but even these will need a fairly large aquarium as they are fast-swimming fishes.

Pangasius sutchi
Asian Shark Catfish
- **Habitat:** Large rivers in Thailand
- **Length:** 450mm (18in)
- **Diet:** In the wild, this species consumes fruit and vegetation, insect larvae, shrimp and various other crustaceans. In the aquarium, it takes bloodworm, foodsticks, frozen krill and Gamma shrimp, chopped earthworms, and spinach
- **Sex differences:** Males have darker stripes and are more slender than females
- **Aquarium compatibility:** Ideal for a large-fish community system, but should be kept in small groups
- **Aquarium breeding:** Not known

Asian Shark Catfishes – now also available in a 'blonde' form – are usually kept as individual fishes in aquariums, which does not encourage them to settle in captivity. They shoal in large numbers in the major Asian rivers, especially in stretches of rapids.

Below: **Pangasius sutchii**
Adapted to live in fast-flowing rivers, the Shark Catfish should be kept in a reasonably large tank.

They can be extremely nervous in aquariums, and will cause a great deal of damage to themselves by striking the cover glass and tank sides, etc., if disturbed. Although they are generally available as youngsters farm bred in the Far East, even small specimens only 50-75mm (2-3in) long are not suitable for inclusion in small systems. This is because the water may be virtually static in the small aquarium, compared to their natural habitat of fast-flowing rivers. You may be able to alleviate this problem to some extent by using a powerful filtration system to create strong water currents through the tank. However, this is really a catfish for larger aquariums.

Not dissimilar to the Africa Schilbe Catfish, this species has an appetite for almost any foods but, it will also eat any fish that it can accommodate in its mouth, so larger companions are recommended.

Family: SCHILBEIDAE
This family, from Africa and Asia, includes the intriguing transparent-bodied Glass Catfish *(Eutropiellus)*. Members of this family have short, front-positioned dorsal fins and long-based anal fins, and most species also have a small adipose fin.

Eutropiellus vanderweyeri

African Glass Catfish

- **Habitat:** Fast-flowing rivers of the River Niger system
- **Length:** 75mm (3in)
- **Diet:** Insect larvae – but will adapt well to prepared flake foods and other aquarium diets
- **Sex differences:** Females are deeper in the body than males
- **Aquarium compatibility:** Relatively peaceful to all fishes.
- **Aquarium breeding:** Not known

This species is often referred to as *E. debauwi,* although this identification is said to be very doubtful. A second species is imported from Zaire which appears similar to the African Glass Catfish but may well be the true *debauwi.*

These catfishes are excellent midwater shoalers for medium-sized to large community aquariums. Although popularly known as the African Glass Catfish, the horizontal dark stripes on the body make it much less transparent than the Asian species *Kryptopterus bicirrhus,* which also has long thin barbels on the top lip. Another definite aid to positive identification is that the dorsal fin in this species is more normally formed, having rays and tissue, while that of the Asian fish is limited to a single ray. You may need to look closely at the dorsal fin to see this, for the first rays are dark, the rest transparent, helping to disguise the fin's true shape. Like many other catfishes, this is a gregarious species and will gradually fade away if kept as a solitary specimen. Keeping it together with a few others of its own kind will help to ensure that it thrives in the aquarium.

Below: **Eutropiellus vanderweyeri**
This catfish is distinguished from closely related species by the stripes in its caudal lobe.

5

Part Five
South American Catfishes

Above: *No community would be complete without a* Corydoras.

Above: Amblydoras hancocki, *a small non-predatory catfish, ideal for the community aquarium.*

The tremendous Amazonian river system of South America is not unnaturally a treasure house of fishes, which include the stately Angelfish and Discus, the brilliantly coloured tetras (along with their ferocious Piranha relative) and an excellent selection of catfishes. In addition to this large catchment area, fishes are also collected in great number from the fringe countries of Argentina, Colombia, Ecuador, Paraguay, Peru and Venezuela. Within the catfish area of interest one group, the Armoured Catfishes of the callichthyidae family, is especially popular with hobbyists; it contains over a hundred species of *Corydoras* alone. All the members of this large family are instantly recognizable by their skin covering of two rows of overlapping bony plates or 'scutes.' South American catfishes range in size from around 25mm to over 2 metres (1in to 6.5ft), so there is plenty of scope to cater for every taste and aquarium size. The pimelodidae family contains many very spectacular species, several of which rival the African *Synodontis* for beauty and interest. The Suckermouth Catfishes, or loricariids, perform a very useful service around the aquarium, ridding it of any soft green algal growths. Failure to supplement their diet with suitable greenfood, however, may result in them turning their attention to equally soft-leaved plants. Whatever your interest – Talking Catfishes, Banjo Catfishes, Driftwood Catfishes – you will find them all featured in this section. Smaller species are ideal for the beginner, while some of the larger varieties present a real challenge to the dedicated enthusiast. An increasing number are being bred in the aquarium, yet another incentive for you to explore the world of South American catfishes.

Above: *Spawning* Corydoras.
Below: *The small Bumblebee Catfish needs plenty of retreats.*

Below: *The scutes of* Brochis britskii *shine in reflected light.*

Family: ASPREDENIDAE Banjo Catfishes

One can but wonder at some of the popular names given to fishes by hobbyists – the members of this family delight in the name of Banjo Catfishes, due to their distinctive physical outline when seen from above. These fairly inactive fishes are characterized by their very long upper barbels, strong spines on their pectoral fins and wrinkled, warty, scaleless skin. Individual species may be hard to distinguish.

Agmus lyriformis

Craggy Headed Banjo
● **Habitat:** Leafy streams and creeks from Guyana to Brazil.
● **Length:** 75mm (3in).
● **Diet:** Insect larvae and invertebrates.
● **Sex differences:** Males are smaller and more colourful than females.
● **Aquarium breeding:** Not known.
● **Aquarium compatibility:** Will thrive in all sizes of tanks but is especially suited to the smaller community aquarium.

The pan-shaped heads and long tails give this group of catfishes their common name, although some species have more eel-like bodies. The small Craggy Headed Banjo, with its distinctive ridges across the head, often catches the eye of new fishkeepers. It is widespread in Guyana and Brazil, where its dark and light brown patterns provide perfect camouflage as it lies motionless on the bed of slow-moving rivers.

Aspredo cotylephorus

Eel Banjo
● **Habitat:** The brackish waters of the mangrove swamps in Venezuela, Guyana and Brazil.
● **Length:** 300mm (12in).
● **Diet:** Shrimps and other small crustaceans.

Above: **Agmus lyriformis**
This sleepy little catfish adds character to the aquarium.

● **Sex differences:** Males are thought to be mottled in black, brown and white; females are relatively plain.
● **Aquarium breeding:** The author has successfully raised *Aspredo* fry in an aquarium from a specimen imported with eggs. The spawning and egg carrying functions have never been fully investigated and remain a mystery even to scientists currently researching the group. It is not certain how or where spawning occurs, nor when and how the

Below: **Aspredo cotylephorus**
The Eel Banjo, as intriguing as its relatives, is much the largest of the three species shown here. Give it plenty of swimming space.

eggs become attached to the stomach. It is thought to be the female which carries the eggs (attached to the stomach wall by miniature lengths of tissue, known as cotylephores or stalks) but sexing of this species (by colour patterning) is uncertain.

● **Aquarium compatibility:** A peaceful, non-predatory species. Will not thrive in small overcrowded communties.

This catfish, formerly classified as *Platystacus,* but recently moved into the genus *Aspredo,* can grow up to 300mm(12in) long, although it is usually imported at 50-75mm(2-3in). It is common in the shoreline seas and river estuaries of northern South America and is best suited to bright, neutral-alkaline systems. (Young fishes acclimatize better than mature forms.) It is known to migrate to fresh water and it is probable that the female carries eggs, attached to the stomach, to safer shallow water.

Bunocephalus amaurus
Bicoloured Banjo
● **Habitat:** Slow-moving rivers and creeks.
● **Length:** 100-125mm (4-5in).
● **Diet:** Insect larvae and small invertebrates and crustaceans.

● **Sex differences:** Males are smaller and more slender than females.
● **Aquarium breeding:** Several eggs are laid freely on the substrate at night and should then be removed to a separate dish or net. Hatching occurs in three days.
● **Aquarium compatibility:** An excellent community catfish.

Almost every South American tropical fish import contains this species, which looks like a cross between a frying pan and a dead leaf! The Bicoloured Banjo will feign dead during the daytime but, like all nocturnal animals, it will come alive in the twilight hours.

Below: **Bunocephalus amaurus**
A great snail eater in the wild, the Bicoloured Banjo will relish small crustaceans in the aquarium.

Family: AUCHENIPTERIDAE Driftwood Catfishes
The fishes in this family, commonly known as Driftwood Catfishes, have an elongated body shape. Other physical characteristics are the dorsal fin, set well forward, the broad indented caudal fin, and the eyes, which are situated at the very front of the head. Body patterning is variable from species to species, ranging from the spectacular to the fairly drab.

Auchenipterichthys thoracatus
Midnight Catfish
● **Habitat:** Small inland rivers and creeks.
● **Length:** 100-125mm (4-5in).
● **Diet:** Insect larvae and small invertebrates and crustaceans.
● **Sex differences:** Males are more distinctively patterned than females with rows of white body dots, and they have an elongated

tip to the anal fin which is used in spawning.
● **Aquarium breeding:** Fertilization is internal and the eggs are deposited to hatch within several days. No successful aquarium breeding has been recorded.
● **Aquarium compatibility:** Peaceful with fishes of equal size.

This small Driftwood catfish is regularly imported from the

Peruvian Zamora region and can be distinguished by its rows of white specks on a dark blue body. As with all members of this family, it is extremely nocturnal.

Liosomadoras oncinus
Jaguar Catfish
● **Habitat**: Brazilian rivers and streams.
● **Length**: 150mm (6in).
● **Diet**: Small crustaceans, fish and assorted invertebrates.
● **Sex differences:** Males are more ornately patterned than females.
● **Aquarium breeding:** Not known, but the spawning method is presumably the same as for other Driftwood Catfishes.
● **Aquarium compatibility:** Fine with fishes of equal or greater size.

One of the most beautiful of all South American catfishes, the Jaguar Catfish can be recognized by the yellow blotches on a brown body. It is unique in that it possesses characteristics of two different catfish families. On the one hand, it is scaleless, as are all of the auchenipterids, while on the other, it possesses an outer gill spine and a long-based adipose fin, which are distinctive traits of

Left:
Auchenipterichthys thoracatus
The starry iridescences on its dark back give this Midnight Catfish its common name. The elongated tip to the male's anal fin is a spawning aid and can be clearly seen when the fin is extended.

the doradids, South American Talking or Thorny Catfishes. Scientists have argued as to which family it truly belongs, but current research places it in the *Auchenipteridae* family. From a fishkeeping point of view, the Jaguar Catfish has proved fairly easy to keep; it will accept a broad range of conditions and a wide variety of foods.

Above: **Tatia aulopygia**
These delightful dwarf catfishes will thrive in the smallest community aquarium. To make them feel even more at home, furnish their tank with plenty of sunken logs or pieces of bogwood to provide hideaways.

Tatia aulopygia
Black Pigmy Driftwood
● **Habitat:** Small rivers and creeks.
● **Length:** 75mm (3in).
● **Diet:** Small invertebrates and crustaceans.
● **Sex differences:** Males have an extended anal fin.
● **Aquarium breeding:** Internal fertilization; eggs are deposited about 24-48 hours later.
● **Aquarium compatibility:** An ideal small community catfish.

This jet-black catfish has two colour forms, one plain black, the other speckled with white flecks. Both forms are sometimes imported from South America. These slender, torpedo-shaped catfishes live in and around submerged logs and riverbanks.

Left: **Liosomadoras oncinus**
The Jaguar Catfish is quite a shy species but is a beautiful aquarium catfish. Its spotted body markings are very similar to those of its feline namesake.

Family: CALLICHTHYIDAE Dwarf Armoured Catfishes

These so-called Armoured Catfishes are among the best-loved aquarium fishes. Almost every community aquarium contains at least one member of the *Corydoras* genus, small-sized catfishes, which spend their time searching around the aquarium floor for food. Callichthyids are characterized by the covering on their bodies; they have rows of overlapping bony plates, called 'scutes', which provide a protective 'armour' to the body. Many species of the active *Corydoras* genus also breed in the aquarium, the female carrying the eggs between her pelvic fins to a selected site, where hatching occurs. Like all catfishes, members of this family should not be seen as mere scavengers, but given food as and how they require it; in the case of these fishes a feeding just before 'lights out' will not come amiss since they continue their activities after darkness falls. During the day, many will hide from view.

Aspidoras pauciradiatus

False Corydoras
- **Habitat:** Southern Brazil.
- **Length:** 25mm (1in).
- **Diet:** Very small invertebrates.
- **Sex differences:** Males are more slender than females.
- **Aquarium breeding:** Eggs are placed at random and can be difficult to hatch.
- **Aquarium compatibility:** Peaceful.

This commonly imported catfish is the best-known *Aspidoras* species and also one of the smallest. It was originally described in 1970 as a *Corydoras* because of its body shape, but can be distinguished by its long head. Its requirements are similar to those of *Corydoras* except that it can be more delicate on introduction to the aquarium. These fishes may rest motionless on the substrate and refuse to feed if confronted with adverse water conditions, such as low pH and poor filtration.

Above: **Aspidoras pauciradiatus**
A superb miniature species for the small aquarium, this catfish seems fairly hardy once it has settled in the aquarium and is feeding. This species is easily confused with catfishes from the Corydoras *genus.*

Brochis britskii

Britski's Catfish
- **Habitat:** Weed-choked slow rivers in the Mato Grosso region of Brazil.
- **Length:** 100mm (4in).
- **Diet:** Insect larvae and assorted crustaceans.
- **Sex differences:** Females are larger than males.
- **Aquarium breeding:** Not recorded, but probably as for *Corydoras*.
- **Aquarium compatibility:** Peaceful.

This superb Brazilian species has the emerald green *Brochis* sheen enhanced by a reddened hue in the caudal fin. It is very similar in appearance to *B. multiradiatus* from Ecuador and Peru, but lacks the latter's long snout.

Brochis britskii have been collected in the Rio Guapore in the Brazilian Mato Grosso region. They live in slow-moving, heavily planted rivers (3-6m/10-20ft deep), where the water is soft and has a pH of around 6.9-7.2.

Brochis splendens

Emerald Catfish
● **Habitat:** Rivers in Peru, Ecuador and Brazil.
● **Length:** 75-100mm (3-4in).
● **Diet:** Small insect larvae and assorted invertebrates.
● **Sex differences:** Females are larger than males.
● **Aquarium breeding:** Egg layer as *Corydoras*.
● **Aquarium compatibility:** Peaceful.

Species in the *Brochis* genus can be distinguished from *Corydoras* by the presence of more dorsal

Below: **Brochis britskii**
This catfish prefers deeper water and thrives on a shredded shrimp and insect larvae diet.

Above: **Brochis splendens**
Now a firm favourite, this robust species is an ideal addition to the community aquarium. Its longer-based dorsal fin prevents Brochis *being mistaken for a large* Corydoras *species.*

rays. The Emerald Catfish, sometimes mistakenly known as *Brochis coeruleus*, is the most commonly imported species of the three described here. *Brochis* show a preference for deep aquariums (45-60cm/18-24in in depth) and are more active when kept in groups of between four and six specimens. They delve into the substrate for food more than most species of *Corydoras* and will also eat small shredded prawns and chopped earthworms.

243

Brochis multiradiatus
Hognosed Brochis
- **Habitat:** Small rivers in Ecuador, Brazil and Peru.
- **Length:** 100-125mm (4-5in).
- **Diet:** Insect larvae and assorted crustaceans.
- **Sex differences:** Females are larger than males.
- **Aquarium breeding:** Not recorded but most probably as for *Corydoras*.
- **Aquarium compatibility:** Peaceful.

First discovered in Ecuador, this long-nosed, large-dorsal-rayed species has more recently been imported from Peru. It is considered to be one of the most beautiful of the smaller catfishes.

The long head and snout length of the Hognosed Brochis enable it to dig into the substrate in search of food, especially live bloodworm and *Tubifex*, which may have been missed by other fishes. They thrive in bright, neutral water.

Right: **Brochis multiradiatus**
The rarest of these three Brochis *species, the Hognosed form is happiest in a neutral to alkaline system with non-aggressive fishes.*

Corydoras acutus
Black Top Catfish
- **Habitat:** Peruvian rivers.
- **Length:** 75mm (3in).
- **Diet:** Insect larvae, aquatic worms and most small crustaceans and invertebrates.
- **Sex differences:** Males are more slender than females.
- **Aquarium breeding:** Egg laying among plants.
- **Aquarium compatibility:** Peaceful.

The Black Top is one of the snouted species of *Corydoras* that arrive in shipments along with the very popular *C. julii* catfishes. The Black Top Catfish has a long snout which it uses to dig into the substrate, sifting the gravel for food that other fishes may have missed. It shares the black dorsal spot with *Corydoras julii* and, when juveniles are mixed, it can sometimes be difficult to distinguish the two species. Like many of the Peruvian species, it seems to prefer bright, neutral waters, and will thrive in a properly maintained aquarium.

Right: **Corydoras acutus**
A robust and peaceful species.

Corydoras adolfoi
Adolf's Catfish
- **Habitat:** Clear water offshoots of the Rio Negro in Brazil.
- **Length:** 50mm (2in).
- **Diet:** Insect larvae, aquatic worms and most small crustaceans and invertebrates.
- **Sex differences:** Females are slightly more robust in shape when carrying eggs.
- **Aquarium breeding:** Indiscriminate egg laying.
- **Aquarium compatibility:** Peaceful.

One of the most beautiful species of *Corydoras*, Adolf's Catfish is distinguished by its orange patch and high price! However, the patterning on the body, especially the black mask across the eyes, is quite common to a number of *Corydoras* species, notably *C.arcuatus, C.melini, C.metae,* and *C.panda*. Positive identification of these species is usually assisted by some other factor, such as extra markings on the body or dark patches appearing in the dorsal fin. *Corydoras adolfoi* was discovered recently in the whitewater offshoots of the blackwater Rio Negro in Brazil, where it lives alongside another mimic, *Corydoras imitator*.

Right: **Corydoras adolfoi**
This attractive species requires bright neutral water conditions and will thrive when offered a shaded aquarium and shredded shrimp.

Corydoras ambiacus

Spotted Catfish
● **Habitat:** Peruvian and Colombian rivers.
● **Length:** 75mm (3in).
● **Diet:** Insect larvae, aquatic worms and most small crustaceans and invertebrates.
● **Sex differences:** Females are larger than males.
● **Aquarium breeding:** One of the few species of *Corydoras* not yet spawned in the aquarium.
● **Aquarium compatibility:** Peaceful.

This species is well known to fishkeepers, although the scientific name is not commonly used. Although plentiful in the wild, and commonly imported, the Spotted Catfish has not been spawned in the aquarium. It is not generally fussy about its water conditions, but the key to breeding may well prove to be the provision of clear, neutral water.

Below: **Corydoras ambiacus**
A robust and adaptable species, ideal for the community aquarium. Examine the patterning carefully to make a positive identification.

Right: **Corydoras arcuatus**
Good filtration will alleviate the risk of infection, which can result in barbel loss in this species.

Corydoras arcuatus

Skunk Catfish
● **Habitat:** Peruvian and Brazilian rivers.
● **Length:** 50mm (2in).
● **Diet:** Insect larvae, aquatic worms and most small crustaceans and invertebrates.
● **Sex differences:** Females are slightly larger and deeper bodied than males.
● **Aquarium breeding:** About 20-30 eggs are laid among plants.
● **Aquarium compatibility:** Peaceful.

The Skunk Catfish, also known as the Bowline Catfish, has a distinctive, black upper body stripe that passes through the eye. This strong pattern provides camouflage to disguise it from aquatic and terrestial predators in the clear waters – from above the fish resembles a piece of debris. In the aquarium the Skunk Catfish will thrive in water that is neutral to slightly alkaline in pH value.

Corydoras delphax

False Blochi Catfish
- **Habitat:** Colombian rivers.
- **Length:** 75mm (3in).
- **Diet:** Insect larvae, aquatic worms and most small crustaceans and invertebrates.
- **Sex differences:** Males are smaller than females.
- **Aquarium breeding:** Egg laying as with other *Corydoras* species, but rarely spawned in an aquarium.
- **Aquarium compatibility:** Peaceful.

Below: **Corydoras delphax**
A native of fast-flowing waters, the False Blochi Catfish will thrive in a large community aquarium with well-oxygenated water.

This Colombian species was originally incorrectly identified as *Corydoras blochi*. Although it has been known to aquarists for a long time, it was not scientifically described until 1983. It is one of the most frequently imported species and is a mainstay of Colombian tropical fish exports. Despite being a reluctant spawner, it has proved to be very hardy and adaptable and is an ideal species for the non-predatory community aquarium. A range of colour forms exist. One is dark, almost black, and speckled with a pale saddle patch from the dorsal to the middle body region. Another form, which also has a saddle patch, is without the speckled pattern.

Corydoras elegans

Elegant Catfish
● **Habitat:** Creeks and small rivers of Peru, Brazil and Ecuador.
● **Length:** 50mm (2in).
● **Diet:** Insect larvae, aquatic worms and most small crustaceans and invertebrates.
● **Sex differences:** Males are more highly patterned than females.
● **Aquarium breeding:** Very easily spawned when mature and the eggs are fairly robust, with very high hatching rates.
● **Aquarium compatibility:** Like most small *Corydoras* species, it is quite peaceful.

Above: **Corydoras elegans**
This small catfish is distinctive as one of only a handful of species in which males are more ornately patterned than females. This species is easy to sex and breeding successes are common. Males are confused with C. nanus.

This species is quite widespread in South America, although the majority of imported specimens are from Peru.
  Corydoras elegans has generally proved extremely adaptable to a wide range of water conditions and is an excellent choice for the smaller community system.

Above: **Corydoras julii**
This beautiful Brazilian species is easily maintained in slightly acidic waters. It is best suited to the small community aquarium.

Corydoras habrosus

Salt and Pepper Catfish
● **Habitat:** Colombian and Venezuelan rivers.
● **Length:** 25mm (1in).
● **Diet:** Insect larvae, aquatic worms and most small crustaceans and invertebrates.
● **Sex differences:** Females are slightly larger than males.
● **Aquarium breeding:** Will spawn in planted aquariums.
● **Aquarium compatibility:** Peaceful.

This tiny Venezuelan catfish (adult at 25mm/1in) is one of the smallest species in the genus. It is known in Colombia as *Corydoras cochui* (a valid Brazilian species according

Left: **Corydoras habrosus**
These pigmy catfishes are best kept in groups of six or more; they are happiest and most active when shoaling together.

to current research) and this has caused much confusion in fishkeeping circles.

Corydoras julii

Julii Catfish
● **Habitat:** Brazilian rivers.
● **Length:** 50mm (2in).
● **Diet:** Insect larvae, aquatic worms and most small crustaceans and invertebrates.
● **Sex differences:** Males are smaller than females.
● **Aquarium breeding:** This species has not spawned in the aquarium.
● **Aquarium compatibility:** Peaceful.

This delightful and attractive Brazilian catfish – its silver-white body adorned with fine black dots – is much confused with the Peruvian species *Corydoras trilineatus*.
Corydoras julii is a small, delicate species suited only to small, peaceful community aquariums. It is not too demanding of specific water quality and will thrive in acidic to neutral pH levels.

Corydoras leopardus

Leopard Catfish
● **Habitat:** Colombian and Brazilian rivers.
● **Length:** 75mm (3in).
● **Diet:** Insect larvae, aquatic worms and most small crustaceans and invertebrates.
● **Sex differences:** Males are more slender than females.
● **Aquarium breeding:** Has not spawned in the aquarium.
● **Aquarium compatibility:** Peaceful.

At 75mm (3in), the Leopard Catfish is larger than the two species with which it is sometimes confused; *Corydoras julii* and *Corydoras trilineatus*. All three species have a black dorsal spot and the same basic body pattern.

Above: **Corydoras leopardus**
Another peaceful community catfish that is very adaptable to a broad range of water conditions and different sizes of aquariums.

Corydoras melanotaenia

Green Gold Catfish
● **Habitat:** Colombian rivers.
● **Length:** 75mm(3in).
● **Diet:** Insect larvae, aquatic worms and most small crustaceans and invertebrates.
● **Sex differences:** Males are distinctly more slender than females.

Below: **Corydoras melanotaenia**
Green Gold Catfishes are fast swimmers and will, therefore, be happiest in large community aquariums. Provide them with bright, slightly alkaline water.

● **Aquarium breeding:** This species is very closely related to the Bronze Corydoras (see pages 166-7), but is not as easily bred. Spawning can be induced by adding cool water to the aquarium. Egglaying, as with all *Corydoras* catfishes.

● **Aquarium compatibility:** Peaceful.

The Green Gold Catfish has often been confused with the Bronze Corydoras, *Corydoras aeneus,* but its common name highlights the difference in colour pattern. It is also longer in the head and body than *Corydoras aeneus*. This small, shy, fast-swimming species would be a welcome addition to the community aquarium.

Above: **Corydoras melini**
This catfish shares the eye stripe and body pattern with several other Corydoras *species, including a newly discovered Brazilian form,* Corydoras davidsandsi.

Corydoras melini

False Bandit Catfish
● **Habitat:** Colombian and Brazilian waters.
● **Length:** 50mm (2in).
● **Diet:** Insect larvae, aquatic worms and most small crustaceans and invertebrates.
● **Sex differences:** Females are more robust than males.
● **Aquarium breeding:** Egg production rarely exceeds 20-30 and these are placed in and among plants, where they can be easily overlooked on the undersides of the leaves.
● **Aquarium compatibility:** An excellent community species.

This species is easily confused with *Corydoras metae*, with which it shares the Rio Meta Basin waters. If you look closely, you will see that the stripe continues into the tail fin in *C. melini*, whereas in *C. metae* the pattern rounds off at the base of the tail.

Corydoras metae

Bandit Catfish; Meta River Catfish
● **Habitat:** Colombian rivers.
● **Length:** 50mm (2in).
● **Diet:** Insect larvae, aquatic worms and most small crustaceans and invertebrates.
● **Sex differences:** Females are slightly larger than males.
● **Aquarium breeding:** About 20-30 eggs are placed on plants and/or on the aquarium glass.
● **Aquarium compatibility:** Peaceful.

The Bandit or Meta River Catfish, which is illustrated overleaf, is one of the most popular Colombian species. It has a lookalike, aptly called *Corydoras simulatus*, which can be identified by its longer snout. The two species are imported together and it is worth keeping an eye on new batches of catfishes in the aquarium shop to see if you can distinguish between *Corydoras metae* and its mimic.

Above: **Corydoras metae**
A bright water catfish which shares *the same rivers as* C. melini, *and its mimic,* C. simulatus.

Corydoras nattereri
Natterer's Catfish
- **Habitat:** Coastal rivers of Brazil.
- **Length:** 50mm(2in).
- **Diet:** Insect larvae, aquatic worms and most small crustaceans and invertebrates.
- **Sex differences:** Females are more rotund than males.
- **Aquarium breeding:** One of the easiest of the wild forms to spawn. Fry have a low fatality rate.
- **Aquarium compatibility:** Peaceful.

Below: **Corydoras nattereri**
Extremely robust and easily bred; this species will adapt to a broad range of water conditions.

This blue catfish is imported from southern Brazil in great quantities and has been spawned by many fishkeepers. It is a very robust and undemanding species which will live quite comfortably in both acidic and slightly alkaline water.

Corydoras Panda
Panda Catfish
- **Habitat:** Peruvian rivers.
- **Length:** 50mm(2in).
- **Diet:** Insect larvae, aquatic worms and most small crustaceans and invertebrates.
- **Sex differences:** Females are slightly larger than males.
- **Aquarium breeding:** Spawning takes place over a 12-24 hour

period and about 20-30 eggs are placed on the glass. These are best hatched in a separate dish or breeding trap (see Breeding section.

● **Aquarium compatibility:** Peaceful.

This catfish has recently been imported from Peru by enterprising wholesalers. The attractive 'panda' eye mask and tail spot make it one of the most sought after of all catfishes, but, because of its rarity, it is very expensive. Pairs or larger groups can be kept in a community aquarium with bright, clear, neutral water. Once they reach maturity you can isolate a pair to a small breeding aquarium (see Breeding section).

Below: **Corydoras panda**
Now widely available, these striking catfishes have become firm favourites with enthusiasts.

Corydoras pygmaeus
Pigmy Catfish
● **Habitat:** Rivers in Brazil and Peru.
● **Length:** 25mm (1in).
● **Diet:** Fine invertebrates and organic foods.
● **Sex differences:** Males are smaller and more slender than females.
● **Aquarium breeding:** There are many reports of Pigmy Catfishes spawning and fry being raised in community aquariums without any direct intervention by fishkeepers.
● **Aquarium compatibility:** Small species such as this are best kept in small community aquariums or in breeding tanks as larger fishes are likely to mistake them for food! Often confused with *Corydoras hastatus,* the body stripe in this species is quite distinctive. The Pigmy Catfish, found in midwater shoals of thousands in the wild, will only thrive if kept in groups in the aquarium. This tiny fish will accept a wide range of conditions and is adaptable to extremes in water hardness.

Below: **Corydoras pygmaeus**
The best-known pigmy species and easily bred in the aquarium.

Corydoras robineae

Mrs Schwartz's Catfish; Flagtail Corydoras
● **Habitat:** Whitewater tributaries of the Rio Negro.
● **Length:** 75mm (3in).
● **Diet:** Insect larvae, aquatic worms and most small crustaceans and invertebrates.
● **Sex differences:** Males are more slender than females.
● **Aquarium breeding:** There are no records of successful breedings of this relative newcomer to the aquarium.
● **Aquarium compatibility:** Peaceful.

The Flagtail Corydoras has been imported in fairly large numbers in recent years. Only discovered in 1983, it is now firmly fixed in the enthusiasts' list of great species.

It possesses a distinctive caudal pattern, which it shares with its larger relative, *Dianema urostriata*, the Flagtail Catfish.

Corydoras sodalis

False Network Catfish
● **Habitat:** Small offshoots of large creeks and rivers in Peru and Brazil.
● **Length:** 50mm (2in).
● **Diet:** Insect larvae, aquatic worms and most small crustaceans and invertebrates.
● **Sex differences:** Males are more slender and less robust than females.
● **Aquarium breeding:** Not known, but is likely to be typical of most species of *Corydoras*.
● **Aquarium compatibility:** Peaceful.

Above: **Corydoras robineae**
Spectacularly marked fishes soon become favourites with hobbyists and the recently discovered Flagtail Corydoras has lost little time in doing just that. Unlike its near-relative, Dianema urostriata, *it lives on the aquarium substrate.*

Corydoras sodalis is invariably confused with *Corydoras reticulatus*, the Network Catfish. *C. sodalis* has a shorter, more rounded profile, lighter reticulation, and only light pigment in the dorsal fin. Keeping these two species together in the aquarium is, thankfully, not a problem, as both thrive in neutral to slightly alkaline waters and are relatively robust and undemanding.

Dianema longibarbis

Porthole Catfish
● **Habitat:** Peruvian and Brazilian creeks, ponds and rivers.
● **Length:** 100mm (4in).
● **Diet:** Small invertebrates.
● **Sex differences:** Males are more slender than females.
● **Aquarium breeding:** *Dianema* are the only catfishes in this family in which spawning remains a mystery.
● **Aquarium compatibility:** Peaceful.

The Porthole Catfish resembles an elongated *Corydoras* and shares the peaceful character of its cousins. Some fishkeepers have suggested that *Dianema* may spawn in the bubblenest fashion of *Hoplosternum*, but this has not been proven.

Above: **Corydoras sodalis**
There are a large number of 'lookalikes' among Corydoras *species. Similarly marked fishes probably group together for mutual shoal protection. This attractive pair of False Network Catfishes will live happily alongside* Corydoras reticulatus, *which they closely resemble in size and patterning.*

Above: **Dianema longibarbis**
Despite the reference to this catfish's long barbels in its name, and the amount of spotting on its body, the Porthole Catfish is most easily distinguished from its relative, D. urostriata, *by the lack of patterning in its caudal fin.*

Hoplosternum thoracatum

Bubblenest Catfish

● **Habitat:** Large rivers and swamps from northern South America (Guyana-Surinam) to Brazil.
● **Length:** 200mm (8in).
● **Diet:** Crustaceans and small invertebrates.
● **Sex differences:** Males have thickened pectoral spines and are slightly smaller and darker in colour than females when in breeding condition.
● **Aquarium breeding:** The male constructs a bubblenest in which the fertilized eggs are placed.
● **Aquarium compatibility:** Peaceful.

This speckled catfish is especially attractive in juvenile colours; in

Above:
Hoplosternum thoracatum
Below: *This* Hoplosternum *bubblenest has been created around leaf debris on the surface.*

adults, the speckled pattern begins to fade. It is one of three species of *Hoplosternum* known to fishkeepers and is particularly popular among catfish breeders.

Family: DORADIDAE Talking Catfishes
The Talking, or Thorny, Catfishes are closely related to the scaleless Driftwood Catfishes, except that, unlike the latter, they possess a single row of bony plates along the body flanks. Smaller forms in this family include the well-known *Platydoras* and *Amblydoras*, which are non-predatory towards other fishes and are thus ideal for the community aquarium. The larger forms are almost prehistoric in shape and in their possession of scute thorns (body spines) although they are harmless opportunist feeders living on fruit, snails and seeds. Smaller forms, such as *Agamyxis*, have been known to spawn in the aquarium, but this is an extremely rare occurrence.

Agamyxis pectinifrons
Spotted Talking Catfish
● **Habitat:** Widespread throughout South American rivers.
● **Length:** 125mm (5in).
● **Diet:** Crustaceans and invertebrates.
● **Sex differences:** Females are deeper bodied than males.
● **Aquarium breeding:** It will spawn among floating plants in the aquarium.
● **Aquarium compatibility:** Safe with fishes of equal size.

This Brazilian catfish is black with yellow or white spots across the body. As with all doradids, this species is inactive during daylight hours although you can encourage the fishes to appear by introducing freshly shredded shrimps and prawns. Use rocks and pieces of bogwood to construct hiding places for these fishes. Their popular name arises from the sounds these fishes make by rotating the pectoral fins. The sound is amplified by the swimbladder.

Below: **Agamyxis pectinifrons**
No two specimens of this intriguing catfish are identical. Some are lightly patterned with spots, in some the spots form lines, and others are finely peppered.

Amblydoras hancocki

Hancock's Catfish
● **Habitat:** Widespread in rivers from Guyana to Brazil.
● **Length:** 100mm (4in).
● **Diet:** Crustaceans and invertebrates.
● **Sex differences:** Females are deeper bodied than males.
● **Aquarium breeding:** Scanty reports suggest substrate 'nest' spawnings, although habitat observations by Hancock, published in 1829, state that these catfishes spawn in the rains after making a nest of leaves, and that parental care is shown. From recent reports it seems likely that this species will also spawn in floating plants.
● **Aquarium compatibility:** Safe with fishes of equal size.

The author has seen huge numbers of this species collected in the Essequibo River in Guyana, and awaiting export. Hancock's Catfish is undemanding and seems to adapt easily to a wide range of water conditions. However, bright, neutral and soft water and a densely planted aquascape will create ideal conditions.

Platydoras costatus

Humbug Catfish
● **Habitat:** Widespread in rivers from Peru to Brazil.
● **Length:** 200mm (8in).
● **Diet:** Snails, insect larvae, etc.
● **Sex differences:** Females are larger than males.
● **Aquarium breeding:** Not recorded.

Above: **Amblydoras hancocki**
A tough smaller doradid, this species is found in great shoals in the main Guyanan rivers.

● **Aquarium compatibility:** The Humbug Catfish can be extremely territorial towards its own kind and is likely to dispute ownership of caves, nooks and crannies with other nocturnal catfishes. However, it is not over aggressive and will do little more than outspread its pectoral and dorsal fin spines and this is only dangerous when directed at scaleless fishes disputing territory. This striking black Talking Catfish has a 'humbug' white stripe across its lateral line, which makes it popular among fishkeepers. It is exported in large quantities.

Below: **Platydoras costatus**
The best-known doradid, the Humbug Catfish, like most catfishes, is extremely nocturnal.

LORICARIIDAE Suckermouth and Whiptail Catfishes
This family contains more species than any other catfish family, with a great diversity in terms of size, shape and colour. *Hypostomus* and *Pterygoplichthys*, for example, can grow to between 300 and 600mm (12-24in), whereas the tiny *Otocinclus* is adult at only 50mm (2in). These fishes have a wide distribution, encompassing Central as well as South America, and are characterized by their possession of a sucker mouth underneath the head. Some species are also heavily plated. The males of most species are parental towards eggs and fry, and successful aquarium breeding is common. Large forms spawn in riverbank burrows, however, and this site is difficult to recreate successfully in the aquarium.

Ancistrus dolichopterus
Bristle-nosed Catfish
● **Habitat:** Widespread in rivers throughout South America.
● **Length:** 125mm (5in).
● **Diet:** Algae, plants, fruits and small invertebrates.
● **Sex differences:** Males develop distinctive head bristles in the breeding season.
● **Aquarium breeding:** Frequently spawned in community aquariums. Indeed, it is not unusual for the fishkeeper to discover a secret spawning when the youngsters appear from under bogwood at a week or so old. Males are wonderfully parental towards eggs and fry but in the community aquarium it is best to remove fry to a shallow aquarium and feed them with plenty of greenfood.
● **Aquarium compatibility:** Although they can be territorial among their own kind, these catfishes are generally peaceful towards other community fishes.

Ancistrus dolichopterus is one of over 50 species of *Ancistrus* known but identification of individual specimens is almost impossible without an array of scientific data. Bristle-nosed Catfishes are superb community aquarium scavengers and, being robust and extremely adaptable, are suited to most water conditions. In the wild they survive in shallow pools which almost dry up outside of the rainy seasons. They feed on algae, which is plentiful in the wild, and this habit is useful in the aquarium, where they can be used to clean the aquarium glass of excess algae. You will need to supplement their diet with greenfoods, such as shredded spinach leaf, green beans, peas and lettuce.

Below: **Ancistrus dolichopterus**
The male of this species (left) can usually be identified by his cheek bristles when mature.

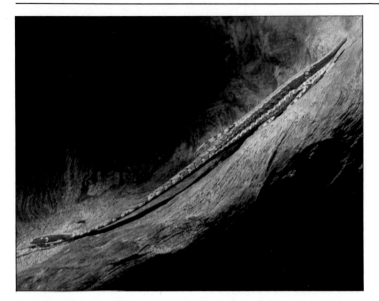

Farlowella gracilis
Twig Catfish
- **Habitat:** Colombian rivers.
- **Length:** 200mm (8in).
- **Diet:** Algae, plants and organic material.
- **Sex differences:** Males are more slender than females.
- **Aquarium breeding:** Accounts of successful spawnings in the aquarium are uncommon. The female places eggs on long-stemmed plants or on the aquarium glass and the male guards them until they hatch.
- **Aquarium compatibility:** Peaceful.

Not only are there almost 60 species of *Farlowella* known, most of which are difficult to differentiate from each other without close examination, but there are also

Above: **Farlowella gracilis**
Spawnings of these extraordinary and popular fishes are still not common in the aquarium and this catfish continues to represent a challenge to catfish enthusiasts.

several related genera, *Sturisoma* and some species of *Rineloricaria*, which appear remarkably similar. All have long slender bodies and excellent camouflage, as their common name suggests. These fishes prefer an aquarium between 45-60cm (18-24in) deep and will thrive in bright, acidic to neutral water. They will indicate poor water quality, especially low oxygen conditions, by poking their snout above the surface of the water, but will generally prove easy to maintain once they are established in the aquarium.

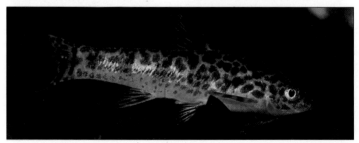

Otocinclus flexilis
Peppered Suckermouth
● **Habitat:** Alongside the Peppered Catfish (*Corydoras paleatus*) in Brazil and Argentina.
● **Length:** 50mm (2in).
● **Diet:** Algae, plants and invertebrates.
● **Sex differences:** Males are more slender than females.
● **Aquarium breeding:** Not recorded.
● **Aquarium compatibility:** There are many reports of hungry *Otocinclus* sucking at the body mucus of other fishes and causing infections. This semi-parasitic behaviour may well cease if plenty of healthy greenfood, such as peas, spinach and lettuce, is provided for these fishes.

Otocinclus flexilis are imported alongside, and resemble, *Corydoras paleatus* (page 169). They are found in huge shoals and are best kept in small groups (although this is not recommended in a heavily planted aquarium as they can destroy soft-leaved plants). They will eat algae on hard-leaved plants (which is beneficial to the plant) and on the aquarium glass, but you should supplement this diet with a continual supply of greenfoods,

Below left: **Otocinclus flexilis**
This small catfish shares both its pattern and habitat with Corydoras paleatus, *see page 169.*

such as peas, lettuce, spinach and green beans, and soaked flake (which sinks to the substrate quickly). They will thrive in a broad range of water conditions, and should be kept in a small to medium-sized aquarium.

Panaque nigrolineatus
Royal Plec
● **Habitat:** Peru, Colombia, Venezuela and the Amazon Basin.
● **Length:** 600mm (24in).
● **Diet:** Plants, fruits, algae and general aquatic debris.
● **Sex differences:** Males have thickened and bristled pectoral spines in maturity.
● **Aquarium breeding:** Not known.
● **Aquarium compatibility:** Territorial with its own kind but otherwise peaceful.

This Brazilian and Peruvian giant Suckermouth is an impressive fish; it is large, and has distinctive 'pinstripe' patterns and red eyes. There appear to be several pattern variations in juveniles, but it is not clear if all belong to this species. New imports can be extremely hollow-bellied and it is important to offer them a high-fibre diet and similar foods, such as spinach, to help them recover from malnutrition.

Below: **Panaque nigrolineatus**
These fishes require large amounts of shrimp and greenfood but may be difficult to feed as they mature.

Right:
Parotocinclus amazonensis
The beautiful False Sucker thrives in a densely planted aquarium.

Parotocinclus amazonensis

False Sucker
● **Habitat:** Coastal rivers of southern Brazil.
● **Length:** 50mm (2in).
● **Diet:** Algae and invertebrates.
● **Sex differences:** Males are more colourful than females.
● **Aquarium breeding:** Eggs are placed on the leaves of plants.
● **Aquarium compatibility:** Peaceful.

The False Sucker, with its beautiful red-edged fins and long body, is a favourite with enthusiasts. It looks like an *Otocinclus*, but has an adipose fin. New specimens can be difficult to establish but thrive in the community aquarium if provided with bright, neutral soft water and finely shredded spinach.

Peckoltia vittata

Clown Plec
● **Habitat:** Brazil.
● **Length:** 75mm (3in).
● **Diet:** Algae, assorted plant material and invertebrates.
● **Sex differences:** Males are slightly smaller and more colourful than females.
● **Aquarium breeding:** Not known.
● **Aquarium compatibility:** Generally peaceful although they can be slightly territorial.

These dwarf Suckermouths are very attractive, usually well marked with stripes and spots, and are sought after by enthusiasts. Although it lacks the rarity value of the Striped Plec, the attractive Clown Plec is a firm favourite in catfish circles. Its small size and adaptability to almost any range of water conditions, add to its popularity with the fishkeeper. According to recent reports, there are nineteen different species of Peckoltia. Positive identification often depends on knowledge of their actual place of capture.

Below: **Peckoltia vittata**
A popular species best suited to small community aquariums.

Pterygoplichthys gibbiceps

Sailfin Plec

● **Habitat:** Widespread in the Peruvian and Brazilian Amazon.
● **Length:** 450mm (18in).
● **Diet:** They feed avidly on lettuce, peas, spinach, whole prawns and pellets.
● **Sex differences:** Males are more colourful and slender than females.
● **Aquarium breeding:** Not possible in the aquarium. Commercially, this species is spawned in Asian dirt ponds in the same manner as the Snow King.
● **Aquarium compatibility:** Mature specimens are very territorial and can inflict fin damage to others of the same species if confined in too small an aquarium.

Now being farmed in the Far East,

Above:
Pterygoplichthys gibbiceps
A superb companion for large community cichlids and characins.

this brick-red beauty is one of the top ten most popular catfishes. Adult Sailfins are suited only to large aquariums although juveniles can be kept in more modest-sized tanks providing they are transferred to a larger aquarium as they outgrow their surroundings. Sailfins are highly recommended for the fishkeeper seeking a suitable companion for large South American Cichlids (*Aequidens*, *Geophagus* and *Cichlasoma*) and larger Characins (*Metynnis* Silver Dollars and *Anostomus*-type Pencilfishes).

Below: **Rineloricaria lima**
This species can be kept safely with even very small fishes.

Rineloricaria lima
Common Whiptail Catfish
- **Habitat:** Brazilian rivers.
- **Length:** 180mm (7in).
- **Diet:** Algae, greenfoods and small aquatic invertebrates and pellets.
- **Sex differences:** Males are more distinctively patterned and more slender than females when viewed from above. Sexually mature males display bristles on the cheek or side of the head.
- **Aquarium breeding:** This species is regularly spawned in the aquarium in the same way as *Rineloricaria lanceolata*, the Whiptail Catfish.
- **Aquarium compatibility:** Peaceful.

Rineloricaria lima, R. stewarti from Guyana to Brazil, and *R. fallax* and *R. lanceolata* from Brazil, are probably the best known of the ten or so species of *Rineloricaria* imported. All make perfect aquarium catfishes. *Rineloricaria* are ideal substrate haunters for the community aquarium. They rarely, if ever, leave the gravel and should therefore be offered tablet food, or presoaked flake, which will sink directly to the aquarium bottom. This will ensure that they do not miss out on general feedings.

Sturisoma aureum
Giant Whitptail
- **Habitat:** Colombian rivers.
- **Length:** 300mm (12in).
- **Diet:** Algae, greenfoods and small aquatic invertebrates.
- **Sex differences:** Difficult to sex until males develop cheek bristles. However, these may be shed after the breeding season.
- **Aquarium breeding:** Eggs are placed on the aquarium glass or long-leaved plants. The males remain with the eggs until they hatch.
- **Aquarium compatibility:** Slightly territorial with their own kind but peaceful with other species and ideal for the community aquarium.

This catfish is also known as *Sturisoma panamese* and, with *S. barbatum*, is one of the most popular large non-predatory catfishes. It has fin extensions almost as long as its body. The species is very easy to breed and the 50mm (2in) babies, all fins and spindle body, retain their attractive brown and beige striped patterns when they are fully grown.

Below: **Sturisoma aureum**
This intriguing species is imported in large quantities from Colombia.

PIMELODIDAE Naked Catfishes
These scaleless predators are widely distributed throughout South America. The larger forms inhabit wide, fast-flowing rivers and are characterized by a wide gaping mouth and a broad tail, which aids speed through the water. Smaller forms have tiny eyes, and shoal in huge numbers over the beds of large and small rivers. The family has continued to challenge catfish breeders, as no attempts at spawning or fry raising have yet proved successful.

Brachyrhamdia imitator
False Corydoras
● **Habitat:** Venezuelan rivers.
● **Length:** 75-100mm (3-4in).
● **Diet:** Insect larvae and various invertebrates.
● **Sex differences:** Females are deeper bodied than males.
● **Aquarium breeding:**
Unpublished information based on habitat observations and aquarium behaviour suggests that most pimelodids are egg scatterers, but documented details are very scarce.
● **Aquarium compatibility:**
Peaceful with fishes of their own size although slightly territorial with each other. They should be fine in a large aquarium.

This is one of three species known to science (the other two, *B. marthae* and *B. meesi*, were discovered and described by the author). They are imported with *Corydoras delphax* and *Corydoras melanistius*, whose patterns they share. Why they 'imitate' *Corydoras* patterns, i.e. in terms of any possible biological or environmental benefit (or similar), is a mystery, although much has been written on the subject. They are active, fast-swimming fishes, and well suited to large aquariums.

Below: **Brachyrhamdia imitator**
This catfish mimics Corydoras *so perfectly that certain species are hard to separate at first glance.*

Leiarius marmoratus
False Perrunichthys
● **Habitat:** Peruvian and Brazilian Amazon.
● **Length:** 450-500mm (18-20in).
● **Diet:** Small fishes, crustaceans, invertebrates and fruits.
● **Sex differences:** Males are more slender than females.
● **Aquarium breeding:** Not known.
● **Aquarium compatibility:** Give this species plenty of space, because of its large adult size and territorial nature, and avoid keeping two specimens together, as they are likely to fight.

For many years, this species was confused with *Perrunichthys,* which is similar but has fewer dorsal rays. For such a large fish the eyes are relatively small; the maxillary barbels from the upper mouth are very long, sometimes reaching past the end of the long-based adipose fin. This type of predatory catfish requires a large aquarium with a good water flow from power filters, and plenty of swimming space. Once mature, feed such large predatory fishes no more than twice a week.
Note: *Leiarius marmoratus* is illustrated overleaf.

Above: **Leiarius marmoratus**
Another large predatory catfish suitable for the 'bumper' aquarium. This species has often been confused with Perrunichthys.

Below: **Microglanis iheringi**
Unlike its larger, predatory Asian namesake, this dwarf pimelodid is ideal for small community tanks with plenty of hiding places.

Microglanis iheringi
Bumble Bee Catfish
● **Habitat:** Widepread in Peruvian, Venezuelan and Colombian rivers.
● **Length:** 100mm (4in).
● **Diet:** Small aquatic invertebrates.
● **Sex differences:** Males are smaller than females.
● **Aquarium breeding:** Not known.
● **Aquarium compatibility:** Peaceful with fishes larger than itself.

This tiny catfish, with its brown and yellow/beige banding patterns, is not to be confused with the Asian Bumble Bee Catfish, which is much larger. It is very secretive but will make brief skirmishes to the front of the aquarium to feed.

Phractocephalus hemioliopterus
Red Tail Catfish
● **Habitat:** Widespread across the Peruvian, Guyanan and Brazilian Amazon.
● **Length:** 1000mm (39in).
● **Diet:** Fish, crustaceans and larger aquatic invertebrates.
● **Sex differences:** Not known, although it is thought that males possess a brighter red tail and are

more slender than females.
● **Aquarium breeding:** Not known.
● **Aquarium compatibility:** Must be kept alone, as they will attempt to consume any living creature (and some inanimate objects, such as heaters and suction clips) that they can fit into the mouth.

The Red Tail Catfish is almost a legend among catfish enthusiasts; public aquarium specimens have lived for more than 20 years. Examination of the stomachs of specimens collected in the huge rapids of the Madiera River in Brazil revealed freshwater crabs, fruits and seeds.

Pimelodella cristata
Graceful Catfish
● **Habitat:** Widespread.
● **Length:** 200mm (8in).
● **Diet:** Small aquatic invertebrates.
● **Sex differences:** Males sometimes display dorsal filaments and are more slender than females.

Below:
Phractocephalus hemioliopterus
The emperor of the Amazon and a spectacular public aquarium fish.

● **Aquarium breeding:** Not known.
● **Aquarium compatibility:** Predatory with smaller fishes.

This common species, also known as *P. gracilis* and *P. geryi*, is frequently confused with its larger cousin, *Pimelodus*, but is recognizable by its elongated adipose (second dorsal) fin. Mature specimens of *Pimelodella* may predate on small fishes, but well fed individuals will become rather lazy and rely on manufactured foods. Few fishkeepers are aware of the size they can attain, as aquarium specimens rarely grow beyond 100mm (4in).

Pimelodus maculatus
Spotted Pim
● **Habitat:** Rivers from Brazil to Paraguay.
● **Length:** 150mm (6in).
●**Diet:** Small fishes, insect larvae and assorted aquatic crustaceans.
● **Sex differences:** Not known.
● **Aquarium breeding:** Not known.
● **Aquarium compatibility:** Predatory towards smaller fishes.

This is one of the more attractively patterned *Pimelodus* catfishes,

Above: **Pimelodella cristata**
The Graceful Catfish is a nocturnal predator; feed well on manufactured foods and keep away from small community fishes.

with a silver body similar to that of the Polka-dot, but with grey/brown rather than black spots. It seems to have a wide distribution from southern Brazil extending into the Paraguay River in Paraguay. In Brazil, it is known as *P. clarias*. Unfortunately, this attractive fish is frequently ignored by aquatic books. The type of colour pattern appears to vary from one habitat to another, some areas producing fishes with smaller spots than others. The Spotted Pim is only suitable for the large aquarium with fishes of a similar size.

Pimelodus pictus
Angelica Pim; Polka-dot Catfish;
● **Habitat:** Peruvian and Colombian rivers.
● **Length:** 125-150mm (5-6in).
● **Diet:** Small fishes, insect larvae, and assorted aquatic crustaceans and invertebrates.
● **Sex differences:** Males are smaller than females.
● **Aquarium breeding:** Not known.
● **Aquarium compatibility:** When introduced to the community aquarium, small fishes, such as neon tetras, may disappear at

Below: **Pimelodus maculatus**
An attractive, though rarely seen, species which can be kept safely with fishes larger than itself.

Above:
Pseudopimelodus raninus
This nocturnal predator should not be kept with small community fishes, because of its predatory nature, but is fine with larger fishes.

night, consumed by a hungry *Pimelodus*. Although it will be less predatory if well fed, it is best to keep the *Pimelodus* in an aquarium with larger fishes (see pages 17-19).

This silver-bodied, black-spotted catfish, from the Meta River in Peru and Colombia, is the most popular non-*Corydoras* catfish available to fishkeepers. There are two forms known; the Colombian species has a few indistinct body spots, while the one from Peru is covered in many clearly defined spots. Because of the great number of *Pimelodus* species known, the tentative identification of these species by fish collectors has not been scientifically verified.

Below: **Pimelodus pictus**
The most popular South American catfish with the exception of the all-time favourite Corydoras. *However, it is very predatory and so best kept with larger fishes.*

Pseudopimelodus raninus
Big Bumble Bee Catfish
● **Habitat:** Peruvian and Brazilian Amazon.
● **Length:** 150mm (6in).
● **Diet:** Small aquatic invertebrates.
● **Sex differences:** Males are more slender than females.
● **Aquarium breeding:** Not known.
● **Aquarium compatibility:** Predatory with smaller fishes.

This is basically a giant *Microglanis*. *Pseudopimelodus* is undemanding of water conditions but should not be kept in an overcrowded aquarium or bacterial skin infections may result. This catfish is a night-time predator and will consume any unfortunate fish that will fit into its mouth. There are several *raninus* forms, which have been broken into subspecies.

Part Six
Livebearing Fishes

Above: *Rio Nacome in Honduras, one of the known habitats of the widely distributed livebearer, Poecilia sphenops.*
Below: *A colourful wild Guppy. Selective breeding has capitalized on this natural variation.*

Although many hobbyists are familiar with Guppies, Swordtails, Platies and Mollies, the natural habitats of these fishes also provide homes for other livebearing species. In recent years, many such other species have been imported and a strong following has built up, with national and local specialist groups keeping and breeding these different fishes. This involvement has strong conservationist and ichthyological benefits: knowledge of fishes' reproductive methods is always important and the fact that species can be distributed within the hobby without the need for an ever-increasing collection of wild stock must be a bonus. These wilder forms are completely natural species

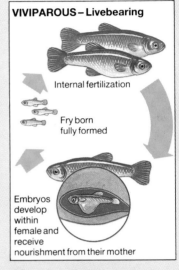

TROPICAL AQUARIUM FISHES

and, so far, have resisted any divergence into 'aquarium-developed' strains. Some of their reproductive methods are very sophisticated, with the unborn young depending upon their mother for 'before birth' nourishment. Not all livebearing fishes have remained in their natural habitats: Man has introduced several species into other tropical areas for his own benefit – these fishes have a healthy appetite for mosquito larvae, for example, and so assist greatly in keeping down the spread of these malaria-carrying insects. In this 'closer look' at livebearing fishes, we examine some of the less common 'enthusiasts' fishes. All are presented in A-Z order of scientific name in their respective families and genera.

VIVIPAROUS – Livebearing

Internal fertilization

Fry born fully formed

Embryos develop within female and receive nourishment from their mother

Above: *In so-called 'viviparous' (livebearing) fishes the mother provides nourishment for the developing embryos.*

Family: ANABLEPIDAE/Genus: ANABLEPS

These fascinating fishes from the brackish waters of Central and South America are highly specialized surface feeders. Their eyes are divided horizontally so that when swimming at the surface they can see clearly both above and below the water. An aquatic vivarium would be ideal for them.

Anableps anableps

Four-eyes

● **Habitat:** Slow moving brackish waters throughout southern Mexico and into the northern parts of South America.

● **Length:** Up to 30cm (12in) but 23-25cm (9-10in) is more typical.

● **Diet:** In the wild these fishes feed on insects landing on the water surface; in captivity, they will take most foods fairly greedily, although some individuals appear not to like fish. Flying insects caught using a net on the car bumper are useful, as are crickets, mussels and home-made meat-based foods.

● **Features:** *Anableps anableps* is unmistakable in appearance, with a long body – brownish with violet stripes on the sides – a flat head and large frog-like protruding eyes. The cornea, pupil and retina are divided horizontally by a layer of tissue which allows the fish to see both above and below the water level as it cruises at the surface. The males have a fleshy tubular penis-like organ supported by curved anal finrays. In common with *Jenynsia lineata*, these fishes are 'one-sided' (see text on opposite page).

● **Basic care and breeding:** This brackish species will live in full seawater. A specific gravity of 1.010 is suitable. They are good jumpers so be sure to provide a sturdy cover on the aquarium. This will also help to maintain the necessary high humidity. Also provide a large shallow water area and a gravel beach area to enable them to come out. The ideal temperature is in the region 24-28°C (75-82°F). Good filtration is essential in the aquarium to cope with the waste and uneaten food from these large fishes.

Populations seem to be heavily biased numerically towards females, so finding a male may not be easy. Anableps usually produce two small broods of between three and five fry per year; occasionally up to 20 may be seen. These measure about 3-5cm (1.2-2in) at birth.

Above: **Anableps anableps**
Protruding 'bifocal' eyes allow this fish to see above and below water.

Above: **Jenynsia lineata**
An elegant bottom-dwelling species

that will adapt to a wide range of water conditions. Male at right.

Genus: JENYNSIA
Although only one species is known to aquarium hobbyists, members of the genus *Jenynsia* are distributed across South America south of the Amazon. Their distinctive feature in terms of reproductive biology is their curious trait of being 'one-sided'.

Jenynsia lineata
One-sided Livebearer
● **Habitat:** Two strains seem to exist: one lives in brackish pools and slow-flowing rivers in southern Brazil, Uruguay and northern Argentina; the other strain lives in high-salinity lagoons, where evaporation has raised the salinity to above that of sea water.
● **Length:** The sexes are very different in size; males reach 3-4cm (1.2-1.6in) and females 9-12cm (3.5-4.7in)
● **Diet:** Most aquarium foods.

● **Features:** A slender silvery grey body with fine black markings in lines along the sides; there may be an orange mark close to the anus of young virgin females.
● **Basic care and breeding:** These are slow-moving, bottom-dwelling fish. Older males and large females can be rather aggressive. Like the Anablepids, these are one-sided fishes; the male has a rather short gonopodium slightly curved at the tip and can only curve it one way. Similarly, females have a genital opening which is directed to one side. Therefore, a left-handed male can mate only with a right-handed female and vice-versa. A number need to be kept together to find 'matching pairs'.

Once a pairing is successful, broods of about 20-30 fry are seen at intervals of about 28-35 days. The fry are quite large and, like the Goodeids, will thrive on live foods, such as grindalworms and crushed snails, plus small pieces of ox-heart. The best temperature for ensuring successful breeding in the aquarium is in the region of 25°C (77°F).

Left: **Anableps anableps**
These fishes need a spacious tank or vivarium with a shallow beach.

273

Family: HEMIRHAMPHIDAE

The Halfbeaks fill the type of niche in Southeast Asia occupied by the Poeciliidae in Central America. They are schooling fishes living in the surface layers of rivers and streams, in both fresh and brackish waters. The males have a well-formed andropodium developed from the anal fin, although it is less mobile than the gonopodium of the Poeciliidae and means that the fish must get closer when mating to ensure transfer of 'sperm packets'.

Dermogenys pusillus

Malayan Halfbeak; Wrestling Halfbeak
● **Habitat:** Fresh and brackish water of streams and ponds in much of Southeast Asia.
● **Length:** Females up to 7cm (2.75in); males up to 5.5cm (2.2in).

Above: **Hemirhamphodon pogonognathus**
This Toothed Halfbeak from the forest streams of Singapore will thrive in the surface waters of a well-planted tank. This is a colourful male.

Above: **Nomorhamphus sp.**
These Beakless Halfbeaks have a relatively short extension of the lower jaw, which in males (here the upper fish) curves downwards.

Right: **Dermogenys pusillus**
This is the most commonly kept member of the Halfbeak Family. This is a fine female specimen.

● **Diet:** These fish need live food such as *Tubifex* worms fed via a floating worm feeder and floating insects; they are top feeders and cannot feed from the bottom. Flying insects caught with a hand net or using a net fixed on the car bumper are suitable.

● **Features:** Halfbeaks have a characteristically long pointed lower jaw which is fixed in position; the male's anal fin is modified and appears folded. Both sexes have a silvery blue iridescence.

● **Basic care and breeding:** Keep these interesting fish in a moderately planted tank of about 50-100 litres (11-22 gallons) at a temperature of about 26°C (79°F). Some floating plants are important. Cover the tank securely since halfbeaks live in the upper waters and are keen jumpers. As with other livebearers, use hard water in the aquarium, perhaps with some added salt – 0.5-1.5gm per litre (0.5-1.5 teaspoon per gallon) – particularly in softer waters. Proprietary buffers can be used to keep the pH above pH7.

For breeding, use a tank set up as described above and be sure to include some floating plants; these provide a refuge for the female to escape the over-enthusiastic attentions of the male.

The most suitable sex ratio is one male for two or three females. This avoids the fighting which often breaks out between males (hence 'wrestling') and prevents one female being too harassed by an overly attentive male. Pregnancy lasts between five and seven weeks, and 10-20 young are usually produced. These fishes are very cannibalistic, so if possible move pregnant females to a smaller but similar tank to give birth. Do this very carefully since the pregnant females – with a prominent gravid spot and bulky appearance – are prone to lose their broods. After the birth, move the female back to the main tank.

Raising the broods can be difficult at first; the fry feed on newly hatched brineshrimp, moving later on to the same food as the parents. The fry begin to develop the beak after about four to six weeks.

● **Other genera:** Another genus of interest in this Family is *Nomorhamphus*, the Beakless Halfbeaks of the Indonesian island of Sulawesi. They grow much larger than *Dermogenys* – to about 11cm (4.5in) – and although the lower jaw does have an extension, it tends to curl downward and in the males takes on the appearance of a pronounced goatee beard. They are good feeders, taking anything that moves, living or not. Breeding is difficult but along similar lines to *Dermogenys*.

The Toothed Halfbeaks, *Hemirhamphodon* species, are also worthy of mention. Like the other members of the Family, they come from Indonesia. *H.chrysopunctatus* from the soft acid, blackwaters of the Borneo jungle and *H.pogonognathus* from the forests near Singapore. They are larger than *Dermogenys*, although not as large as *Nomorhamphus*, and the andropodium is longer than in the other genera. General care of *H.pogonognathus* is similar to that of *Dermogenys* except that it is more strictly a surface feeder. The aquarium needs of the recently discovered *H.chrysopunctatus* are not yet fully understood. Never mix these genera of Halfbeaks since fighting will occur.

Family: GOODEIDAE

In overall shape the Goodeids are similar to the Platies, but with a somewhat deeper body and a very narrow caudal peduncle; the females have a well-rounded anal fin. All the species come from Mexico. Their distribution in the wild centres on the highland catchment area of the Rio Lerma, where the Family is represented in a variety of ecological niches, from pools to fast-flowing streams. Goodeids are fairly adaptable to temperature and are not too difficult to keep in the aquarium.

Because of the different system of embryo development in Goodeids, the fry are born significantly larger than those of other similarly sized livebearers. Often the trophotaenia, which act as a type of placenta, can be seen hanging from the rectum at birth.

Ameca splendens
Butterfly Goodeid

● **Habitat:** The Rio Ameca Basin in western Mexico.

● **Length:** The males are quite a bit smaller than females; 6.5cm (2.5in) as opposed to 9cm (3.5in).

● **Diet:** Typically vegetarian with a preference for such plants as *Synnema* (Water Wisteria) and *Ceratopteris* (Indian Fern). If the fish will accept it, offer them flaked diet with fresh green foods as supplements; this seems more acceptable to them if they are introduced to it as fry. Midge larvae may be eaten more avidly than *Daphnia* (water fleas).

● **Features:** The male is particularly attractive, with blue-green iridescent flanks and a yellow-orange underside. A black band runs along the side and breaks up on the caudal peduncle. On the tail there is a definite vertical black band and a bright yellow one. The female is relatively drab, with less iridescence. These fishes will thrive in a wide range of temperatures – 18-30°C (65-86°F) – and water conditions in the aquarium.

● **Basic care and breeding:** Courtship is obvious, combining displays with mild aggression. After a successful mating, a brood takes six to eight weeks to develop into large well-developed fry, up to 1.5cm (0.6in) long at birth. The birth may take 10-60 minutes. Adults are not cannibalistic and so the urge to hide shown by most livebearer fry is not seen. The fry are ready to eat the same food as their parents from the very first day (see notes on diet).

Left: **Ameca splendens**
This male has the typical iridescent markings and yellow edging on the tail. A highly adaptable species that will breed readily in the aquarium.

Characodon audax

Black Prince
● **Habitat:** Streams and ponds in western Mexico.
● **Length:** Males reach up to about 3cm (1.2in) and the females up to 5.5cm (2.2in) in length.
● **Diet:** As with all the Goodeids, some green food is well worthwhile, although flaked foods are a good basis for their day-to-day diet.
● **Features:** Males are greeny/gold mottled with grey, and have black fins. Females are a drab greeny/grey with two black spots on the caudal peduncle, a silvery belly, and a good strong gravid spot when they are due to give birth.

A generally peaceable species, although the males are fairly territorial and can be aggressive towards each other in the tank.
● **Basic care and breeding:** The optimum temperature is 24°C (75°F). The water hardness is less important than pH, which should be 7.6-7.8. Salt is not absolutely necessary but is probably worthwhile in softer waters.

Broods of 10-20 fry about 6mm (0.25in) long are produced approximately every six weeks. Ideally, place the female in a trap in shallow water about seven days before she is due to give birth; this allows the fry to reach the surface to fill their swimbladders. First feeding with grindal- and microworms leads quite well on to commercial flaked foods.
● **Other species:** *Characodon lateralis*, the Rainbow or Red Rainbow Goodeid, is fairly aggressive and consequently makes a poor community fish. They seem happier in a relatively overgrown, dark tank and when kept together in a large group. In this situation no one fish is vulnerable to a high level of victimization. Avoid trapping the females; they often drop the fry prematurely. Best results are usually achieved in well-planted 'species' tanks, when broods of up to 12 can be expected.

Below: **Characodon audax**
A male specimen with the typical jet black fins. Males are territorial and will show aggression to one another.

Girardinichthys viviparus
Amarillo

● **Habitat:** Found only in a single, virtually stagnant pool in a Mexico City park. The water is very hard and alkaline (pH9), is green with algae and has occasionally been found frosted.

● **Length:** Males are 3.5cm (1.4in); females 6.5cm (2.5in).

● **Diet:** Their natural environment is rich in live food and captive diets need to mimic this; algae growing on plants, *Daphnia*, brineshrimp, grindal - and microworms are all suitable foods for this species.

● **Features:** Both sexes are basically grey with slight black barring and a black belly; the dorsal and anal fins of males are edged with black.

● **Basic care and breeding:** The Amarillo has so far been very difficult to maintain, needing hard mature water at a temperature of 21-23°C (70-73°F). They seem to be very delicate and particularly sensitive to netting. Therefore, drive them quietly into a cup or small plastic container for tank transfers.

It is best to establish new tanks with fry, since adults take less well to transfers. Use only light aeration or none at all and keep the lighting at low level. Excess aeration and bright light encourage too much algal growth and increased levels of waste products in the tank, which may account for the reports of fin rot in fry and death of adults. The best approach is to use a large aquarium – 120cm (48in) long – heavily planted and filled with well-matured water filtered through foam filters. Ideally, maintain a low stocking rate to parallel the natural situation as closely as possible, although this approach is not easy in small tanks.

Colony breeding in a well-planted aquarium seems best. Alternatively, move the female to a nursery tank about 10 days before she is due to give birth. Since this may prove rather stressful, it is best to leave her alone unless she is likely to be harassed. The gestation period is six to eight weeks. Remove the female after the babies are born to protect her from the males.

Above: **Girardinichthys viviparus**
This species needs mature water and a roomy 'natural' aquarium environment to thrive and breed.

Below: **Goodea atripinnis**
An attractively marked species that may prove aggressive in the aquarium. The male is at top.

Goodea atripinnis
Black-finned Goodea

● **Habitat:** Streams and lakes in the area of the Rio Lerma in western Mexico.

● **Length:** Males reach 8.5cm (3.3in); females 13cm (5in) or more.

● **Diet:** Members of this genus are filter feeders, eating plant and animal plankton, but in captivity they will eat a range of vegetable matter and some live foods.

● **Features:** Both sexes have a long, laterally compressed body, olive-green in colour tinged with pink and a slight bluish iridescence. The fins are yellowish but darken in colour in response to stress and moods. Females have a typically rounded anal fin.

● **Basic care and breeding:** This is a difficult fish to breed; best results are likely to be achieved in a nursery tank or a well-planted species tank at a temperature of 20-24°C (68-75°F). After a gestation period of six to eight weeks, the female produces about 20-40 young. Feed these on newly hatched brineshrimp and on 'green water' from a tank left out in the sun to develop an abundance of suspended algae. Certain commercially produced fine diets for fry are also acceptable.

Ilyodon xantusi

● **Habitat:** Fast-flowing streams among the highlands of the Pacific coast of Mexico.

● **Length:** The sexes are about the same size, quite large for Goodeids, at approximately 10cm (4in).

● **Diet:** These are very much algae eaters; a tank receiving direct sunlight or an excessive amount of artificial light and too little vegetation may look unsightly but it will suit these fishes perfectly.

● **Features:** The male is striking in appearance, with a blue iridescence and a golden belly. A diffuse black line runs along the flanks to a tail edged in black; a chequer-board black pattern covers the remainder of the body.

● **Basic care and breeding:** Keep these fishes in a well-lit tank with plenty of aeration and water movement caused by power filters. Provide rocks, bogwood and a few clumps of plants to give the fish some shelter and provide suitable surfaces for the growth of algae. Enriching the water with blackwater extract will further encourage the algal growth needed for success. After a gestation period of about 55 days, 20-35 fry are produced. At this point the trophotaenia (wormlike extensions that absorb food from

Above: **Ilyodon xantusi**
A splendid male of this attractive species. Provide plenty of algae.

the ovary wall) are still present, but these usually wither away within the first 24 hours after birth. The young feed well and become sexually mature at four to five months.

Below: **Skiffia bilineata**
A long-established aquarium species, previously Neotoca. *Female.*

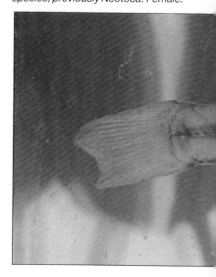

Skiffia bilineata

Black-finned Goodeid

● **Habitat:** Rivers in volcanic areas of Central Mexico.

● **Length:** Males up to 3.5cm (1.4in); females 6cm (2.4in).

● **Diet:** Vegetable matter and some live food.

● **Features:** The sexes are similar. The dorsal fin starts halfway down the olive-grey body and, like many Goodeids, the belly is tinged yellow. Along the flanks is a narrow blue-green iridescent zone with a dark longitudinal line running from the snout to the caudal peduncle, where it is crossed by dark bars in males. Mature males develop black fins.

● **Basic care and breeding:** Best results will be obtained in a well-planted, large aquarium. Maintain the temperature at 22-25°C (72-77°F) and as near to pH7 as possible. The gestation period is six to eight weeks, and 5-40 young may be produced in a typical brood.

Xenotoca eiseni

Red-tailed Goodeid; Orange-tailed Goodeid

● **Habitat:** Streams in Mexico.
● **Length:** Male up to about 5cm (2in); females up to 7cm (2.75in).
● **Diet:** A wide range of foods, from dried foods to live and green foods; they will also browse on algae.
● **Features:** A deep stocky body with a narrow caudal peduncle. The front of the male fish has a bluish band and there is a bright orange band around the caudal peduncle; the tail is a yellow-orange in colour.
● **Basic care and breeding:** It is fairly tolerant to aquarium conditions, although it will thrive best in moderately hard water. It is a reasonably quiet fish, but can be a fin nipper in a community tank. Breeding traps are not needed since the fry are rarely bothered by the parent fishes. Providing plenty of food for the parents in a well-planted aquarium usually affords the fry sufficient protection. Generally broods contain between 20 and 60 good-sized fry.

Right: **Xenotoca eiseni**
A male specimen showing the typical orange coloration at the base of the tail. Hardy and adaptable.

Family: POECILIIDAE
This Family includes 26 genera and over 138 species, one species of which, *Tomeurus gracilis*, is not necessarily a livebearer. Officially it is an egglayer but on occasion under certain conditions becomes a livebearer! In this Family, the gonopodium is made up from the 3rd, 4th and 5th anal fin rays. *Poecilia* and *Xiphophorus* are the major genera and these are discussed in separate sections. First, we look at a range of other Poeciliid fishes.

Alfaro cultratus
Knife Livebearer; Alfaro's Livebearer

● **Habitat:** Running streams in the Atlantic coastal regions of the Central American countries of Guatemala, Costa Rica and Panama.

● **Length:** The male generally reaches about 5cm (2in); the female in the region of 6-8cm (2.4-3.2cm).

● **Diet:** It will accept flaked foods readily, especially when tempted with live foods. Being a surface feeder, it will relish midge larvae.

● **Features:** The fish is very slender, with the spine clearly apparent through its translucent body. The two rows of scales on the lower edge of the caudal peduncle give it a characteristic knife edge appearance. The colour is a yellow-green, pale on the belly and with a greenish purple iridescence above the anal fin.

● **Basic care and breeding:** This shy but aggressive fish needs a well-planted tank for shelter and benefits from the movement created by a small power filter. Maintain the temperature at 25-28°C (77-82°F) for successful breeding. After a gestation period of between 28 and 32 days, a brood of 30-100 small fry is produced. If the adults can be prevented from eating the fry, they grow quite rapidly. Although it is possible to trap the female about 10 days before she is due to give birth, this causes serious stress to these nervous fishes. Using a nursery tank or tank division is preferable

Left: **Alfaro cultratus**
The characteristic 'blade-like' row of scales along the rear lower edge of the body are visible on this male.

Belonesox belizanus

Pike Livebearer; Pike Top Minnow
- **Habitat:** Still waters, marshes and lakes along the Atlantic coast of Central America: Southern Mexico into Yucatan and Honduras.
- **Length:** This is the largest Poeciliid, the males up to 10cm (4in), and the females 18cm (7in).
- **Diet:** *Belonesox* is carnivorous, even on its own species. Females may eat small mates, so keep them alone except under supervision. They seem to need virtually all live food, including insects, earthworms and fish, although it may be possible to cajole them into taking flakes or home-made heart-based foods.
- **Features:** Greyish silver with tiny black dots in rows along the upper body and a black spot in the tail. A

Above: **Belonesox belizanus**
A female displays a wide-opening jaw, bristling with sharp teeth.

dark lateral line shows along the side of the fish depending on mood. The pointed snout and small sharp teeth of this sleek fish are instantly recognizable features.

Above: *The brownish grey waters of Rio Atoyac in Mexico, a typical habitat for* Belonesox belizanus.

● **Basic care and breeding:**
Naturally shy, the Pike Livebearer seeks out plant cover in which to lurk for its prey. Keep it in a tank on its own, therefore; a community aquarium would equate to a restaurant to such a fish and would not remain a community for long. Keep it in a large aquarium at a temperature of about 25-28°C (77-82°F), ideally with some salt in the water – 0.5-1.0gm per litre (0.5-1.0 teaspoon per gallon) – although this is not essential.

These fishes can be sexed at three to four months old, and become sexually mature at six to nine months. After a gestation period of 30-50 days, 20-80 fry 1.5cm (0.6in) long are produced. Feed the fry initially on *Cyclops* and day-old guppies, and give them immediate protection from their mother. Using a heavily planted nursery tank is the best strategy, since this gives the fry a chance to reach some shelter; remove the female from the nursery tank as soon as she has given birth.

Left: **Belonesox belizanus**
A superb pair of these streamlined voracious fishes. Female at top.

Brachyrhaphis rhabdophora
A male, with the broad dorsal fin and black gonopodium typical of its sex.

Brachyrhaphis rhabdophora

● **Habitat:** Costa Rica, Atlantic and Pacific slopes of the central mountain ranges.

● **Length:** Males can be up to 4cm (1.6in); females 7cm (2.75in).

● **Diet:** Plenty of live foods, such as insects and grindalworms, with the addition of flaked food.

● **Features:** These fishes are a similar shape to Guppies but with a thicker caudal peduncle and smaller fins; males have a fan-like dorsal fin.

● **Basic care and breeding:** This is a hardy but rather aggressive fin-nipping fish, not ideally suited to a community aquarium. Keep known fin nippers and males separately, both from each other and from a community aquarium. For successful breeding, maintain the aquarium at 21-30°C (70-86°F). There is a gestation period of 28 days between broods of about 25 fry. Females are very quick to eat fry, but unfortunately these fishes are not good in breeding traps. The small broods mean that it can be difficult to detect any swelling and there is no gravid mark. Because of this, it is best to breed this species in very heavily planted aquariums. The fry can be difficult to sex because the female has a black mark on her anal fin easily mistaken for the male's black gonopodium. They are fairly slow growing and take seven to nine months to reach maturity, although not full size.

Below: **Brachyrhaphis episcopi**
An attractive species from Panama that will thrive in the aquarium. This is a fine pair. Provide a separate nursery tank to rear the fry.

Brachyrhaphis episcopi

The Bishop

- **Habitat:** Still waters in coastal Panama.
- **Length:** The male is 3.5cm (1.4in) and the female 5cm (2in).
- **Diet:** Live foods: *Daphnia*, insects and grindalworms, etc., plus some flaked food.
- **Features:** Two long red lines with green between run from the flat head along both sides of the elongated body. The scales have a dark border, giving them a netlike pattern. The male has a sickle-shaped red anal fin.
- **Basic care and breeding:** For best breeding results provide a well-planted brackish water aquarium with a good growth of algae and maintain it at a temperature of 25-30°C (77-86°F). The broods of 6-20 fry need cover from their parents. A separate nursery tank is ideal since the fry are difficult to rear. Be sure to provide an excess of small brineshrimps and *Daphnia* to get them feeding without delay.

Gambusia affinis

Western Mosquito Fish; Silver Gambusia; Spotted Gambusia

● **Habitat:** The basins of the San Antonio and Guadalupe rivers in Texas. There are two local varieties or subspecies, *G.affinis affinis* (western form), and *G.affinis holbrooki* (eastern form).

● **Length:** The males grow to about 4cm (1.6in); the females up to approximately 6.5cm (2.6in).

● **Diet:** True to their name, these fishes love to eat surface-dwelling insects, particularly mosquito larvae in vast amounts. Fortunately, they will also take flake foods and vegetable matter.

● **Features:** They have a noticeably flat head, which confirms their surface-feeding habit. The female is a fairly dull olive-green with scattered black spots. The colour of the male is very variable, being basically yellowish with a pale belly and often with a lot of black markings, especially on the dorsal fin, tail and under the eyes.

● **Basic care and breeding:** These are fairly easy fishes to breed,

provided that the fry can escape the attentions of their hungry mother. A temperature of 20-22°C (68-72°F) is suitable, and salt can be added to the aquarium water (0.5-1.0gm per litre/0.5-1.0 teaspoon per gallon) *Gambusia* becomes sexually mature at just a couple of months old, probably because of pressure from predation, since they are very vulnerable living at the water surface. The gestation period is 30 days, the female producing 10-100 fry (average 23 fry). This species responds well to being placed in a

Above: **Gambusia affinis affinis**
A pair of these surface-dwelling fishes, the female noticeably larger.

trap for aquarium breeding.
   Although this species was the first livebearer available to the aquarium market, it is unsuitable for inclusion in community tanks because of its aggressive nature.

Below: **Gambusia affinis holbrooki**
Here, the male of the subspecies shows an abundance of black. Other specimens may be clear.

Gambusia marshi
● **Habitat:** Lives in large rivers of northeastern Mexico.
● **Length:** Males up to 3cm (1.2in); females up to about 5cm (2in).
● **Diet:** A simple, mixed diet of commercial flaked foods and some live foods is taken avidly.

● **Features:** A slim grey body with a black speckling above the lateral line. The adults develop a yellowish sheen, which is particularly prominent in the females. Some strains are darker and the sheen appears blue. The fins are rounded and may have a black edging. The

Above: **Gambusia marshi**
An active species that can prove to be a fin nipper in the aquarium.

gonopodium is relatively long.
● **Basic care and breeding:** This species is fairly straightforward to maintain, preferring water at about 22-27°C (72-81°F). This is an active fish and, like many such active species, can be a fin nipper. Therefore, it is best to keep it in a species tank rather than in a community aquarium. After a gestation period of 21-28 days, it produces at least 10-40 fry.

291

Girardinus metallicus

Girardinus

● **Habitat:** Cuba and Costa Rica, in small streams and ditches.

● **Length:** The male grows to 5cm (2in); the female up to 9cm (3.5in).

● **Diet:** This species eats well in captivity, taking most dry and flaked foods, live foods, algae and vegetable matter.

● **Features:** Quite a deep-bodied fish with a broad flat head and large dorsal fin. The body is typically a yellowish grey with an olive-green tinge and blue iridescence on the sides, overlaid with sickle shaped bars, those on the female being indistinct. The males are black underneath and this may extend down the front of the gonopodium.

● **Basic care and breeding:** For good breeding results maintain these fishes at a temperature of 22-25°C (72-77°F). The gestation period is about four weeks, and the female needs to be isolated in a trap or nursery tank to produce her 10-60 fry, and then replaced in the main aquarium. Although generally peaceful, these fishes eat their fry.

Heterandria formosa

Mosquito Fish; Dwarf Top-Minnow; Dwarf Livebearer

● **Habitat:** Fresh and brackish waters, North Carolina to Florida.

● **Length:** A tiny fish, the smallest livebearer, the male reaches 2cm (0.8in) and the female 3.5cm (1.4in).

● **Diet:** Despite its common name of Mosquito Fish, it eats primarily green matter.

● **Features:** The basic colour is olive-green, with a dark brown line running down each side of the body. The fins are yellowish in colour, the dorsal fin being marked with a single spot. The male has a very large gonopodium.

● **Basic care and breeding:** Keep these fishes in a species tank at a temperature of 20-24°C (68-75°F) in hard, slightly alkaline water. *Heterandria* continually produce a few fry rather than distinct broods, which allows them to bear larger fry – up to a third of the size of their mother – with a better chance of survival. (This process is called superfoetation.) Because of this 'production line' system, there is no

point in trapping the female. Ideally, use a well-planted 'species' tank for breeding and either leave the fry with the mother or remove them to another tank for greater safety when the opportunity arises.

Above: **Heterandria formosa**
A tiny livebearer best kept in a species tank. Male at bottom.

Below: **Girardinus metallicus**
The female of an iridescent species.

Heterandria bimaculata

Two-spotted Heterandria

● **Habitat:** Rivers and streams along the Atlantic coast of southern Mexico into Yucatan. Also in Guatemala, Honduras and Belize.

● **Length:** Males up to 7cm(2.75in); females up to 15cm(6in)

● **Diet:** Normal aquarium dried foods and vegetable matter.

● **Features:** The body is an attractive shade of pale rosy mauve-blue, with black edges to the scales. There are two spots: one just behind the gill cover and one on the caudal peduncle. The former is often small and may be missing in small fish.

● **Basic care and breeding:** This slim-bodied species can be very aggressive, making it unsuitable for a community tank with small fishes. Females can pose a serious threat, even to their own mates. This species is quite prolific, producing up to 100 fry at intervals of six to eight weeks. Provide a well-planted breeding tank; otherwise, the female will eat her own offspring.

Left: *A stream in eastern Mexico, a typical habitat of* Heterandria bimaculata. *This species has also been collected from the fast-flowing waters of Rio Atoyac, shown in the photograph on page 285.*

Below: **Heterandria bimaculata**
An active and aggressive species with a large mouth and appetite to match. This photograph highlights the rich coloration of both male (bottom) and females. Not suitable for a community of small fishes.

Right: **Limia melanogaster**
*In this pair, the female shows a very
prominent gravid spot. These fishes
are ideal for a community aquarium.*

Limia melanogaster

*Blue-bellied Limia; Black-bellied
Limia*

● **Habitat:** The warm, still and
rapidly flowing waters of Jamaica
and Haiti.
● **Length:** Males reach up to 4.5cm
(1.8in); females up to 6cm (2.4in).
● **Diet:** Varied aquarium foods but
with plenty of vegetable material.
● **Features:** The back is olive-
green in colour, and the large scales
over the rear part of the body are
royal blue crossed with dark bars.
The male's dorsal fin is blue-black
and the caudal fin yellow-orange
edged with black. The female has a
large blue gravid spot, which often
persists after birth.
● **Basic care and breeding:**
Ideally, keep these fishes at a
temperature of 24-26°C (75-79°F) in
a well-planted aquarium. They
produce about 20-60 quite large
young after a gestation period of
about four weeks. Fed on plenty of
live food and high-protein flakes, the
fry develop quite quickly into
peaceful adults that make good
community fishes.

Limia nigrofasciata

*Hump-backed Limia; Black-barred
Limia*

● **Habitat:** Slow moving or static
bodies of water in Haiti, generally
with a heavy plant growth.
● **Length:** Males up to 5cm (2in);
females up to 7cm (2.75in).
● **Diet:** Mainly vegetable matter
plus flaked food and live foods
● **Features:** The male and female
fishes are similar in colour; the
upper part of the body is olive-green
with a blue iridescence below. There

Below: **Limia nigrofasciata**
*Note the characteristic black
streaks with a hint of iridescent blue
on the flanks of this male specimen.
A prolific species in the aquarium.*

are black streaks on the body, and the underside is black. The hump develops in adult sexually mature males (9-12 months old); the dorsal fin also enlarges as males grow older, thus emphasizing the hump.

● **Basic care and breeding:** Maintain the temperature at about 24-26°C (75-79°F). The males pester heavily gravid females, so the best system is to use a well-planted 60cm (24in) tank as a breeding tank for a single pair and to move the male before the female is due to give birth. Broods of 10-50 fry are born approximately every 21 to 33 days, although this is very variable. Although rather delicate at first, the fry mature fairly quickly and are able to breed at three months old.

Limia vittata
Cuban Limia
● **Habitat:** Streams along the coast of Cuba, often in brackish water.
● **Length:** Males up to 6cm (2.4in); females up to 10cm (4in).
● **Diet:** A variety of aquarium foods, including vegetable and dried foods.
● **Features:** The overall coloration is olive-brown with a bluish sheen on the scales and many dark speckles and bars in a longitudinal band. The belly is a silvery pink and the fins pale yellow in colour. In the best males, and occasionally females, gold patches develop on the body. Since those that develop large patches seem short lived and sterile, it may be that these are the yellow equivalent of the melanomas in Platy/Swordtail crosses.
● **Basic care and breeding:** Cuban Limias are easy to breed and very prolific in well-planted tanks with some algal growth. They generally produce 20-60 young after a three to five week gestation period. This species prefers higher temperatures of about 25-28°C (77-82°F), and most breeders add salt to the water at the rate of 0.5-1.0gm per litre (0.5-1.0 teaspoon per gallon). The fry thrive on flaked foods and live food, taking a higher protein level than the adults.

Above: **Limia vittata**
This female shows just a trace of yellow markings. Such gold patches are more common in males.

Phallichthys amates amates

Merry Widow

● **Habitat:** Pools and slow streams in Guatemala and Honduras south to Panama.
● **Length:** Males grow to 4cm (1.6in); females to 7cm (2.75in).
● **Diet:** All types of aquarium foods, including algae.
● **Features:** A silvery yellow fish with a black line running through the eye. An iridescence can develop which outlines the scale edges. The male may have black vertical bars and a very distinctive black edge to the dorsal fin.
● **Basic care and breeding:** This species is easy to maintain and breed. Keep it at a temperature of about 25°C (77°F) in a well-planted tank and in the company of at least a couple of its own species, although other quiet community fishes are also suitable. The 10-60 fry will need a plentiful supply of brineshrimp and then *Daphnia*. They grow slowly and are not mature until they are about six months old.

Phallichthys amates pittieri

Orange-dorsal Livebearer

● **Habitat:** Pools and slow streams in Costa Rica and Panama.
● **Length:** A little larger than the related Merry Widow, the male reaches a length of up to 5cm (2in) and the female up to 8cm (3.2in).
● **Diet:** Wide ranging dried and live foods, including algae.
● **Features:** The body is olive-green in colour fading to golden yellow on the belly. A dark line runs vertically through the eye. The male has faint vertical blue lines on the sides of the body, and a large gonopodium turned down at the tip, reaching almost to the tail.
● **Basic care and breeding:** Maintain at 20-25°C (68-77°F). After a gestation period of four to six weeks, a brood of 10-50 fry is produced. These fishes become sexually mature in six weeks.

Below:
Phallichthys amates amates
A fine pair; the male shown at top.

Above:
Phallichthys amates pittieri
A male specimen. Undemanding.

Phalloceros caudimaculatus

Caudo; One-spot Livebearer; Dusky Millions Fish

● **Habitat:** Fresh and brackish waters in Argentina, southeastern Brazil, Paraguay and Uruguay.
● **Length:** Males up to 3cm (1.2in); females up to 5cm (2in).
● **Diet:** Wide ranging; they will eat most dried and live foods.
● **Features:** A basic golden olive-green with one or more dark spots and/or markings on the body, and often a black border to the dorsal fin. Quite elongated in shape.
● **Basic care and breeding:** This fish is hardy and undemanding, although rather sensitive to water changes. It will thrive in fresh or brackish water at 20-24°C (68-75°F). After a gestation period of 21 to 28 days, approximately 20-80 young are produced. Given the opportunity, the parents will eat their young so protect them in a breeding trap or nursery tank.
● **Varieties:** *P.c.auratus* – Golden One-spot Livebearer. *P.c.reticulatus* – Spotted Livebearer. *P.c.reticulatus auratus* – Golden-spotted Livebearer. Strangely, none of these truly lives up to its name; 'caudimaculatus' means one spot on the caudal peduncle and none of them is strictly limited to one spot.

Below:
Phalloceros caudimaculatus
This is the reticulatus *variety of the species, with an abundance of black markings. Male shown at top.*

Genus: POECILIA
These are generally medium-sized fishes and, as with most livebearers, the males are a little smaller than the females. The basic colour of most of the group is a green – or brown – tinged olive-yellow, the females being somewhat paler than the males. Black is a common colour in those members that were originally classified as *Mollienisia*, a colour now seen to perfection in the black forms developed from *Poecilia sphenops*. Some species have greatly enlarged dorsal fins, setting them apart from the Limias, which have more obvious humped backs and more flattened sides.

Many species come from coastal areas and so normally inhabit waters with some salt present. A number can even be kept in tropical marine tanks (as can *Gambusia affinis* if acclimatized first). They are largely herbivorous and therefore need green foods in the aquarium, although they will also take some live foods. Keep these fishes in slightly hard, alkaline water at a temperature of 25-28°C (77-82°F) with sea salt added at a rate of about 1gm per litre (1 teaspoon per gallon).

Keeping them in community tanks at lower temperatures often puts them under perpetual stress and leads to diseases; therefore it is best to keep them in a species tank, where they can be seen at their best in ideal conditions.

Poecilia formosa
Amazon Molly
● **Habitat:** Mexico and southern Texas.
● **Length:** Up to 7.5cm (3in).
● **Diet:** A wide range of vegetable-based foods, plus dried foods and a little live food.
● **Features:** Although drab in appearance, this fish is keenly kept by enthusiasts.
● **Basic care and breeding:** It is in relation to breeding that the Amazon Molly is well known. The natural hybridization between *P.latipinna* and *P.mexicana* (or the closely related *P.sphenops*) results in an all-female population of *P.formosa*. These then reproduce gynogenetically, which means that although they mate with males of either parent species the males do not contribute towards the resulting embryo, all offspring being female clones of the mother. The eggs are simply activated by fertilization.

Poecilia picta
Black-banded Poecilia
● **Habitat:** The waters of the Demerara River in British Guyana, Trinidad and Brazil.
● **Length:** Males up to 3cm (1.2in); females 4cm (1.6in).
● **Diet:** Like most of its relatives, this species will thrive on a predominantly vegetarian diet with flakes and some live food.
● **Features:** The male is basically

Above: **Poecilia formosa**
A natural all-female clone notable for its unusual breeding heritage.

yellowish green, dotted with large blue spots under a bronze sheen. The dorsal fin, yellow edged with blue and with a blue spot at the base, is set well back. The female is green with a mottled bronze patch in front of her dorsal fin.
● **Basic care and breeding:** This can prove a difficult fish to breed successfully; it needs salt in the water and plenty of plant cover. The gestation period is 28-31 days and the female produces only 6-15 fry per brood. It is vital to trap the female because the fry are very small and they stay close to the bottom of the tank when born.

Poeciliopsis scarlli
Flier
● **Habitat:** The coastal freshwater canals and irrigation ditches north of the Guerrero/Michoacan State boundary in Mexico. These are mud-bottomed waters with no

submerged plants but an abundance of algae.

● **Length:** Males up to 3.5cm (1.4in); females up to 4cm (1.6in).

● **Diet:** The dietary requirements of this species have not been fully established. However, it will accept algae, livefoods and flakes.

● **Features:** Adults of both sexes are greyish yellow with fine vertical stripes and blue eye rings. The leading ray of the dorsal fin is black. The body shape is streamlined and the set of the pectoral fins is said to make it look ready to take flight – hence its common name of 'Flier'.

● **Basic care and breeding:** This recently discovered fish, named after a British fish collector, seems to prefer relatively low water temperatures of 22-23°C (72-73°F) and a pH value close to 7 (neutral). Small numbers of fry – four to six – are normally produced at intervals of 9-14 days. Cannibalism does not seem to be a problem in this fish.

Above: **Poecilia picta**
A male fish showing the distinctive markings in bright blue and yellow.

Note: The popular species from this genus, *Poecilia latipinna* and *Poecilia sphenops,* are included in Part Two (see pages 188-9). Both are generally regarded as 'cultivated' rather than wild species. This is borne out by the various colour varieties of these species – gold, black and speckled – that have been developed from aquarium stock. Another species, *Poecilia velifera,* is similar in appearance, behaviour and requirements to *Poecilia latipinna*, the only differences between the two being the number of dorsal rays they possess and their size – *P. velifera* is slightly larger.

Below: **Poeciliopsis scarlli**
A relative newcomer to the hobby. The female is shown here.

Genus: XIPHOPHORUS Swordtails and Platies
These fishes, now classified as one genus, originally belonged to two;
Xiphophorus and *Platypoecilus*. The discovery of 'linking species' in 1932
(P.xiphidium), 1943 (P.pygmaeus) and 1960 (X.milleri) resulted in
Xiphophorus, the name first proposed in 1848, becoming the established
genus for all these species. These have been popular aquarium fishes for
many years and selective 'line-breeding' has established many
internationally recognized colour strains. Some of these cultivated forms
– *X. helleri, X. maculatus* and *X. variatus* – are included in Part Two (see
pages 192-5). In recent years, however, there has been an intense revival
of interest in 'other species' of livebearing fishes. Here we examine some
'wild' member species of the *Xiphophorus* genus in two groups; the
Montezumae complex and the Maculatus complex.

The Montezumae complex

These species are grouped
together by virtue of their showing
more physical characteristics of
the 'swordtail' side of the
Xiphophorus genus than of the
'platy'. All have an elongate body
form and the sword-like extension,
however small, to the caudal fin.
(One species, *Xiphophorus milleri,*
does not have a sword at all, but
shares other characteristics.)
These species are easily
recognized by the dorsal fin, which
is similarly marked throughout.
The species in this complex are:

X.milleri. This species from a small
tributary of Lake Catemaco is an
important fish in scientific terms
because it 'bridges the gap'
between *Xiphophorus* and
Platypoecilus. Both sexes have a
gravid spot and are similar in shape
to the male Swordtail, but without
the characteristic sword.

X.montezumae (Montezuma
Swordtail). There are two
subspecies, both from pools and
slow-moving streams:
X.m.montezumae and, with a

Above: **Xiphophorus cortezi**
*This attractive fish is a shorter
sworded subspecies of*
X. montezumae. *Easy to maintain.*

Below right: **Xiphophorus milleri**
*A female specimen of this species
from eastern Mexico. The small
male does not develop a sword.*

smaller sword, *X.m.cortezi* (which is also known as *X.cortezi*).

X.pygmaeus (Pygmy Swordtail). There are two subspecies: *X.p.pygmaeus* lives along the banks of fast-flowing streams in the Rio Axtla, Mexico. It has virtually no

Above: **Xiphophorus montezumae**
This is an amenable species. The sworded male is shown here.

sword. *X.p.nigrensis*, on the other hand, lives in more static waters and pools in Rio Panuco, Mexico and has quite a respectable sword.

Centre: **Xiphophorus p.pygmaeus**
A pair of the yellow form of this subspecies – male shown at top –

from the fast-flowing waters of Rio Axtla in Mexico. Typically, the male fish shows no sign of a sword.

Above: **Xiphophorus couchianus**
*Originally from the springs around
Monterrey in northeastern Mexico,
their numbers in the wild have*
*declined because of loss of habitat
and interbreeding with other*
Xiphophorus *species. In this pair,
the male is shown at bottom left.*

Above: *A typical river in Vera Cruz, eastern Mexico, the natural habitat of several* Xiphophorus *species.*

The Maculatus complex

These fishes are grouped together by their similarity to the deeper-bodied Platy. They are classified by more exact anatomical details.

X.couchianus couchianus (Monterrey Platyfish). Listed as endangered, and probably extinct in the wild. It originates from the headwaters around Monterrey, Mexico. The subspecies *X.c.gordoni* (Northern Platyfish) is also listed as endangered.

X.xiphidium (Swordtail Platy; Purple Spike-tail Platy). This species is similar in shape to *X.maculatus*. The male grows to 4cm (1.6in); the females to 5.5cm (2.2in). The basic coloration is olive-green, becoming pale underneath, and with a purple-blue iridescence. The female has a dark band along the lateral line and yellow patches above and below it at the caudal peduncle. In the male the tail is darker with a yellow crescent, and the bottom few rays extend into a spike. Both sexes have an apparent gravid spot!

The optimum temperature for keeping this species is 24-26°C (75-79°F) and they seem to do best on a high-protein diet. A well-planted tank is vital to give some protection to the 15-20 fry. These placid fishes are eminently suitable for a community tank.

Below: **Xiphophorus xiphidium**
An easy going species that will mix with community fishes. The male is much smaller than the female.

GENERAL INDEX

Page numbers in **bold** indicate major references, including accompanying photographs. Page numbers in *italics* indicate captions to other illustrations. Less important text entries are shown in normal type.

INDEX TO SPECIES

INDEX TO PLANTS

Index compiled by Stuart Craik

FURTHER READING

Alderton, D. *Looking After Aquarium Fish*, Ward Lock Ltd, 1983

Allen, G.R. *Inland Fishes of Western Australia*, Western Australia Museum, 1982

Andrews, Dr. C. *A Fishkeeper's Guide to Fish Breeding*, Salamander Books Ltd, 1986

Baensch, Dr. U. *Tropical Aquarium Fish*, Tetra Press, 1983

Carrington, Dr. N. *A Fishkeeper's Guide to Maintaining a Healthy Aquarium*, Salamander Books Ltd, 1986

Dawes, J.A. *The Tropical Freshwater Aquarium*, Hamlyn Publishing Group Ltd, 1986

Dawes, J.A. *A Practical Guide to Freshwater Aquarium Fishes*, Hamlyn Publishing Group Ltd, 1987

Hunnam P., et al. *The Living Aquarium*, Ward Lock Ltd, 1981

Jacobs, K. *Livebearing Aquarium Fishes*, Studio Vista, 1971

Jacobsen, N. *Aquarium Plants*, Blandford Press Ltd, 1979

James, B. *A Fishkeeper's Guide to Aquarium Plants*, Salamander Books Ltd, 1986

Jenno, A. *Aquarium Technology*, Barry Shurlock, 1976

Loiselle, P.V. *The Cichlid Aquarium*, Tetra Press, 1985

Leggett, R. & Merrick, J.R. *Australian Native Fishes for Aquariums*, J.R. Merrick Publications, 1987

Merrick, J.R. & Schmida, G.E. *Australian Freshwater Fishes*, Macquarie University, 1984

Mills, D. *Illustrated Guide to Aquarium Fishes*, Kingfisher Books, 1981

Mills, D. *You & Your Aquarium*, Dorling Kindersley Ltd, 1986

Mills, D. *A Fishkeeper's Guide to the Tropical Aquarium*, Salamander Books Ltd, 1984

Mills, D. *A Fishkeeper's Guide to Community Fishes*, Salamander Books Ltd, 1984

Muhlberg, H. *The Complete Guide to Water Plants*, E. P. Publishing Books Ltd, 1982

Ramshorst, Dr J.D. van, *The Complete Aquarium Encyclopedia of Tropical Freshwater Fish*, Elsevier-Phaidon, 1978

Sands, D. *A Fishkeeper's Guide to African & Asian Catfishes*, Salamander Books Ltd, 1986

Sands, D. *A Fishkeeper's Guide to Central American Cichlids*, Salamander Books Ltd, 1986

Sands, D. *A Fishkeeper's Guide to South American Catfishes*, Salamander Books Ltd, 1988

Scott, P.W. *A Fishkeeper's Guide to Livebearing Fishes*, Salamander Books Ltd, 1987

Spotte, S. *Fish & Invertebrate Culture*, Wiley-Interscience, 1979

Sterba, G. *The Aquarist's Encyclopedia*, Blandford Press, 1983

Thabrew, Dr.V de, *Popular Tropical Aquarium Plants*, Thornhill Press, 1981

Ward, B. *The Aquarium Fish Survival Manual*, Macdonald & Co. (Publishers) Ltd, 1985

Whitehead, P. *How Fishes Live*, Elsevier-Phaidon, 1975

Wilkie, D. *Aquarium Fish*, Pelham Books Ltd, 1986

Zupanc, G.K.H., *Fish and Their Behaviour*, Tetra Press, 1985

PICTURE CREDITS

Dick Mills: 23, 34

Arend van den Nieuwenhuizen: 10-11(B), 36(T), 41, 43, 61, 63, 72, 73, 76, 77(B), 78(T), 79, 80-1, 82-3, 83, 84, 85, 86(T), 88, 90-1(B), 93, 94-5(T), 96, 98-9, 100-1(B), 102-3, 104, 106(T), 107, 108(B), 110(T), 112(T), 117, 118, 119, 120, 122, 123, 124, 126, 127(T), 128, 130, 132-3(T), 136-7, 143(B), 144, 145, 146, 148-9, 153(B), 154-5(T), 156-7, 158-9, 160-1, 162-3, 164-5(T), 166-7(B), 168(T), 169(B), 172, 173, 174-5, 176(T), 178-9, 181(T), 186, 187, 188-9, 191, 192-3, 194-5(B), 197(B), 207, 219(T), 237(T,C), 238(B), 246, 255(T), 256(B), 257, 258(B), 259, 264, 266(T,C), 269(B), 272(C), 272-3(B), 274(C), 276(T), 298, 299(B)

Barry Pengilley: 69, 86-7(B), 129, 131, 134-5, 140, 147, 183, 185

Laurence Perkins: 198

Eduard Purzl: 282-3(B), 284-5(B), 292-3, 297(B), 302, 303(B)

Bernard Pye: 214-5(BC)

Mike Sandford: Title page, 105, 109, 184, 213(T), 231(T), 236(B), 258(T), 260(T), 261, 274(T)

David Sands: 167(T), 168(B), 196(B), 202, 204, 208(T), 210, 212, 214(T,C), 215(T,C), 216, 217, 218, 219(B), 222, 223, 224(T), 225, 226, 227, 228, 229, 230, 231(B), 232, 233(B), 236(T), 237(B), 238(T), 239, 240-1, 242, 243, 245(T,C), 247, 248, 249, 250, 251, 252(B), 253, 254, 260(B), 262, 263, 265, 266-7(B), 268(B), 269(T)

Ian Sellick: 196(T)

W A Tomey: 11(T), 39, 65, 78-9(B), 95(B), 114-5(T), 133(B), 138, 150-1(T), 155(B), 165(B), 195(T), 245(B), 296-7(T)

Keith Waller Associates © Salamander Books Ltd: 11(BR)

Terry Waller: 300

Uwe Werner: 10(T), 170-1(T), 196-7(BC), 197(T,C), 200-1, 203, 205, 206, 208(B), 209, 211, 213(B), 236-7(BC), 270(T), Back endpaper

Lothar Wischnath: 299(T), 303(T,C), 304-5(T)

Rudolf Zukal: 224(B)

PRINTED IN BELGIUM BY

proost
INTERNATIONAL BOOK PRODUCTION